Nick Pointing

found his way in to writing through the Word and Island Life magazine a gap year back packing the globe h Zealand Classic cars publication.

CW00551216

Nick studied HND GraphicCommunications after serving with the Royal Navy. Time at sea with Prince Andrew and shore time manning the mast as Button Boy at the Royal Tournament and Edinburgh Tattoo opened a world of adventure and eventually ending up as a Tour guide on H.M.S. Victory.

Complete with a Blue Peter badge this made for a creative career. Overseas deployments fuelled his ambition to travel further a field including a charity cycle ride across Borneo. Employed as a Manager for Marks & Spencer and married to his wife Carolyn, Nick was presented with a challenge of a life time.

Carolyn Pointing

wife and mother of two children, ran her own business as a local Postmistress. As a hobby, she was a competent confectioner and her birthday and wedding cakes were in high demand.

Raising money for charity and fulfilling her ambition for adrenalin, Carolyn took to the skies in a 2000 ft parachute jump and to the seas for a challenge in water skiing.

Not content as a visual merchandising manager she took up her current employment as a police officer with Hampshire Constabulary and hasn't looked back.

Child hood memories of her favorite film sparked an e-bay collection of all things Chitty Chitty Bang Bang and so embarked on a quest for the real thing.

Motley Play Hut Books MPH
Published in Great Britain by Motley Play Hut Books
Newchurch, Isle of Wight, Great Britain.

Printing history
Published in hardback 2011
Published in paperback 2011
Printed by Motley Play Hut Books
Copyright @ Nick Pointing 2011
The moral rights of the author has been asserted
Copyright Designs and Patents Act 1998.

A CIP catalogue record for this book
is available from the British Library

ISBN 978-0-9568851-0-4

Maps by Kevin Morey
Copy editor: Carol Anderson
Editor: Tony Maasz

Photography: Carolyn Pointing
Cover design: Nick Pointing

Typeset in Times
Printed and bound in Great Britain.

Port Out Starboard Home

Overland to Australia on a Wing and a Prayer

Nick & Carolyn Pointing

Published by
Motley Play Hut Books

Port Out Starboard Home
Overland to Australia on a Wing and a Prayer

Contents
Introduction
Acknowledgements

Port Out Starboard Home
Overland to Australia on a Wing and a Prayer

Introduction

The world of travel certainly does a lot for the soul: it's inspiring, humbling and very influential on one's own standing in life. Viewing scenery from afar is fine, but real travel allows a person to touch it, smell it and live it. Travel creates an unusual hierarchy. The countries travelled through, the sheer number and variety of exotic locations score respectable points, as does the duration of travel. The mode of transport gives added weight and so does the accommodation used. On a Spanish package holiday for a week the traveller hardly causes a raised eyebrow, but to some, driving overland for a year and a day increases one's position in the respect league. You are viewed as either a travel geek or travel god. When I bumped into a Frenchman who walking round the world I realised that by travelling down under in a kid's movie car, I was probably a geek.

We all have dreams and ambitions and top of mine was to write a book. I chose travel simply because I had something to write about. It could have been simple: wife wakes up, wife asks me to build her Chitty Chitty Bang Bang, I do then we drive it to Australia. Fortunately for the book it was slightly more complicated than that,

so here goes.

Acknowledgements

This project would not have been possible without the moral and practical support of many people, from the time that the idea began to take shape in my mind to the moment we drove off the Fishbourne Ferry on our arrival back home.

First, I must thank my closest friends and family, who believed in what we were doing, especially our parents for flying the flag of approval and the support they gave. To John Reynolds and his Land Rover mechanic, to Phil and his team at Niton Undercliff Garage for buying into the whole project and for getting Chitty through the MOT. To Bob Lacy, the 'very nice' AA man and my good friend Scott Matthews who also helped the adventure take shape. They looked beyond the problems and amazingly had complete faith in us. So did Dave Khan, who came to our defence when his work colleagues gathered round at the showing of our internet web page and laughed and jeered at an impossible idea.

I would also like to thank all those friends and acquaintances who admired our idea of planning to build a replica Chitty Chitty Bang Bang and drive overland to Australia, although their eyes glazed over and they smiled through their teeth, thinking we were completely off the planet, but were far too polite to say so. These people only hardened our resolve. I want to thank all those non-believers, all the characters who crossed our paths, who ridiculed us and thought we were barking mad. All those people who were brave enough to be vocal in their opinions, stating the task was impossible: 'You will never build a replica Chitty, it's technically beyond you, and as for driving to Australia, you are both crackpots living in cloud cuckoo land.' 'You won't make it out of Newchurch, let alone drive it halfway round the flippin' world.' That group of inward-looking realists truly gave us the inspiration to prove them wrong.

Grateful thanks goes to our support crew Steve and Julia for having the guts to put their money where their mouths were and get on and do it. Without the support they gave us in the planning and by sticking to their word to follow us down under the journey might not have been undertaken.

Lastly, the top honour for worthy support falls to my wife for her inspiration and genuine faith in me, for endless patience and cups of tea and for being brave enough to forgo hairdryers, pretty clothes and en-suite bathrooms on a year-long Chitty trip into the unknown.

A week before embarking on our adventure I opened a fortune cookie in a Chinese restaurant and mine simply said: 'If you think you can, you probably can.'

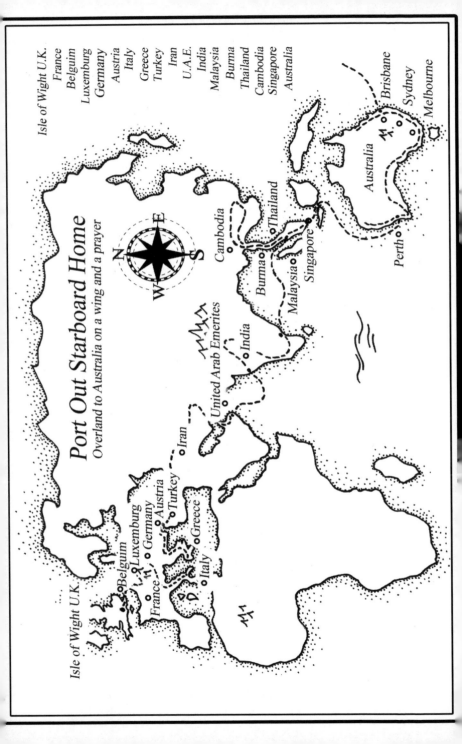

Port Out Starboard Home
Overland to Australia on a wing and a prayer

Chapter 1 **E**sfahan by nightfall

The Iranian sun was dropping in the sky and dusk was just around the corner. Iran's top temperature that summer was 54°C, but thankfully that wasn't today. Carolyn constantly rearranged her hijab scarf as the wind through Chitty's cab was relentless. 'This bloody thing,' she said with vigour. The scarf had dropped down around her neck and was flapping like a windsock. I could see the frustration on her face and chose not to remind her of the men in passing cars looking in and taking photos on their mobile phones. The drive had been particularly long – over four hundred kilometres – as we intended to make Esfahan by nightfall, which was really pushing the original 1973 Land Rover motor. I knew one litre of oil was good for only 200 kilometres because it leaked through every gasket and every joint possible. Black smoke continued to belch out of Chitty's exhaust, plaguing my ozone-friendly conscience, but my vague attempt to rectify the carburettor problem had only made things worse. My thoughts were soon interrupted by a rather rude and abrupt two-way radio call from Steve in the Land Rover Discovery behind. 'So have you found somewhere then? You know you have passed the last potential camping site.'

Oh have I? I thought. 'Well, why didn't you say so,' I moaned.

As we approached the city outskirts, the sweat was cooling on our skin and the air was turning chilly. We were both very tired and hungry and stressed by the need to find a hotel in the dark which met with our support vehicle's approval. My concentration was waning, which was not good with a constant supply of Iranian onlookers waving, taking photos and driving so close that they could count the fillings in my teeth. Fortunately, the road was straight and the five or so cars escorting us were in good spirits. The car in front wasn't a Toyota, but a rebadged Hillman Hunter, and, in fact, most of the cars were of the same ilk. Four Iranian women squashed on the back seat politely waved and smiled while the car to our left was full of men shouting, 'Hello, what model. Where from?' in broken English.

'What was that?' I said as I jumped in shock at the sound of a truck horn fixed to the car waiting behind for a photo.

The clean straight road soon gave way to a jumbled wasteland lined with small but never ending garages and workshops. Trucks, dismantled cars and old oil drums littered the sides of the road. The area became closely built up and soon we were joined by teenage boys on two motor scooters. They rode three up and as they wove in and out of the cars they waved and grinned. Two scooters became five and it wasn't long before the word was out and roughly twenty circled us like a pack of hyenas. We smiled and waved but my driving and my attention were stretched to their limits. One lad riding close put his hand on Chitty's front wing while another cut inside with his pillion passenger standing with one leg stretched out ready for boarding. The situation was becoming fraught with danger – not that they saw it like that. Carolyn shouted out, 'Let go of the car', which was clearly received with disapproval. Focused on not running somebody down, I drove slower but the mood darkened. A scooter carrying three lads and having the guts screamed out of it pulled up alongside; the waving had gone, along with the smiles.

The young teenage driver, with thick, black hair and dressed in formal shirt open to the waist, was on a mission.. Manoeuvring closer, he spoke in Farsi with matching hand gestures and you didn't have to be a rocket scientist to work out that he wanted us to go away, although I imagined in his local tongue it was more direct that that. The two lads on the back reached out and started kicking Chitty's tyres. The situation was getting out of hand. Iran had received us with open arms but now we were in for a bit of a shock. I pushed the accelerator to the floor but fifty miles an hour was our limit and we couldn't shake them. Every time I caught their eye, hand gestures and tyre kicking followed. It was dark and I felt increasingly insecure. I needed to find a hotel. Eventually, the entourage of teeny bikers fizzled out and the stress of nearly killing one of them became that of finding a hotel with secure parking.

We were now caught in a constant stream of city cars and we were being swept along with the flow. We needed to get out of it. The bright lights of busy shops caught my eye and on a snap decision I pulled over. As I parked up, the car in front stopped and so did two or three behind. 'Hop out and go and ask in that shop if there is a hotel here,' I said to

Carolyn. Before she managed to get out, twenty or so men congregated around the car. Then three mopeds pulled up and without putting their feet down they leant against Chitty's front and rear wings. Unsure of the response I smiled; they smiled back but took it upon themselves to rearrange the brass wing mirrors and open and close the glovebox. Twenty men had now become fifty, but no women. The only English spoken was 'model, what model'. 'Chitty Chitty Bang Bang' fell on deaf ears. However, 'Land Rover' seemed to meet with approval.

Carolyn was taking far longer than expected and by now the road was completely blocked. The circus had come to town and scarily we were the main attraction. Smiling, waving and grunting, as nobody understood a thing, I surveyed my surroundings. The tree-lined avenue was divided into four lanes separated by a hedged central reservation. Traffic and enthusiastic Iranians all eager to catch a glimpse of our four-fendered friend soon congested the road. This was the main artery into the city and all lanes were blocked. Cars parked up at random all over the place, doors left hanging open, Kids weaved in and out on mopeds and people stood on car bonnets straining for a better look.

It was overwhelming and all very intimidating. The police turned up to see what all the fuss was about. Their frosty arrival soon gave way to interested smiles on the offer of a Chitty photo card showing our route and a picture of the original Land Rover.

Just as I started to relax and enjoy the attention, a taxi screeched hard on its brakes. The driver was so intent on rubber-necking our car that he crashed straight into a stationary motorbike, knocking the rider clean off. The bike hit the floor with a huge wallop and the sound of metal hitting tarmac resonated through the air. The rider, bewildered, found his feet and made straight for the taxi driver. Fuel spilt from the bike's tank and ran towards the kerb, tempting the teetering ash to fall from the end of a cigarette welded to the mouth of a well-weathered old boy crouching to my right.

We were no longer the centre of attention; the focus was now on the rider, a smartly dressed man in his forties. With fire in his eyes he dragged the taxi driver out of his seat; verbal abuse turned into fisticuffs and a well-placed punch, clean on the side of a slightly unshaven face, took the taxi driver and a group of bystanders to the floor.

The fifty men, who had originally been looking at us and then had turned to look at two Iranians fighting, were now looking at us again. The old man, now standing on the kerb to my right, slapped me on the forearm then pushed a clenched fist against me into my shoulder. I continued to make no eye contact with anyone, looking down but very aware of the flamboyant hand signals going on. The whole situation was turning into a riot and as far as all concerned it was our fault. I started the engine but had nowhere to go, my path was blocked solid and Carolyn was still in the shop. The police were busy manoeuvring traffic, two or three teenage boys started jeering and shaking Chitty sideways, my heart was racing; I gripped the steering wheel and started to fear for my life. No one was smiling, the mood had turned sour and with all this going on around me I asked myself how on earth did I find myself here?

Chapter 2 **S**tretch of the imagination

It was unusual for Carolyn to lie in, she always maintained it was a waste of a day, although coming in from work at 3 a.m. it seemed pretty fair to me. A rufty tufty, cat rescuing and community tea-drinking policewoman of four years, lack of sleep and food was of no concern to her. I couldn't make 10 a.m. without an all day breakfast, let alone with sleep depravation. I did the decent thing, carefully rearranged her teddy bears and made a cup of tea.

Carolyn had an obsession with all things Chitty Chitty Bang Bang. A bit of an eBay queen, Carolyn had pulled together a small collection of film memorabilia. Once I knew her draw to anything that had Dick Van Dyke in it I made it a priority for a birthday or Christmas present. In fact, knowing what to buy her apart from diamonds and kittens wasn't easy, so I latched on to this big style. It started with a Corgi model toy car and went on to include everything from the DVD, a couple of original Ian Fleming Chitty books from the 1960s to posters and a surprise trip to see Michael Ball at the London Palladium.

Well, the surprise wasn't Michael Ball but the fact that he was playing the Dick Van Dyke character of Caractacus Potts in the stage show of Chitty Chitty Bang Bang. Apart from a great all-round show, the car looked stunning and managed to trigger real emotion, bringing a lump to my throat over an inanimate object that was about to fly.

The tea was made and Carolyn was still asleep. As I leant over to gently wake her up, clutching two mugs with one hand, I romantically whispered in her ear while pouring tea all over the duvet. Carolyn opened her eyes, looked up at me then down at the duvet, raised an eyebrow but, bless her, said nothing.

Sitting up in bed, most unexpectedly she said, 'So, do you think you could build me the car?'

'What car,' I said. 'A Chitty Chitty Bang Bang car.'

'Yes,' she replied.

I leant forward, looked her in the eye and said, 'Yeh okay.'

'No seriously, do you think you could build me the car?' she said again.

The Sunday morning sun was streaming through the windows and I could feel the spring warmth on my back; the day was bright and full of optimism. 'Well, you obviously think there is a glimmer of hope that I could actually do it, so yes.' What had I just let myself in for?

I'm not an engineer by any stretch of the imagination and my claim to fame is managing ladies' wear and lingerie for Marks and Spencer. I never chose to delve into women's underwear but after leaving the Royal Navy, I found that I was only qualified to track submarines, and there wasn't much call for that on the Isle of Wight. One thing in my favour, however, was a vivid imagination and a bizarre secret desire to build something. Carolyn, like me, is bit of a dreamer but she is also a planner of outlandish adventures. We made an ideal couple for a project like this.

How do you start building Chitty Chitty Bang Bang? It's not as if you can flick through a kit car magazine and pick one off the shelf. I have seen a Batmobile fibreglass kit available on the internet, and the star of Back to the Future was based on a DeLorean. If Carolyn had been in love with the Dukes of Hazard, a General Lee with a fancy paint job would have done the trick. Starsky and Hutch, the 'A' Team and Night Rider – I have seen them all on the internet. There was a programme on Channel 4 called The Car's the Star, listing all the iconic film cars and interviewing owners of various replicas. Sadly, I thought they were all a bunch of anoraks – 'Take a look at yourself,' I hear you say! Well, the thing is Chitty Chitty Bang Bang is a one off. It was never based on anything. They made five or six cars for various parts in the film, including the sea-going version, fitted with aluminium to replace the brass, but only one road-going example. The 1960s Alan Mann Racing Team together with other engineers and top quality craftsmen built the original Chitty Chitty Bang Bang on a bespoke ladder chassis, complete with the three-litre Ford engine. A tough act to follow!

I might be ambitious but the truth was I didn't know if I could really build a replica Chitty Chitty Bang Bang. Maybe Carolyn's faith in me was misguided! How was I going to finance the project? If there is one thing that you learn early to maintain any credibility, it is to not tell anyone what you are doing. However, I forgot to tell Carolyn this …

I was trying to reboot the computer and banging my head on the underside of the stupid chipboard computer table, when Carolyn yelled out over the sound and smell of frying onions, 'Did you hear that?'

'Hear what,' I said.

'I met this bloke who works on classic car trims, he reckons we should go to Beaulieu,' Carolyn explained. Now apart from fighting crime, Carolyn reliably informs me that part of her role (apart from rescuing kittens) is building links with the community – 'Safer Neighbourhoods' and all that! Some might say it is just gossiping, but not a day goes by without her saying, 'Did you know …?' Well today's titbit proved quite useful.

Once I had finished playing around with the start-up disk, the Beaulieu internet site confirmed the dates for the next international auto jumble, and 12 September seemed a pretty good starting point.

***

On the ferry to Beaulieu, I said, 'How did you know about this?'

'Oh,' she said, 'I told Jim the Trim that we were building a Chitty Chitty Bang Bang and that we needed a chassis, so he recommended that we come over here, although he did go on to say that he thought we were as mad as a box of frogs.'

You don't say, I thought to myself.

As it turned out, the National Motor Museum at Beaulieu in the New Forest was one of the best visits we made. The auto jumble covers about ten acres and you can find just about anything. Lord Montagu opens his doors twice a year to the event and if you can't find it there, you probably can't find it. The day was unseasonably hot and in bright sunshine thousands of people jostled between cars and stalls littered with auto bits and bobs reminiscent of an automobile graveyard! Clearly some vendors had just carried out autopsies and the organs were left lying around with dirty 50p stickers on them. One man hidden under a huge cowboy hat and dark glasses had a notice stuck on his back. I expected it to say 'Kick Me', but no it was a request for parts for an old Bugatti. He'd be lucky!

Then bingo, there in the 'You can sell any heap of junk' car mart area was a huge chassis from a 1920s Lee Francis, complete with chain drive. Perfect, just like the film. We had spent hours freeze-framing the DVD for a good look at Chitty and had scoured the internet and movie stills, and this was spot on.

After wrestling with the idea of chopping to bits a 1920s chassis, I noticed a small paper tag attached by string to the steering wheel: 35,000 euros written in soft black pencil. Our hearts sank. This was about £20,000 and £19,900 over our budget!!! I soon realised after looking at brass headlights at £2,000 a pair and an original snake's head horn for £750 that financially we were well out of our league.

Disheartened, we caught the Lymington to Yarmouth ferry home and I rolled on and was ushered by the crew to park close behind a long-wheelbase Land Rover. I took one look and said to Carolyn, 'That's it, that will do.'

Carolyn looked at me with disapproval, 'It's a Land Rover,' she said.

'Yes, but it is one of the only cars still on the road with a chassis. That's perfect – and not only that, they are cheap and you can get the bits everywhere,' I went on.

We had a debate in the car whether it would be long enough, so right there and then, Carolyn jumped out and started to measure the sixteen feet by walking alongside the vehicle. The poor bloke inside was obviously concerned at a female stalking his car, having to wait until Carolyn had finished before he could get out, looking slightly bemused! He retraced her steps and looked intently at his car then darted upstairs presumably to recover with a cup of tea.

Chapter 3 **W**ill it fly?

The Duver in St Helens was the advertised address for a 1973 series 3 Land Rover. After scrutinising the underside, and going against every buyer's top tips, I bought it.. With a few days MOT left to run and £100 lighter, I drove her home. She was in a sorry state but a runner – just! At the first set of traffic lights, I shot to the right as I applied the brakes, nearly taking out a lollipop lady, and on approaching our lane, I hit a pothole and the driver's door fell clean off! It was so embarrassing holding up the traffic while I retrieved it. A little old lady in a Micra would have been great, but no, I had to settle for three lads in their early twenties and a Ford Fiesta with a loud exhaust. Laughing, your not kidding!

We made it home and I parked her up on the space for the garage that we didn't have yet and I went in for a nice English cup of tea, the first of many, and contemplated the whole shenanigans.

For all intents and purposes, we now had a chassis but not a clue what to do with it. The internet is a wonderful thing – when you can get a connection that is – now, surprisingly, there wasn't a great deal to be found when Googling Chitty Chitty Bang Bang. However, I did find out that Ian Fleming, while convalescing from a heart attack, had turned the bedtime stories he told his son, Casper, into a book called Chitty Chitty Bang Bang. Chitty Bang Bang was the name of a series of real life 1920s racing cars owned by Count Louis Zborowski. He raced these cars, with up to twenty-seven-litre aero-engines, at Brooklands, where as a very wealthy man, and certainly an influential character within the early motor racing industry, he was able to exploit Brooklands' rules. Although today the name is synonymous the car, Chitty Bang Bang supposedly comes from a World War I song. It refers to the chit that had to be obtained in order go on leave and the habit of visiting the red light district.

The most productive and useful website was that of Pierre Picton, who is the owner of the original road-going film car. I learnt that he was a stunt driver for the car in the movie and some time after acquired the real Chitty Chitty Bang Bang for himself.

However, at this point I had a wave of doubt. What about copyright?

Am I allowed to do this? I had heard that copyright runs out seventy years after the death of the creator but Chitty was only thirty-five years old. Who owned the copyright anyway? Oh never mind, I would worry about that later, I thought.

It was to be our first full weekend together on Chitty. So this was the plan, I explained masterfully to Carolyn. 'Do you have to stand on a pallet and talk down to me? You are not at work you know,' said Carolyn. I stepped down, not so masterful now, 'So this is the plan, strip it down to the chassis, paint it red,' I explained and then gabbled on about going to Cowes to find a boatbuilder, look for an engineer to make the bonnet and get the local Land Rover dealership to sort out the engine. Easy – if only! The least of my concerns was the engine and gearbox; a mechanic could sort that lot out once Chitty was built. Oh, and the brakes, clutch, differentials and prop! Well, just about anything that is standard Land Rover – that was just a matter of routine. I could even have a diesel motor fitted, I thought. Then I wondered what it would all cost but I decided not to wonder any more.

***

Ben was the elder of our two children at twelve; Michelle was eleven. Ben always got involved with our latest projects, embracing them to the full; Michelle on the other hand was far more interested in socialising and the latest fashions. They both looked on at a sorry Land Rover – Ben, full of enthusiasm, grinned and leapt straight into the passenger seat eager for a ride around the garden; Michelle stood unimpressed with her hands on her hips, her blonde hair catching the sun as she flicked it back and turned towards the house in response to a highly important text message. Ben, full of imagination, said, 'So, how will you make it fly?' This was not good timing as Michelle was still in earshot. I said optimistically, 'Oh, I will cross that bridge when we get to it, Ben.' Michelle instantly stopped in her tracks, turned and with a look that only a younger sister can give, said, 'Oh get real, Ben.'

Over the next few weeks, Ben took plenty of rides in the old bus, once with no roof at all when we all kidded ourselves that we were on safari going through the long grass. Another time, when we had stripped the Land Rover to a rolling chassis and engine, I stuck the spare wheel on the frame, sat on a cushion on for a seat ,and Ben hung on the back for dear life. We managed to churn up the lawn pretty well, but we did have fun.

Our garden is larger than the average but soon the borders were littered with Land Rover parts. Not knowing too much about Land Rovers but aware they had a great following I assumed that I could sell the bits.

I am always the one who pays for an extortionate advertisement and manages to exceed the fifteen words minimum. They were only scrap bits from a 1973 banger but I seem to have written a series of chronicles. In the end I finally resorted to the free ads. Free to a good home – no, free to any home – but there were no takers.

In the end I took every unwanted part down to the dump. 'Excuse me sir,' says a bearded man with John Lennon glasses. 'You throwing that away?' Well, blow me, somebody wants it, I thought. 'You should have stuck an ad in the paper, mate,' he said.

***

September was now drawing to a close. The weather to the west looked grim and the blue tatty tarpaulin covering Chitty's chassis was about to take off. The Steptoe theme tune was ringing in my ears, now that the pallet garage was complete. Its only snag was that it was so narrow, it was either the car or me.

We all get that feeling of being watched, and this day was with good reason. A neighbour stood half behind his washing line in a feeble attempt at a disguise, and was clearly bemused by my actions.

I would paint the chassis red while holding a Corgi model Chitty Chitty Bang Bang out at arm's length, one eye shut like an artist with a pencil. It seemed perfectly normal to me to establish the correct size and proportions in this manner. I could visually mark off points as to where the bonnet would start and end, where the windscreen would sit, and how far back the boat tail should go.

Once I had finished a painting session, I would change persona by dressing in my business suit and disappearing off to Marks and Spencer and work.

Marks & Spencer is based in Newport, close to the local industrial estate and handy to specialist firms and engineering works. As I finished off my tie, I remembered the four sections of steel I had prepared for the bonnet frame. I had spent hours measuring, making templates and scouring photos. All I needed now was a local firm to run them through their industrial rollers, bending them round into a nice curve. I walked into a small workshop, rather hot under the collar after rushing over during my lunch break. Clutching bits of metal and wooden templates, standing in my M&S suit, I heard a voice say, 'So Nick, how can I help you?' How did he know my name? He repeated 'So Nick' as he pointed to my management name badge. 'Oh yes,' I said politely. 'Ah, well, I am building a replica of Chitty Chitty Bang Bang and I wondered if you could roll these for me.'

'Sorry, what do you want?' the completely bald man in overalls asked in an 'I'm very busy' tone of voice.

I walked away wishing I had never mentioned Chitty and my confidence in getting it done was waning.

I was late for work and feeling hot and sweaty from running. I passed a garage door which said 'Newport Steel'. On a whim, I popped my head around it and saw a huge bloke angle grinding. Among the cascade of glowing sparks, he caught sight of me from the corner of his eye, stopped what he was doing and with a friendly smile said, 'Yes, me ol' mate, what can I do for ya?' The whim paid off, this guy turned out to be a supplier of all things metal from aluminium to brass. He would cut to any size, so I took his card and thought of a pathetic excuse for being late back for work.

Chapter 4 **U**nskilled knicker seller

Upstairs, getting changed, Carolyn shouted out 'Why is there a load of breasts in your car?' I had asked the visual merchandising manager – window dresser to me and you – to save me some cardboard, and the selection I needed to make a rough bonnet came courtesy of lingerie

I had a few ideas in my head but that's all they were – ideas. I needed to pick a few brains, and with a sister married into the motor business, this is where I was going to start.

My sister Nina is a dizzy blonde. Anything logical, practical or mechanical is an alien concept to her. Fortunately, Nina is married to Billy who is a mechanic, but not any old mechanic Billy has his own business dealing in all things hot rod and American.

I had just spent the last couple of hours with him in the North American Motors & Co, workshop picking his brains on how does an unskilled knicker seller like me build a 1960s movie icon. You name it, he has done it. He has chopped the roofs off cars, swapped engines, dropped in V8s tinkered, tuned and repainted. If he didn't know how to build this icon, no one did.

'So Billy,' I said, 'how would I go about building a replica Chitty Chitty Bang Bang?'

All of a sudden, a trolley rolled out from under a 1940s Chevvy and he looked up at me. 'Crikey mate, don't ask me, I'm a mechanic, not a bloody genius,' he said..

***

Chitty was outgrowing the pallet garage. We had acquired numerous bits and bobs and it was becoming impossible to work on her. Although I couldn't justify spending too much on Chitty, I could get my head round a new garage. This was always going to be on the cards and by the next spring the 24 x 20 foot timber workshop was erected. Once relocated, the whole project started to take off and enthusiastically I rang a small firm for their assistance. So, with my four steel rods in hand, I was told that to roll four bits of thin steel, no longer than thirty inches, into a curve apparently takes about half an hour at the most. That was six months ago and I was still waiting. I had rung every month and they were still not done, so this time I was planning on being a little more assertive. 'Oh, hi, hello, um I was just wondering if the Chitty bits are done yet?'

The male on the other end of the phone replied frostily, 'Look, do you know just how busy we are?'

I replied, 'Well, you have had them for over six months and I am paying for the job to be done.' Clearly this conversation had come to an end and as the work hadn't been done, I then continued, 'Look, don't worry, I will come and collect them and get the job done elsewhere.'

***

The spring Beaulieu auto jumble was now the focus of our attention. Although all we had was a rolling chassis, now painted Hammerite red, it seemed fitting to try to gather up a few authentic bits and bobs. The theory being that if we managed to get brass headlights, a windscreen and old leather seats, we could start working these into the project. We compiled a list of period parts, with Lucas, 'King of the Road' gas lamps top priority. As this was our second trip, we now had a good idea where to go and what to look for and we were getting a feel for the prices and working out the traders from the rest.

The day started well with a great find: a genuine brass windscreen from an old MG. You could tell that this chap had been in the business for a long time as he looked a hard-nosed trader and wouldn't budge on his £250 price tag. Emotionally, we wanted it; financially, this was over twice the price we had paid for the whole car! I looked at Carolyn and said, 'Lets face it, we are not very committed, are we? So far, we have parted with a few hundred quid. We are either going for it or not.' We both knew sometime or another we had to bite the bullet. We had been talking a good deal but hadn't truly appreciated the likely cost of the project. Any realistic chance of delivering on such an outlandish scheme needed thousands thrown at it and here we were quibbling over the equivalent of a good night out and maybe the taxi home. Carolyn pulled out four crisp fifty-pound notes and three twenties. 'Oh well, nothing like an impulse buy to cheer me up, especially when it is at a rag-and-bone man sale!' she said. She handed over the notes, pocketed the change, picked up the windscreen and as she tucked it up under her arm she looked me in the eye with delighted glee at her purchase and walked off to the next stall.

The feeling that we were serious was now apparent. By 5 p.m., we had filled our old Mitsubishi with the windscreen, two side lights, a brass Spitfire model plane – no idea what that was for (but we liked it) – a collection of brass nautical steam gauges and a humongous fifty-litre, round, brass fuel tank which Carolyn had had immense fun bargaining for! Priced at £200, she managed to take it away for £50. I knew I had given her a day out for a reason!

***

Spring developed into summer and all we had achieved so far was to spend money. The four bits of steel that I needed rolled into a curve lay across the chassis, the cardboard for a template of the bonnet was still advertising Marks and Spencer's 'Truly You' underwear, and I still didn't have a clue where to start. So true to my fashion, I went off on a tangent and picked up the newly acquired brass tank and took it to a welding and fabrication company to repair its leak. And that was where it remained for three months, awaiting its half hour's job to start.

Chapter 5 **C**hitty Chitty bonkers

The one good thing about not actually starting building was that I had time to spare, and the good thing about that was being able to host a barbecue. A real old-fashioned English barbecue, where everyone spends as little as possible and brings along a pack of sausages or frozen burgers. After choking on the blackest char-grilled feeble excuse for a hot dog, the one no one else wanted, I decided to invite a few friends and colleagues into the garage. I really should have known better, this lot was a right bunch of mickey takers. On opening the doors, a strange conger effect took place as they all filed in one by one, singing 'Chitty Chitty Bang Bang, Chitty Chitty Bang Bang we love you.' Well, they certainly didn't have the vision that Carolyn and I had, that was clear, and not surprisingly they couldn't see the end result as they were looking at a Land Rover chassis with the odd bit of brass placed here and there. Most just humoured us by saying the things they thought we wanted to hear, but it was obvious they reasoned we had fallen out of cloud cuckoo land! If it had stopped there, it would have been fine. However, the next statement from Carolyn's sergeant changed the course of events permanently. Standing about six feet tall and previously in the Marines, he was a very serious-looking guy, with a small scar on his forehead and a very black-and-white attitude.

'You're 'aving a laugh, mate,' he said. 'Chitty Chitty Bang Bang, more like Chitty Chitty Bonkers! You won't build that thing with that, it's impossible.' I could see he was centre stage and although I was the host of this barbecue, this was an opportunity he couldn't miss. I don't suppose a garage full of WPCs helped. Feeling knocked back and a bit of a berk, I was determined to prove him wrong. 'You wait and see,' I said and at that he picked up a period Lucas horn and honked it two or three times. 'You're living on another planet, mate. It will never go, you won't get it through an MOT and all the other jazz.' 'Yes, I will,' I said defiantly. 'I will build Chitty Chitty Bang Bang and when it is done, we will drive it to Australia overland to prove it.' What had I just said? I was thinking on my feet and Australia seemed the furthest place away. Now he must think I am a complete idiot! 'Australia, you'll be lucky, you won't even get that thing off the flaming Isle of Wight,' he replied. I had been humiliated, put in my place and had all my dreams quashed in one foul swoop. I felt low but did my best not to show it. I closed the timber doors and paused for a moment then a different notion took hold: I'll show 'em.

When we decided to embark on a project revolving round a four-fendered friend, I never thought it would be easy, but strangely (and incredibly naively) I never imagined it would be hard either. Carolyn was still new in her role as a WPC, working all manner of shifts; we had two kids in high school full of demands and needs, and I was a floor manager for Marks and Spencer, writing freelance for Island Life, not to mention having just started a three-year HND graphic design course at the Isle of Wight College. Somewhere among all this, I planned to undertake a construction akin to me to building the Forth Bridge. Talk about monkeys on your back, I had a complete troop!

The sales had arrived at Marks & Spencer and it was all hands on deck. It can be a great time: it's busy, you never know what you're going to get next, and the days fly by. I was called to a customer service query on the till and the assistant said to me: 'This lady is bringing back these items of clothing. I have pointed out that they have been worn, the lady has no purchase receipts and they are over seven years old.' I turned to the customer and before I could say anything, she piped up, 'Listen young man, I am a shareholder and so was my husband who is now dead. His clothes aren't any good to me you know', and she pushed forward a couple of creased suits. On refusal, she told me to keep the things and banged down on the counter two brass lamp stands. 'And don't expect me to buy anything else from this shop,' she shouted as she turned towards the exit. Now, that was interesting: two brass lamp stands in the sale, reduced from £80 to £9 and I didn't even know we sold them. Tea could wait. I shot down to the sales floor and bought two – you never know, I thought.

On my way home from work, I pulled into the newsagent's to collect a copy of Land Rover Owner International. A friend had recommended that I read up and familiarise myself with one of Britain's finest. This was an alien world to me and all very agricultural. However, after reading a few editions I realised I was not alone, and the following for this type of vehicle would have done Elvis proud. Not only were there more variations than a karaoke version of 'I Will Survive', but also the list of modifications available was unbelievable. I stumbled over an ad for parabolic springs, guaranteeing a better ride on the road and better off-road performance. It caught my attention because the existing springs and shock absorbers were rusted solid. I had started to focus on getting the chassis up and running because, despite my efforts, not much was happening and I could pay a mechanic to do this. I telephoned a mobile mechanic called Richard Hipkiss – great bloke, ginger-haired, very handy, ever busy but always got time to talk. I outlined the details of swapping over the parts and was greeted with a long pause and then 'Ooooo, Ahhhh. Oh … Well … That's a horrible job, stuck up under a Land Rover,' he said. 'No it's not,' I said enthusiastically. 'It's only a chassis, all clean, painted red and in a nice clean, warm garage.' I tried to paint a glamorous picture and it worked, because he agreed to come over the following Wednesday. Well, if I had put money on him turning up, I would have lost. Wednesday came but the mechanic didn't. Disheartened, I stood in the newly erected garage, scanning the collection of potential Chitty bits and pieces, the brand new shocks and springs and reflected on what I had taken on. Why didn't anyone want anything to do with it? Why was it so hard to get people to help regardless of whether they were being paid or not?

Endless visits and telephone calls enquiring about the repair of the brass fuel tank had been in vain. I hadn't managed to track down anyone slightly interested in rolling my bonnet frame, the mechanic had failed to turn up, and I had made myself look a complete idiot by announcing I would drive down under through a load of countries I knew nothing about. Did I say, 'I don't think it will be hard?' As I had taken the day off, I needed to do something constructive, so I made a cup of tea and put the telly on. The lunchtime news twittered on about the Americans, George Bush and Iran. Completely uninterested, I switched the TV off and then turned it straight back on again. Where in the world was Iran? I had missed most of the report but I had the impression Iran wasn't a place to be in at present. I grabbed my 1920s atlas, courtesy of Great Auntie Lilly who had died twenty-five days before becoming 100, and flicked through the pages: no Iran to be found. On the global map, mostly highlighted in red reflecting the British Empire, I followed the countries through Europe, Persia, India and Asia all the way to Oz. Seemed pretty straightforward, but I couldn't find Iran or Pakistan, though – oh well, I thought, no need to worry then.

The following day Carolyn and I returned home from work, the kids were on sleepovers, and we spent hours bending each other's ear on how crap our respective jobs were. Surely there was more to life than this? All that work/life balance stuff, and the feeling that for someone approaching forty, any job was an inconvenience. We knew in reality that careers and mortgage payments were a good thing, but we just wanted to say it. I then had a great idea. I don't get many so I told Carolyn to savour the moment. We curled up on the settee to watch the first episode of the Long Way Round with Ewan McGregor and Charley Boorman. Two blokes on BMW motorbikes, travelling across Russia, fuelled our imagination. It just gave us the uplift we needed, and with that I rearranged an appointment with Richard the mechanic and shot off to B&Q to buy a welder.

Over the next couple of weeks, I drew hundreds of sketches taken from the paused DVD of Chitty Chitty Bang Bang, downloaded lots of movie stills, and created a file document that an overworked barrister would be proud of.

Despite two further planned dates for the overhaul of springs and shock absorbers, my mobile engineering friend was more elusive than the Scarlet Pimpernel. Finally, to a chorus of 'Hallelujah' singing in my ears, he turned up. Hooray, send out the welcoming committee; open a bottle of champagne; rip down the old sheet '21 Today Sharon' on Coppins Bridge roundabout, and replace it with 'Richard has finally turned up.' Ben was off school and at home with skivalitis and he had strict instructions to look after Richard with directions to the toilet and endless mugs of tea. Being a mechanic, he had been allocated the chipped and oily 'I'm a boob man' mug to make him feel at home.

Mid-morning my phone rang at work: it was Ben, and in an ever-so-sheepish quiet voice he said, 'Um, Dad, I …Um, by mistake I've um … locked the garage keys in the garage. The mechanic came round but we couldn't get into the garage so he's gone.' 'Oh ****' and a selection of choice words, I said under my breath. Unbelievable! You know when you get that subtle feeling that somebody's trying to tell you something? Well, I had it big time. However, it was short lived and the more obstacles that came my way, the more determined I became.

Building things was clearly a struggle; however, dismantling things was a breeze. I had started with Chitty's 'donor' vehicle, then stripped down a scrap Mitsubishi Gallant for steel, nuts, bolts, wiring looms, bulbs, fittings and electronic window motors; I had brutalised a Singer sewing machine and a bathroom cabinet and was now the proud owner of bits from an old piano. Not only was I becoming a complete anorak but also a collectomaniac! I couldn't walk past a skip without breaking into a cold sweat. So many times Carolyn would say, 'What's that bit for?' and I would reply, 'I don't know yet – I just want it.' Stig of the Dump had nothing on me! But this wasn't really progress – I was just kidding myself it was.

The winter rain came and stripping anything down outside was impossible. We retired to a Sunday lunch and an 'I know, let's watch my favourite film' from Carolyn.

The film itself is now very dated, but it is a romantic love story that captures Old England at its best. Caractacus Potts, the renovator of an old sports car, boldly proclaims his task in hand and disappears into the garage for a month of Sundays and gets on with it. I stopped watching the film and started thinking, 'He's right; he's just getting on with it. There is no point in waiting for others; I've got to do it myself.' And so I did. I stopped watching the film midway through, got up and looked at Carolyn and said, 'I'm just going outside – I may be some time.' It was the kick-start I – no, we – needed. If I waited for somebody to do it for me, I would wait for ever. I could learn what I needed to do; my best mate, Scott, was a welder in the aircraft industry and he could teach me, I convinced myself.

Chapter 6 **B**ubble gum welder

I took a week off work mid-summer and jumped right in; the more I did, the more I didn't want anyone else doing anything on Chitty and I became very possessive. The ginger-haired mechanic had become a thing of the past. I completed replacing the suspension myself, albeit it was pretty hard work, and he was right, it was a horrible job.

A chap called Graham Potter runs the Forge in Bonchurch and he gave me some great tips and even lent me a small set of portable rollers to form the four bits needed for the bonnet frame. It wasn't easy to start with – in fact, I messed the first few up and had to cut a new set, but trial and error paid off. I know there will be engineers out there who, if they could have seen me working, would have cringed at my efforts. It would have been like watching a toddler with a chain saw.

I have since decided that I hate welding! This particular morning, I was on a roll – the whole bonnet frame cut to size and in place and it just needed welding together.

Clad in overalls, leather gloves, bobble hat to keep the sparks off my ever decreasing thatch and a black mask that I couldn't see through, I started the seemingly never ending task. Breathing heavily, I struck the metal. You can't look without the shield as it is too bright, but it is too dark behind the pitch black screen so I ended up banging into bits of the car and welding parts that I didn't want too. Every time I started, the end of the wire managed to weld itself to the car and got stuck on. Frustration was an understatement and fumbling about in the dark, I hurled the mask across the garage, tried to pull off the welder, which came free quicker than I anticipated, made contact again and sparked into my eyes. Well, it wasn't too bad – I was lucky, but learnt quickly to be more careful.

Scott, my old welding mate, soon pointed me in the right direction and the frame took shape. He called it 'bubble gum welding', said it was strong enough but just looked like it had been chewed up and spat out. The more confident I became, the more danger I was in. I was halfway along a beautiful weld looking and feeling like a real pro when I could smell burning. It was me! I looked down to discover my overall trouser leg was on fire and working its way up to my groin. I leapt to my feet, shot into the garden and rolled around trying to put out the flames. This was definitely my summer of life-threatening activities. In addition to this incident, while trying to bend the gear lever in a steel vice designed for wood, the gear lever stuck fast but the vice snapped, sending a 3-inch chunk flying past my head as if it had been shot from an atomic accelerator. My fringe lifted but other wise I was okay. I kept telling myself to be careful. I made sure I put on leather gloves when angle grinding, but on one occasion the grinder slipped straight off the bench and into my hand. 'Oh dear,' I said (or words to that effect only with more colour). I dropped the grinder, gripped my hand intently with the other. The cutting disc had made contact with my palm, and knowing that it grinds like a knife through butter, my heart raced. I proceeded to open my hand, finger by finger, fearing the worst, but it was fine Boy, was I lucky.

Somehow I managed to build a complete frame around the engine, ready for aluminium body panels. One of our seven cats had settled down on the lingerie cardboard and this was what I needed to use next. Five hours later, I had cut out a complete section of bonnet made up of eight bits. I copied the shapes on to aluminium sheets and cut them out. Scott, my welding buddy, had instructed me on fixing aluminium to steel using special compounds, as they did in the aircraft industry, which I thought was apt for a flying car. He knew a chap at Sandown Airport working as part of a team restoring World War II Spitfires and suggested he could help mould the shape to fit the frame. I tiptoed into the hangar where the team was working. 'Excuse me, sir,' I said to a man buried deep in a fuselage, 'Is Al about?' It was him. I couldn't have asked for more attention. During his lunch break, he guided me through the rolling process and with his expertise we rolled a beautiful curve, matching the wooden templates, and the bonnet was born.

This was a psychological turning point. Chitty had a bonnet, the piano gave up its brass hinge to join the two main parts, and period latches and an M&S belt from the menswear department held it on firmly. Carolyn and I were so pleased with ourselves that we cracked open a bottle of fine wine to celebrate.

Chapter 7 **R**oyal appointment

'Were you serious about Australia?' Carolyn asked after watching the second episode of the Long Way Round. 'Well, yes,' I said. 'I've always fancied doing some sort of overland adventure, I just never imagined it could be in Chitty Chitty Bang Bang. Why, aren't you?' I asked, hoping for a mutually positive answer. 'I am sort of, but what about the kids and the cats?' she replied. 'They can come too,' I said enthusiastically, not really putting too much thought to it as usual. Then Carolyn said in her usual practical manner, 'Have you ever considered what is really involved? What about the mortgage, who is going to pay it? Who will look after my little babies (meaning the cats) – can I go a whole year without them? What about our jobs, how much will it cost, where will the money come from?' I was desperately searching for answers knowing I was way out of my depth and replied with my old favourite saying 'We could sell something!' How many times had I said that to Carolyn whenever we needed some cash? The fact was we had nothing left to sell. 'We could rent the house out to pay the mortgage – not sure how yet but we will find a way,' I continued.

Carolyn had raised a few serious questions and I really didn't have the answers, but the whole idea just seemed like such a great challenge and, besides, I had told people I was going to do it!

I now subscribed to various Land Rover magazines so that I wouldn't miss a copy, and each month without fail there was somebody going somewhere. I was taken in by the exploits of hardy travellers traversing one part of the globe or another and one thing which seemed common among them all was sponsorship logos. I started to wonder if I could do the same. All the vehicles were incredibly interesting and, for me, also very intimidating. They were the latest Range Rovers or Land Rover Defenders and were kitted out to the highest degree, including roof tents, jerrycans, jacks, winches, fitted water containers with enough to supply a small town, plus duel fuel tanks, etc. The lists were endless and expensive.

My boss – the store general manager – is a practical hands-on guy;

just getting the job done is his motto. No time for networking, bridge building and overdoing it on the PR front. Well, unfortunately for him and fortunately for me, that's just part of the role. He hates it, I love it, so when a charity lunch invitation arrived at the store addressed to the manager it came winging its way to me.

A select few business 'movers and shakers' were invited to attend a charity lunch hosted by Prince Edward – and I (or my manager) was on the list. I instantly rehearsed a verbal script on how I was so much behind charity work because I had done a bit, which was true – but what was it I had done? I recalled doing a charity swim at middle school – yes I know, a bit feeble. However, my grandest claim to charity fame was putting on a show at the Ventnor Winter Gardens in aid of the blind. We raised a few quid and then had to endure the rigours of cycling across a heat-sweltering, mosquito-infested Borneo.

Dressed in my best suit, I arrived promptly at Lugley's Restaurant, with the surrounding area cordoned off and a subtle police presence. The recently taken Chitty photo was carefully stored in my inside pocket just in case the situation arose …

As I twiddled with a canapé and nervously held my glass of sparkling white wine, I went over my lines. If all else failed, I could resort to the fact I served with Prince Andrew during the 1980s on HMS Brazen. I hoped they got on or I really would come unstuck! The catering bit was over and socialising was in full swing. Working his way around the room the Prince came over to talk to Robin Freeman from the Isle of Wight County Press and me. After the pleasantries and formal introductions we launched straight into a conversation about the media. The bloody media, I thought, this is meant to be about charity. I nodded appropriately, added the odd useless comment and smiled where necessary. Then, bingo, charity! He was talking about the contributions to the Save the Church charity fund. This was my chance to outline my potential charity – building Chitty and driving it overland to Australia for which influential sponsorship was the key.

'Well, its funny you should say that,' I said as I reached inside the breast pocket of my suit jacket. In my nervous haste, I caught my suit cuff button on the top of my wine glass, which was now filled with red wine. The glass sprung back and my wine, in slow motion, splattered my tie, shirt, groin and eventually pooled down by my foot. I quickly slide my foot over the spillage and looked up. 'Well, its been very nice talking to you both, keep up the good work, bye-bye,' Prince Edward said as he moved on to the next group.

Talk about missed opportunity, how unlucky was that? I was left feeling a complete idiot. Standing next to Mr Freeman from the local rag I launched into conversation with him. 'So Robin, the media ...' I said and once again reached for the photo of Chitty, thinking I had nothing to lose. I outlined what I had done so far and what I planned to do and this was received with enormous enthusiasm. He gave me his business card and said, 'When it is finished, give me a bell.'

I returned to work, now skipping along like a two-year-old. I was very pleased with myself and my thoughts turned straight to getting on with and finishing Chitty.

Clare Lallow's was well rated in the boat industry in Cowes. The boatyard housed all manner of timber from teak to iroko and everything from halliards to shackles and portholes   Three large sailing boats took centre stage on the ramps. The air was thick with sawdust. I had telephoned earlier to enquire if they had what I wanted – not that I knew what I wanted. After previous humiliations, I had my guard up. Under no circumstances was I going to mention Chitty Chitty Bang Bang! I tiptoed into the workshop over bags of sails and discarded bits of wood until I spied a shortish man about fifty years old bandsawing a long length of redwood timber surrounded in a thick reddish haze and being deafened by the sound of the blade. On completion of his task, he looked up at me and said 'Hello!' 'Hi,' I said, 'I'm looking for Laurie.' 'That's me,' he said, 'Laurie Boarer, how can I help?' Now this was the tricky bit –how was I going to describe what I wanted when I wasn't sure what I wanted or what to ask for and not tell him what I was actually doing! So I started off by saying that I wanted wood for a boat, which wasn't going to sea, but it had to look right and be totally weatherproof. I rambled on and on and I could see this poor chap was rapidly losing the will to live. 'So,' he said with humour in his voice, 'you're building a boat thing. Well, tell me exactly what it is for.' He genuinely wanted to help but couldn't make head or tail of my evasive descriptions. 'So,' he said again and repeated my pathetic explanation of what I was trying to achieve. Eventually, I reached into my pocket for my sketch of the boat tail's side and front views and dimensions. He looked at the drawing and repeated, 'What is it for?' 'Um well, er, if you must know and I expect you will die laughing but I am building a replica of Chitty Chitty Bang Bang,' I muttered sheepishly. 'Well, why didn't you say so,' he said in a reassuring and friendly way as if people built this type of thing on a daily basis. 'What you will need is this,' he went on, pointing to a pile of freshly sawn strips of iroko hardwood. He eventually compiled a list estimating all that was needed to do a proper job. Parting with £500 for what appeared to be a wheelbarrow full of bendy planks, a map, a large tin of 'It will stick anything to anything' glue and a box of brass screws didn't seem a fair swap to me but I was assured that was the price for wood grown in an environmentally friendly manner.

***

Carolyn and I woke to a truly dismal day. The sky was black and rain was lashing the windows. Christmas had come and gone and the New Year was unseasonably mild but extremely wet. Vanessa, a good friend from work, had taken great interest in our project and asked if she could bring her family over for a look. This included her brother Liam, his wife Dawn and their daughter Whitney on holiday from Australia. .

Liam had taken the opportunity to source a few British car parts for his Lotus Seven replica project back home in Perth and he was intrigued to see what I was up to in the garage. Looking at me intently through his square-rimmed extra-thick glasses, he said, 'You know you couldn't get away with this in Oz. Oh, it's a nightmare, especially in Western Australia. Everything you do on a modified car has to be checked, passed and certified.' By the time he had finished, I was extremely concerned that Chitty would never be allowed on the roads. It was going to be hard enough here let alone down under.

We all scurried across the lawn to the garage, coats held over our heads sheltering from the downpour. Liam's wife Dawn, a doctor of psychology, was a lovely lady who asked so many questions and showed such a great interest I couldn't help feeling I was being analysed. After all, here I was, a grown man building something from a kid's film and telling everybody I was planning to drive 12,000 miles across the world in a car which had wings on it.

Liam's engineering eye scanned the car's detail. He was very complimentary as his hand ran along the bonnet. Then he said, pointing to the bonnet mascot, 'They wouldn't allow this.'. 'Or this,' he said as he walked past the brass sidelight protruding from the body. He sent a wave of fear through me as he explained all cars coming into Australia had to go over the pits – this turned out to be an MOT test which was very strict and made no allowances for modified vehicles. Would we ever get in? I thought, a huge seed of doubt having been sown in me.

Chapter 8 **W**hat do you do for a living?

Chitty was slowly but surely taking shape. The old Land Rover chassis was covered with a shiny red coat of paint; a completed full-length aluminium bonnet and a brass radiator grille joined the new shock absorbers and leaf springs. The old MG windscreen sat nicely upon the bonnet, its steel frame firmly fixed in place ready for the timber boat tail. We wrestled for weeks bending timber and fixing in place the slats to form the boat tail. For some strange reason, I dimly thought bending wood around the front of a boat required planks all the same width! I soon learnt that geometry and trigonometry had a meaning in life. God, if at aged twelve I'd known I was going to dabble in pointy bits on a clinker boat, I would have stopped sticking my chewing gum to the underside of the desk and daydreaming out of the window thinking about the nimble lady who flies like a bird as the song goes. Slide rulers, protractors and Pythagoras may as well have been a group of Jurassic dinosaurs as far as I was concerned but here I was trying to work out why one end of the plank needed to be wider that the other and cutting out strips of cardboard seemed the easy option. Maths might have been a bit of an oversight but watching John Noakes on Blue Peter back in the seventies certainly prepared me well for the scissors, cardboard and sticky back plastic.

***

People watching has always been a favourite pastime and now I had added a new dimension: watching people's reaction to our project. Some were incredibly enthusiastic. Of course, others were determined non-believers. However, the ones who intrigued me the most were the unaware bunch

Crouched on the floor, I was forging together various bits of brass using the bases from the lamp stands from Marks and Spencer, together with the original Land Rover glass lights, to make what looked like a set of period-style gas headlamps. Just to my right I was aware of movement. A well-chewed solid rubber ball, covered with congealed dog slobber and freshly cut grass, rolled to a stop near me. A shadow followed and then a voice said, 'Oh, hello, sorry about that.' It was our neighbour who had come to retrieve the dog's toy. I leapt to my feet, full of enthusiasm and prepared to share our well-kept engineering secret with her. 'I bet you are wondering what we've been doing in here?,' I said keenly. 'We are building a replica Chitty Chitty Bang Bang and its nearly finished.' Well, by the look on her face she obviously had never wondered what we were doing in the garage. Chitty took pride of place. Most of the shiny bits were now very shiny; it was imposing, big and with presence – well, I thought so anyway. Pauline scanned the floor, grabbed the ball and said, 'Oh, if it comes over again, just lob it back.'

***

The weekend rushed by as they normally do and I was in work sipping coffee at the Monday morning meeting. The store manager had just disappeared to photocopy something so it was now a conversational free for all. Vanessa looked at me, grabbed my arm and said, 'Guess what.' 'What?' I said. Vic, her husband, who was a gas fitter, had just paid a visit to Coleman's Heating Engineers, she explained, and there, as large as life in the boss's office, was a huge collection of Chitty Chitty Bang Bang memorabilia. Vic only noticed it because he knew what we were up to. John Coleman was the boss and smiled reluctantly when Vic posed the question, 'So does this lot belong to your kids?' knowing full well that John had two teenage daughters. 'Ah, well, no, not really, it is mine,' John replied. Vic said, 'You ain't gonna believe this but I've got a mate who is building the actual car.' Before the manager interrupted us with a handout, Vanessa had told me that John Coleman was a really nice guy, a very clever engineer with a great business. His film collection was top notch and he spent hours on eBay sourcing the rarest finds. He had looked disbelievingly at Vic when he had told him about our Chitty and was incredibly keen to come over and see for himself.

The store manager, totally oblivious to our conversation earlier, listed the key priority for the day. During setting targets and revising sales estimates for ladies' wear I always said as a light-hearted joke that bras had been supported this week so were up and pointing in the right direction and as usual pants were down! It was usually wasted on an eager bunch, so concerned about what they were going to say that they had heard nothing! By the time we had all reluctantly agreed to totally unachievable sales targets for the week, Vanessa had arranged for Vic to introduce John to our version of the fantasmagorical four-fendered collection of wayward parts and we had agreed to meet.

We were feeding the cats and trying to remove a tick from one cat's head and I was explaining to Carolyn in the greenhouse about John and his collection, when we heard the driveway growling as a silver Mazda MX5 pulled up. Vic and John got out of the car. 'They are here,' I shouted. My heart was racing and I was so nervous of this man who was a qualified engineer with years of experience, who just happened to be a Chitty fan. What would he think about my feeble effort?. I would be a laughing stock again. I wished I had never agreed to this meeting.

Carolyn, on the other hand, was so keen to share memorabilia stories, she couldn't wait. She invited them in for a cup of tea and was already pointing out items of her collection. This was a bit of a blessing and it took the attention off my concerns but I could see John was itching to find what lay behind the garage doors. He was a big bloke – a rugby player at weekends – and softly spoken with a genuine look of interest, saying all the right things in the right places. After the formal introductions, I knew that even if Chitty didn't meet his expectations, I would never know. I started to relax and posed a few questions on his engineering credentials. The moment had come. I escorted him to the garage and asked him to wait while I went in to unlock the main doors, hoping to give a full impact view. As they swung open, there was a pause, not a word and John stood and looked. He walked in slowly and stopped. 'God, what's he thinking?' I said to myself. 'He is looking at the detail, I've got something wrong – I knew the horn was too short.' John still said nothing.

Arms folded with one hand up massaging his chin, he slowly walked around the car, pausing to reflect on one aspect or another. I was sure I was being humoured but after two or three minutes that felt like a lifetime he turned to me and said, 'What did you say you did for a living?' 'Oh, um, I run ladies' wear and lingerie for Marks and Spencer,' I said.

There was another long pause and then John took a step back with the car in full view and said, 'You know, I have spent the last ten years thinking about building Chitty Chitty Bang Bang but as an engineer I thought it was logistically too hard. I could foresee all the problems and yet you have done it. I am amazed!' Well I'll be blowed, I had been so concerned and now I felt so proud. John went on, 'The fact that you are not an engineer is why you have done it. You probably didn't see the problems.'

John looked at the car again and noticed we hadn't put the decorative exhaust on yet. 'Have you got the exhaust system sorted?' he asked. 'No, not yet, it is on the list,' I replied. John crouched down looking at the relevant area. 'Can I make it for you?' he asked with enthusiasm. 'It would be a privilege to build a part for the car,' he said. Well, what a day it had been. We received the thumbs up, an offer of help with the exhaust to be made from plumbing copper and found a new friend who had a mutual interest in all things Chitty! Before John left, he gave me a few tips and remarked on how he had been incredibly sceptical when Vic had told him about our project. He said that he had been honestly expecting a cardboard carnival float and now he was going home full of enthusiasm knowing he wasn't the only sad, misguided old fool.

Chapter 9 **R**adio wind-up

Although I had actively tried to enrol media attention for a charity drive by hobnobbing with Prince Edward and the hierarchy at the local press, I wasn't quite ready for it yet. Like all things, keeping a secret is pretty hard and it wasn't long before the Isle of Wight County Press was knocking at our door. Chitty was up and running but she still needed seats, a coat of black paint, four spoke wheels and a set of wings, let alone approval for the modifications through the DVLA and most importantly – an MOT.

We both took the day off from work and were greeted by a young blonde girl doing the story and a photographer. Both of us felt slightly reluctant, as Chitty still wasn't complete, but considered that a small introduction to publicity must be good. We were a little embarrassed by the whole escapade and standing on the front bumper for a photo, not to mention me sitting in the driving seat waving like a lemon with Carolyn sprawled across the bonnet like Miss Glamour Puss in a 1970s muscle car mag.

Friday morning came and the paper was out before work. We each picked up three copies and sent text messages to all and sundry. By the time tea break had passed, a surprising influx of attention came our way.

Carolyn had been driving the police patrol car when her mobile rang. The person on the end of the phone was Alex Dyke from Isle of Wight Radio! He clearly had us in his sights from the front-page feature in the local paper and the caption declaring 'Husband builds wife dream car!' Alex – well known across the island for being extremely controversial – had begged Carolyn to be live on the phone-in at twelve noon that day. She had to shoot back to the nick, get permission from the duty inspector for time out to go on the phone-in and she duly obliged Alex for the next hour. A member of staff had just approached me saying that she had just heard that Carolyn was going to be on the phone-in and with that my mobile rang and it was Carolyn to explain the situation. I rang Isle of Wight Radio, they already had Carolyn on air and Alex talked to the pair of us explaining that he wanted to play devil's advocate and rip the mickey out of us and would we be prepared to go along with it? Well, it all sounded like a good laugh to us so we agreed as any publicity had to be good.

On reflection, the interview was quite demanding and certainly belittled us, and as much as we knew it was a game, it still hurt and we both had to think on our feet. Alex opened the show with a broadside, explaining to the listeners the article in the paper and posing a few direct questions and statements. 'Listeners, here we have a grown man who has built a life-sized kid's toy for his wife. Let's face it, it seems pretty sad to me, a bloke spending all that money and four years for his wife's dream car – and let's face it, it looks more like the dog's breakfast than the dog's dangly. As far as I am concerned,' he continued, 'it still looks like an old Land Rover – look at the wheels, they are not Chitty Chitty Bang Bang wheels, they look like they have come off an old tractor. Come on Nick, isn't this just a total embarrassment?' he asked me. I nervously stumbled over my lines and laughed in replacement of a good answer. I knew it was a wind-up but it was still so hard to hear. Carolyn gave as good as she got and fuelled the debate by reiterating her fascination and obsession with the movie and telling the listeners that she had even gone so far as to name both her children Jeremy and Jemima and that we also had an Old English Sheepdog which we called Edison. Alex didn't know if she was joking or not but she came across as very convincing! He then crafted some pretty engaging questions and you had to be a saint not to bite. 'So, that rough old bit of wood stuck on the back, that looks like an old shed from B&Q, is that what it's supposed to be?' he went on. I was warming up now and started to focus on the charity aspect. 'Well, that's all good stuff,' Alex said, 'but how disappointed your wife must be if that's all you can do. At the least you could have done things properly after saying you were going to build her the dream car it is supposed to be.'

I put the phone down and walked away slightly shell-shocked but also sort of grateful for being worthy of a news story – I think! Was Alex Dyke just winding us up to make a good listening story or had he got a point? Well, it's not even finished yet I kept telling myself. The new wheels we had seen, which were next on the list, would have to be imported from Italy and that would take time. Then we had to spray them red before fitting them.

All of a sudden Carolyn and I had been thrust into a degree of local limelight. I was the talk of the M&S catering unit and Carolyn was being ribbed by the Hampshire Constabulary. Debates were raging about the conduct of the radio station presenter and we were both riding a short but fun wave of local glory.

We settled down to a glass of Hardy's Australian vino and talked about what an experience the day had been. Carolyn grabbed the phone off the wall and listened to the messages of the day. Normally, we would sit and listen to some crap about credit cards, window salesmen or phone offers. However, today, there were ten messages – yes ten – all from news agencies and freelance journalists. Hey, this was novel! How did they get our number as we were ex-directory? The name of the game was that these guys sell local stories to the national press – not that this meant there was anything in it for us as there wasn't – however there were a few shallow promises of possibly a few quid towards our charities.

As green as hell, we agreed to do a national story with the Solent News Agency. It wasn't because they came with offers of fame and fortune but because they were local and the chap handling the story was great. Chris Balcombe introduced himself by explaining his passion for TV and film-related genre as he himself was a proud owner of a 'Dr Who' Dalek and so that subject soon broke the ice! I wrongly had the assumption that only sad lonely men aged over forty and still living at home with their mothers kept or made things like Daleks – a world behind closed doors where grown men exchange rare top trump cards, dress up in storm trooper outfits for an annual Star Wars gathering and swap early editions of the Beano. I had been enlightened. Besides, who was I to talk? Chris wanted to know the ins and outs of everything. He wanted to do the photography but insisted on waiting until Chitty was finished and complete with wings.

The seventh of April 2007 was going to be the grand launch day for Chitty. Carolyn had spent hours on the internet teaching herself how to upholster chesterfield seats. She had tracked down a guy who supplied beautiful red leather at a price and she had managed a pretty damn good job at making them, not to mention her hard work at perfecting the twenty coats of varnish on the timber boat and strengthening the inside with layers of fibre glass.

We had e-mailed hundreds of car wheel suppliers with a photo of Chitty requesting an appropriate alloy which would look the part and fit on an old Land Rover – slim chance but worth a go. Ever since Alex Dyke had raised the issue of tractor wheels on the radio phone-in, it seemed this was everybody's talking point. 'So, what about the wheels, have you found any spoke wheels yet?' was the common question. To be fair it was not the best photo of Chitty in the local press. Nobody except the elite few had seen the car in the flesh so an Isle of Wight County Press photo of a half-finished project was filling endless doubts.

Over the months and years, on a few occasions I was ready to throw it all in at the stick we endured. The mickey was taken on a regular basis and keeping motivated was the hardest task of all. However, a deep determination was setting in and I really wanted to prove something and the launch party was our chance to do just that. As usual, I had grander ideas for the event than we could afford but, more importantly, Chitty had one huge stumbling block. I had spent hours of deliberation wondering whether I should inform the Department of Transport and DVLA about the modification to the old Landy. The problem was this: if they didn't know, it would be taxed and tested as the original car. They would be none the wiser. However, in the event of a crash the vehicle would not as be described and the insurance would be invalid for not disclosing notifiable changes to the vehicle I was really doing my best to avoid contact with the DVLA as this would involve a vehicle inspection and it ran the risk of failing because of safety, e.g. my crap welding, sticky out bits, sharp edges and the Spitfire mascot on the bonnet. It could all be over so easily and then the fat lady wouldn't be singing after all.

Weighing up all the pros and cons and knowing in my heart of hearts it was the right thing to do, I informed the DVLA by a phone call, followed by a letter and photographs, and we were to be blessed with a visit on the Wednesday prior to the launch party.

Worry is a cause of stress and stress makes your hair fall out and if I lost any more hair my black ribboned bowler hat planned for dancing 'Me Ol' Bamboo' at the party wouldn't stay on my head. I talked it over and over with Carolyn and she shared my concerns. It was a Sunday night, the kitchen was piled high with outfits, props, paper cups, plates, napkins, plastic champagne flutes, bottles of booze, nibbles – you name it, it was in there. The back door was blocked with awnings, pagodas and a plastic marquee, all on loan from various in-laws and friends. Chequered flags and bunting lay dormant on the stack of garden chairs ready to go up and everywhere you looked was a clear sign of the effort we were putting into the grand day. A grand day which solely depended on the inspection officer from the DVLA.

Over the last month, six of us, including four friends from work, had been trying to master the dance routine to 'Me Ol' Bamboo', with trying being the operative word! Fortunately, two girls from Marks and Spencer were dancers but the rest of us looked like a bunch of intoxicated Morris Dancers with blisters on both feet and a pack of rabid ferrets down our trousers. We had raised a few expectations and enrolled a mate to dress up as Grandpa Potts and for him to sing the POSH (Port Out Starboard Home) song. He was planned in just before my theatrical brother Stuart and his kids took the parts of Jeremy and Jemima and the Child Catcher. The stage was completed out of a collection of old pallets and once built left just enough room for Chitty to make the grand entrance into the garden from the garage, and also left sufficient space for the vehicle inspector to get in.

Taking yet another day's holiday from work, I waited in for the visit from the DVLA. Carolyn was on her normal rest days from shift and was getting incredibly wound up at the incompetence of the computer. She was bidding on eBay for a very rare Chitty toy model. John Coleman had one and had explained to her why they were so unique. Unlike the original common Corgi 266 model this one was made by Mattel and came complete with an inflatable boat bit, I was enthusiastically informed. 'And it floats,' she hastened to add when my eyebrows raised at a plastic toy measuring six inches being auctioned for a minimum of £200! Somehow, my focus was not on toy cars and eBay but was on the toy in the garage that had taken four years to build so far. We were all four years older, the kids had gone from being kids into almost young adults and we were still not sure if our own Chitty would make it on the road. The whole process was becoming an emotional roller coaster. We had seven cats and a rabbit when we started this project, now we only had four and no rabbit. We had been laughed at, certified, injured, praised and humbled and forged a relationship akin to a family member. We had gambled our reputation, status and characters and our ability to do it. We had set a huge expectation on ourselves and to all who came our way and now we had to make good on our promise. A promise, which for most people was going to be an MFI chipboard country-fete show car, capable of making it to Australia – over the rainbow that, is!

Carolyn slammed her hand down on the computer desk and shouted out, 'Hell, I've been outbid and lost it again to that same sod that's always bidding against me.' I could tell she was pretty hacked off, as she didn't even log off the computer – just pulled the plug out which I hate. 'He must be a right rich git with nothing better to do than to sit on eBay all day long bidding against me,' she said bitterly between her teeth. The eBay guy (or girl) alias 'eb-horse' always seemed to have more ready cash for these items and it frustrated Carolyn no end. On a tight budget with any amount of money going into Chitty, eBay buying was taboo.

The garage was spotless and I had laid out the original Land Rover document and a series of photos of before and after. If the guy could see the entire engine and chassis numbers and was happy with the conversion, we were on to a winner. If not, he would recommend we take a Single Vehicle Approved (SVA) test, and basically then it would be all over. The SVA is a rigid test, which complies with the latest European car safety standards, and I wanted that as much as I wanted to fly long haul sat next to a red-nosed, fever-ridden, airsick, first-time flyer. Throw in a screaming new born who needs a nappy change and you realise the SVA is not a welcome option. I had so much riding on this that I didn't know whether to be over the top and chatty or just to leave him to it. The local press had informed the entire population of the Isle of Wight and for anyone who had missed the fact that some nut had built a Chitty car and made outlandish claims of an overland expedition then Alex Dyke had filled them in on air. Leaping around like a three-year-old needing the toilet, I opened the front door to a mature guy with glasses and a floppy 'Bill and Ben' hat. 'Mr Pointing?' he asked in a bland sort of way. 'I believe you have modified a Land Rover, TGK 681M,' he outlined as he looked down at his clipboard. The rapport was going to be hard and very noncommittal. However, he had a job to do and we had a test to pass. I took him towards the garage and swung open the large timber double doors. Instantly, his demeanour changed. 'Well I never!' he exclaimed. 'I didn't realise I was coming to see Chitty Chitty Bang Bang. I have seen some things in my time but never one like this,' he said in a much warmer manner. 'You don't want this to go through an SVA do you,' he continued with a wry smile on his face. He asked to see all the documents, cross-referencing them with engine and chassis. 'Oh dear,' he said. Oh hell, I thought, what is it? 'You haven't got a chassis number where you should have,' he said pointing out on the front frame. 'Oh dear, oh big dog's doggy doo doo,' I said under my breath. Nobody had told me about this; I thought the riveted description plate on the body was enough. I had no idea it was stamped on the frame too. My optimism was ebbing away; I paused, stood up and just didn't know what to say. 'Well look, I can see it is all in order, you have done a great job. All I can do is submit a positive recommendation to my superiors as the final decision is not up to me,' he said. God, who was it up to then? I thought. He turned out to be a really nice bloke who could see all our efforts but how could he leave me hanging on like this? He said we would know if the car logbook was returned, otherwise there would be a referral for an SVA test. This was worse than being a father of five daughters, praying for a boy in the maternity ward.

Chapter 10 **W**orth the wait

It was now in the lap of the gods but the show had to go on! The seventh of April opened with the stillest of air and cloudless sky. It was totally unbelievable and almost too perfect for words. By 12.30 p.m. over 200 guests filtered into the garden after a successful park and ride scheme which Carolyn had organised courtesy of Lake Taxis and the kind loan of a field at the bottom of the lane belonging to Thompson's Garden Centre. Police signs at the end of our lane had been put in place and every possible in-law, out-law, friend and family member had been enrolled to manage traffic, make tea, pour champagne and usher guests. This was turning into a grand affair and I was increasingly concerned that I had been raising expectations too much. Like most good parties, there is always a gate crasher and we had our fair share because of Isle of Wight Radio turning their personal invitation into a well-aired free for all.

Despite our nightly rehearsals, at the eleventh hour we were one man down and our son Ben boldly donned a bowler hat and quickly learnt a few moves (the ones which had taken us a month to master) and he gave his best shot at the dance routine, no one any the wiser he was an enthusiastic last-minute replacement. The same absconder was also due to dress up as Grandpa and sing POSH so good old brother-in-law karaoke king Steve, who was dressed up to play the part of Master of Ceremonies, stepped into the frame and enlightened us with his version of the song – mainly because he was unsure of the words he made it up as he went along and it was hilarious!

Everybody had been fed and watered and I took to the stage and nervously rambled on. Carolyn held my hand, looking up with a sense of pride. With the rest of the cast, a few songs were sung, 'Me Ol' Bamboo' was danced and the living daylights scared out of anyone under five with the remarkably authentic sibling Child Catcher. The time had come, my sister's kids, dressed in fluorescent ground crew jackets courtesy of Bembridge Airfield and holding table tennis bats, prepared to taxi us out of the garage-cum-hangar to an explosion of fire crackers. We had set the scene well and built up the anticipation by being suitably dressed in period attire, Carolyn in her slightly adapted wedding dress, large brimmed hat with pink satin scarf tying it down, and me in my granddad collar shirt, waistcoat and jacket. I honked Chitty's large snake's head horn and started the engine to the cue of the theme tune music to the film blasting out across the garden via the hired PA system. As the doors flew open, the fire crackers ignited and showers of confetti were exploded into the air. The atmosphere was electric and I squeezed Carolyn's hand as a tidal wave of emotion engulfed us both, only to be rewarded by a huge intake of breath and aaaahs of surprised appreciation from the onlooking crowd.

We gently rolled out of the garage to faces of genuine amazement and almost disbelief. The 'Aaaah' vocal surprise gave way to a rapturous round of applause. The hair on the back of my neck stood straight up and tingled as a huge sense of pride and satisfaction overwhelmed us both. The sense of vindication was enormous; yes, who's laughing now I thought. Both Carolyn and I had tears of emotion welling up. There were only a few moments in life that equalled this – be it marriage or the birth of your child – and today was in that league. It was one of the best days of our lives.

The wings were open and set in place and the new alloy spoke wheels sprayed Ferrari red looked the business. Carolyn's summer hat complete with pink satin scarf reflected the light beautifully and contrasted well with my nephew and niece who were sat in the rear seats in the role of Jeremy and Jemima, both holding brightly coloured huge lollipops and candy sticks. Through word of mouth the local Island Life magazine photographer and editor turned up, along with the island's Solent TV film crew. They brought a sense of occasion with them and gave order and structure to the day In an unplanned moment, my brother-in-law Steve – a qualified aircraft inspector – pulled out a fictitious airworthy certificate signed and stamped for Chitty and presented it grandly to us. He congratulated us on our achievement and explained our 'uncertain and, in particular, our no-idea-what-to-do-plans' for driving to Australia. He made a point of saying we were raising money for the local hospice, MS Society and the World Wildlife Fund and, for those who were interested, a donation would be gratefully received on the way out. What a bloody good idea I thought, it hadn't crossed my mind.

Once the confetti bomb dust had settled, literally, and the party was over, we were tinged with a bit of sadness. All the food was eaten, paper cups littered the garden and a shiny example of four years' hard work sat roped off alone among a minefield of streamers, bunting and exploded party poppers. A gentle breeze blew scone-crumbed napkins across the lawn and I reflected on the day and the challenge we had ahead of us. Today's crowd had been clearly expecting a lot less, but now the day had almost passed, they were expecting a lot more. They were fostering the notion we might actually make good on our promise and drive to the land of the didgeridoo! However, a wall of blind fear was now upon us and I sat on the running board, posing many questions to myself. Will Chitty ever get approval from the DVLA ? God, will it pass an MOT? Never mind the mechanics, what about the engine, I have only ever driven it five miles from St Helens to home and that was four years ago! Can I really drive a 35-year-old Land Rover 15,000 miles through countries I haven't got a clue about in a vehicle that has no roof, no doors and no security for God's sake? The task ahead was enormous. 'Time for another cup of sobering tea,' I said to Carolyn.

Chapter 11 **M**edia mayhem

Carolyn made a polite telephone call to the Solent News Agency and explained to Chris Balcombe that the wings were finished and ready for a photo shoot.

Chris was a tall, handsome man (Carolyn's summing up) with short, dark brown hair and was dressed in a formal suit and clad in camera bags. Chris had an instant rapport with us and really didn't match the image I had of a sad old man with a dalek! His excitement at seeing Chitty was getting the better of him. It didn't help when Carolyn made tea and shared her collection of film memorabilia with him.

I opened the garage doors in my usual 'let's get the full impact' style and Chris lifted his camera and said 'Wow!' He was on a mission, maintaining a flavour of professionalism, but underneath I could see he was like a cat with two tails! Chitty was poised with wings abreast and looked fab. Chris turned to Carolyn and said, 'Right, have you got something white to wear?' Off she duly went and returned, beautifully dressed in her wedding attire, looking most apt as the style of dress was like that of Truly Scrumptious's! Chris then swivelled on his heels to look at me. 'Off you go then, your turn,' he said. I pulled out my brown corduroy jacket, donned a stripy, grandpa collar-style shirt and found an old maroon waistcoat. 'Perfect,' he said as I made my way across the lawn towards him and the array of camera equipment. How sad I thought, these were all my own clothes and ones that I still wore!

***

Monday morning blues were lightened as Carolyn had been put directly through, which was normally taboo. 'Its here, its here,' she said, hardly managing to contain herself. 'Chitty has passed, she has passed her test, what a clever girl,' she continued. 'What is here, what has she passed?' I said, questioning her as the mad tone increased in her voice. 'The DVLA have passed her, the log book is back and she is now classed as a brown and silver Land Rover tourer!' she said. I told her that at that precise moment

I was a little busy and that I would ring her at lunchtime. However, I was ecstatic with the news, Chitty was legal and all she now needed was her MOT. I couldn't wait so rang Niton Undercliff Garage and booked Chitty in for her once-over, which seemed far more important to me than scrutinising sales and justifying the benefits of seam-free pants.

For a week, I worked on Chitty until midnight and one night I managed to stay in the garage until 3 a.m. completing her braking system. The garage was a cold lonely place at that time of the night but I was determined to pass first time. Driving Chitty to Niton was her first day out on the roads and I was so worried that I asked my brother Tad to follow me. En route near Whitwell, Carolyn alerted me to a strange grinding sort of noise and was leaning out of the side trying to determine where it was coming from. The noise then turned into a loud knocking sound coming from the rear and I eventually pulled over into someone's drive, devastated that we hadn't even made it the ten miles to Niton. I tried to explain the noise to my brother and was sure it was a major fault. How am I ever going to save face claiming to be able drive across the world and I can't even get the car a short distance across the Isle of Wight. Meantime, Tad had given Chitty a quick once-over and then started to laugh uncontrollably. 'You silly sod,' he said, 'You haven't done the rear near-side wheel nuts up.' I looked down to see that the rear wheel was leaning out with five nuts only just on. In my MOT haste, I forgot to do them up! What a plonker I thought and started to laugh too.

The Isle of Wight County Press followed the story outlining our progress but nothing prepared us for the media onslaught once we hit the nationals. Chris Balcombe had crafted a great story along the lines of 'Husband makes wife's dream come true ...', an eccentric love story with great supporting photos. We rushed out and bought several copies of the Daily Telegraph, Daily Express and Daily Mail and savoured our fifteen minutes of fame. The Telegraph had photos of Carolyn in her police uniform together with an article entitled 'Built on a Wing and a Prayer'. How true that was. . They also outlined all the bits used to make the car including a singer sewing machine and a bathroom cabinet. It was so intriguing to read about yourself Well I never, I thought as I read on through the newspapers, I was now younger and had changed my career to a police officer! Chitty had foldaway aluminium wings instead of wood and it was capable of reaching speeds of up to 100 mph! They were hopeful! All the articles were fantastic and it really tickled us with their flexible stories. Then the phone started ringing. In fact, the day we hit the press, it rang approximately every fifteen minutes. It was unbelievable. Such a wake-up call. Again, how did they get our home telephone number, we were ex-directory, or supposed to be! How on earth did they get hold of Carolyn's mobile numbers and mine? All of a sudden our identity, our security was exposed. We felt vulnerable We were experiencing an extremely small taste of the paparazzi. Luckily for us this was just for one day and our story was great. Having said that, everybody who crossed our path was kind, courteous and very helpful. Offers of magazine articles and contracts filled the day. Photographers requested historical images from our pasts and signatures were required for done deals. All was laid bare: our identity, past history, future plans, location and personal details were entrusted to the media and we were left with a sense of bewilderment. To be the focus of so much attention was exciting and scary. Our inbox of e-mails filled with requests for shows, fetes and carnivals, not to mention hiring out for weddings! An invitation to take part in the Lily Savage Show on TV was in the bag. It was all very humbling. By lunchtime, the TV crews from the BBC and ITV had turned up and Carolyn and I were frolicking around the garden back in period costume and performing like a couple of circus horses.

The day ended like no other. Surrounded by newspaper cuttings we set the DVD and settled down to another fifteen minutes of fame, watching ourselves on Newsround and the regional news..

The evening news opened with the capture of a group of Royal Navy sailors by the Iranian military. There it was again, Iran in the news; I really must find out where this country is I inwardly thought to myself. Anyway, the phone rang, 'I've just seen you on telly!' my sister said without taking a breath. 'I know, I will be signing autographs later,' I joked. She informed me of the e-mail she had just sent with a link to news items containing us. With the TV news over, we booted up the computer only to find online newspaper reports from all over the world of our story; we managed the USA, China, Pakistan, India, Japan and

Australia. Unbelievable! Yet another startling reminder of the media machine. There was also a message that raised concerns, serious concerns – a nerve-tingling shockwave resonated through me. The e-mail said, 'I have just read the article of the Chitty Chitty Bang Bang car constructed by yourselves please call me on —.'. Why was I so concerned? It was from the Mayflower Theatre in Southampton, which was due to present the stage show this summer. I called Carolyn over and explained the issues with copyright. 'It's a brand,' I said, 'you can't just go around exploiting someone's brand.' I was flapping around like a scene from Alfred Hitchcock's The Birds, metaphorical feathers were everywhere.

Carolyn looked completely unfazed and said, 'Stop flapping, they probably want to use us for promos or something.' 'Oh get real, they are backed by MGM. They're not going to be interested in us. And besides, look at this e-mail from Susie Picton.' Susie Picton had a point, a good scary point. She was the wife of Peter Picton, the owner of the original car. Chitty Chitty Bang Bang had been in his care for forty years and had established a pretty good business from weddings to fetes. Susie didn't mince her words. 'I hope you have got permission to build your car from MGM. They take these things very seriously and can result in a law suit,' her e-mail read. It was another hurdle. If the Mayflower Theatre has an issue, maybe I could tell them it is not an exact copy. Perhaps Susie rang them and complained, maybe she rang MGM – oh, and maybe I am just overreacting. Susie mentioned a law suit – maybe I am not overreacting!

We had a great day, a true boat full of emotion. It seemed we had come so far, overcome so many obstacles and had been rewarded with an exciting media circus. The 'Picton' e-mail certainly took the wind out of our sails but we would cross that bridge another day. The mid-week hysteria gave way to a somewhat bland and empty weekend. We were yesterday's news and our smug little faces were only fit to wrap up cod and chips, with a pickled egg thrown in for good luck. We had been dropped like a school bag on a Friday afternoon.

Then the phone rang. It was Carolyn's mother who was on holiday somewhere the other side of the world, totally oblivious to the fact that her daughter was surrounded by fame (but not yet fortune – maybe that would come!). 'I am just sitting down drinking my morning coffee in glorious sunshine, reading the Telegraph, and I can't believe my eyes – you are in it with Chitty and have got a full page spread!' she marvelled. Carolyn went into the spiel of the last few days from when Chitty was in the County Press and how the week had snowballed from then on. I dread to think how much the phone call cost, but it is not every day your daughter appears in the nationals!

Another day had arrived so I gingerly responded to the Mayflower Theatre's e-mail. Instead of ringing them I left it up to them to contact us, not wanting to tempt fate and all that. Bloody Hell, the phone rang, God, I had only just sent the e-mail; they are obviously more on the ball than I thought. 'Hello, is that a Nick or Carolyn Pointing?' The voice sounded a young but vibrant type. 'Uh, yes, Nick speaking,' I said. 'Hi, I am a researcher for Good Morning Britain with Fern Britton and Philip Schofield and we wondered if you guys would like to bring your Chitty Chitty Bang Bang on the show next week.' This totally stumped me. 'Are you not from the Mayflower Theatre then?' I said, somewhat shocked and confused. 'Sorry?' the voice said. 'Oh, um yes, that sounds terrific,' I quickly said trying to hide my doubts and guilt about what I was going to say to the Mayflower. My heart was pounding but I was relieved at the conversation. This sounded really exciting although unreal and unbelievable. A call to be on the morning tele; all we did was build a car; what a lot of fuss over us; it just didn't sink in. Then it dawned on me, Chitty still needed an MOT and driving to London ..... hell that's a long way. Then Carolyn piped up, 'Get a grip, you have announced to the world that you are going to drive it to Australia!' She was right, have faith. It was time to rebook the MOT. I was reaching for the phone when it rang again; why does that always happen? 'Hello,' the voice said. 'Can I speak to Mr or Mrs Pointing please.' 'Yes. Speaking' I said. 'Good morning, my name is Robin, I am from the Mayflower Theatre,' the male said. Oh my God, run, hide, put the phone in the cupboard, pretend I am out, do something, I twittered on in my head. Then I needed to think of what to say, go through my lines. Chitty is built on a Land Rover, it is wider than the normal Chitty, we have never called it Chitty Chitty Bang Bang, it is our 'Chitty'. The male continued, 'We have read your article in the newspaper regarding your extraordinary building of a replica Chitty Chitty Bang Bang and would like to enquire whether we could forge some links in a promotional manner. The stage show is due here in June and providing the car is brand worthy and subject to approval with MGM, we would like to use your car if possible.'

Now, they would like to use our car and no mention of copyrights. Subject to approval, what was that all about? 'Wow that's fantastic. Yes, we'd be more than happy to help out,' I said. 'How do we get approval from MGM?' I went on.

Robin explained the stage show had been running at the London Palladium for a number of years now and the producer was a chap called Michael Rose. He was the driving force behind the whole project and worked very closely with the Broccoli family in America who own the rights to James Bond and Chitty Chitty Bang Bang. The stage show was on tour and heading to Southampton to run for the summer season. They would send a theatre representative to photograph our car for Mr Rose to scrutinise. A huge weight has just been lifted off my shoulders. It was a potential rubber stamp turning us from poachers to gamekeepers. This really was a serious proposition and we couldn't believe our luck. It was coming together thick and fast and we both wondered how we were ever going to have time to go to work! With my serious M&S manager's head on, I considered all the possibilities, MGM and the theatre links might just be enough to generate a bit of sponsorship. We must get Chitty roadworthy first, though.

Chapter 12 **F**lying high on celebrity status

Before starting work, Carolyn followed me down to Niton Undercliff Garage for the MOT and to ensure a lift home. The drive was an incredible experience. I stopped for petrol and the world stopped too! The forecourt at Safeways filled with cars and mobile phone photography. It was novel and overwhelming; something that we had built was generating so much interest, even the cash assistant left her bubble for a photo! 'You're doing this for charity, is that right?' a plump lady with three kids said. 'There you go, pop that in your tin' and she handed over a £5 note. 'Thank you very much,' I replied. How kind people can be. Apart from the waving and smiles, I have never seen so many double takes and pointing fingers, not to mention mouths moving to the speech of Chitty Chitty Bang Bang.

Phil from Niton Garage said he would give me a ring when it was done. Carolyn dropped me off at work for a bit of normality and went back home as her shift was starting at 2 p.m. Very soon normality turned into disaster when I couldn't stand the suspense any longer and I telephoned Phil at the garage for an MOT progress report. 'Bit of bad news, mate,' he said in a caring doctor/patient kind of way. 'The brakes need sorting, the steering box is knackered, you've got an oil leak from the rear diff and the props have got excessive play.' I really didn't want to be hearing this but it had to be done. 'Can you do it by next week, as I'm off to London in it.' 'I will do my best, it all depends on parts though; the brakes won't be a problem, we can tighten up the prop but it's the steering relay box which is the nightmare,' he said not too convincingly.

We were certainly having our fair share of highs and lows. I never thought it would be easy. Visiting my parents the following evening, Carolyn and I explained our ongoing adventure over a cup of coffee made with powdered milk. Why did we always burn our lips? We should know by now that we can't just gulp it down, as it doesn't have that drop of cooling milk.

My dad is a big bloke, with a great mop of hair and always with a smiley face. He listened intently, every now and again remarking, 'Ha ha,

I think this story is wonderful, you couldn't make it up if you tried!' My mother, so interested in our travel plans, raised practical questions like, 'So I assume if you plan to drive to Australia you will have a support vehicle with you.' Support vehicle, is she mad? we both thought. It was not something that we had even considered but maybe we should; another thing to add to the list of our 'maybes' and to 'think abouts'. Carolyn was engaging in conversation on how she managed to fit into her old wedding dress. My brain was working overtime.. Where would we find a support crew? Do we actually need a support crew? Let's face it, we couldn't pay them and who had got a suitable 4 x 4 vehicle in their backyard and were just waiting for an opportunity to take a year out and drive across the world, all self-funded? And what wife is going to let their chap do that? The odds on finding that couple were slimmer than a vegetarian winning the meat raffle. I could see my parents' genuine concern and considered their comments. I tried to convince them that all would be okay. We would put an advert in a Land Rover mag or something similar to see if we got any bites; perhaps someone was going to be doing the exact same trip and we could join up.

Mum probed me on the route again. 'Have you got an atlas? Then I can show you,' I said, thinking oh my God, I will now have the world laid out in front of me. I will have to be decisive and quickly consider all possibilities. I bluffed my way across the globe, saying, 'Well we will probably go through Europe, Turkey and um, oh, uh, Greece before that and then maybe Iran …' 'Iran?' Mum piped up. 'Are you crazy? You will be stuck on the end of a rocket launcher and sent to the moon if you go through there!'

Working Saturday gave me the previous Wednesday off and I found my self back at Niton Garage. All was going well, although the mechanic couldn't access the steering box. They daren't touch any of my handy work and requested that I remove the front bonnet and grille so they could start. By nightfall, I was somewhat financially lighter but relieved and grateful for their efforts. The County Press photographer turned up, to the embarrassment of the mechanics, to record the moment and I held the new MOT certificate as if it was made from gold. I kissed the print in celebration that our Chitty was now legally on the road. After a taxing moment, the road licence was paid and we were ready for anywhere and that anywhere was going to be London. In preparation for the big day, I topped up the oil, which I knew would eventually find its way to the garage floor, and gave the whole vehicle a once-over for any loose nuts and bolts!

The 6 a.m. ferry from Fishbourne was booked and we turned up at 5.30 a.m. still half asleep and freezing cold. Chitty was laden with wings, a tartan fleece blanket and a flask of tea. We sat in the car queue with flying jackets on, bobble hats and motorcycle gloves with the tartan blanket over our legs and we were still freezing our nuts off. We genuinely looked like a couple of OAPs on a day's outing to the seaside, complete with blue lips and quivering voices! I looked at Carolyn and she smiled through eyes watery with the ice-cold wind. 'You are going to have to put a heater in here,' she said, 'and build a roof.' It was a daunting thought, off to London in a car with no roof and God, if it rained, we were going to get soaked and look pretty stupid. With almost an hour's crossing on the ferry and two hours' drive to the South Bank through all the commuter traffic, we only just made it for 9 a.m.

The journey was an event in itself with a constant stream of in-car photography. The dual carriageway allowed cars in succession to wave, photograph and video while we struggled to top 50 mph. At the studio, the floor manager escorted us to the river bank where we waved and looked down from the car against a blue screen as we were filmed superimposed flying over London with Philip Schofield periodically saying 'They are nearly here!' As we were ushered upstairs, Philip himself greeted us with a bright and cheery, 'Good morning, look at you two!' Carolyn was positively weak at the knees as she fancied the pants off him and, in replacement of coherent English, she ugged a bit as I wiped the dribble from under her chin! Philip with a beaming smile said, 'I've been watching you two down there and do you know what? You are both quite normal!' Ha ha we laughed. I think it was a compliment! After make-up and breakfast – how good was that – we sat in the green room and watched the various interview guests disappear and reappear on the TV monitor. Once the first couple of chat show guests had done their turn, I realised why Philip's comments were so apt – we were normal!

The first bloke, or lad should I say, was a 20-year-old eunuch who had had his testicles removed by choice as he was uncomfortable being a man or a woman as the case might be. I sat cross-legged watching that one; the next couple were celebrating their love for each other, he was twenty-two years old and she was a 65-year-old grandmother; the third was a psychic who could predict the weather! Slightly nervous, I went to the gents and stood next to Russ Abbot at the urinal! What an atmosphere and God I wanted to sing it! It's always an unwritten law in the male toilets to look straight ahead and never look left or right and keep your mouth shut. During hand washing, I sparked up a conversation and what a jolly fine fellow he was.

Our moment of stardom had come. Fern Britton made it all so easy, she was as friendly and as motherly as she was portrayed on the television and with a warming and genuine interest in us. Russ Abbot joined us at the car, chipping in as appropriate as he starred as Grandpa Potts in the London version of the stage show Chitty Chitty Bang Bang.

We drove back down south with the biggest cheesy grins, humming to the CD soundtrack. 'Can you hang on a sec while I get a photo,' said the cabbie who had just abandoned his taxi at the lights, holding up the endless traffic of Westminster. Soon London Transport was grinding to a halt too. 'Oi mate, don't mind if I get a photo for my daughter, she loves the film' The imposing Routemater stopped rather abruptly and engaged reverse, crossing his and the right turn only lane, lining up for the perfect shot. The big red bus had caused a symphony of reversing bleeps and honking horns. The light changed green for the fourth time and as we pulled away a flash Merc pulled alongside, a distinguished man leant over and said, 'I helped make that film' and then he was gone.

Still flying high on celebrity status and back home on the Isle of Wight, today's mail only added to the free fall of attention. Carolyn did the usual 'you, me, you, me, both' letter sorting and the both pile consisted of an invitation to the Grand Press Launch of Chitty Chitty Bang Bang stage show at the Mayflower Theatre in Southampton. How excited we were after everything that we had experienced during that day in London. For every person who doubted us, there was justified reward and we really couldn't believe how lucky we were for the kind of attention and respect we were getting. We are only down-to-earth normal people – Philip Schofield said so!

Chapter 13 **S**upport crew two

It was now May and we really needed to start to think about planning our overseas jaunt. Carolyn and I had talked so much about what we were going to do but so far had actually done nothing towards it. In comparison, we had just spent four years building Chitty and planned to be away for a year, leaving ourselves only five months to organise the whole affair – not too bright I would say. Both her work and my bosses had come to terms with the fact we wanted to take a career break in September but we didn't even know what visas we wanted. We took time out from acting like Mickey and Minnie Mouse and planned a serious night of research. The internet – full of overland adventures – posed as many questions as it solved and we discovered that we needed a carnet for the car which effectively was its passport into all the countries and would cost a small fortune from the RAC. Without this, Chitty would be going nowhere. Most visas need at least three months to apply for and receive and unless we took a trip to the 'Big Smoke' we needed to think about hiring an agent.

Medical injections were also a high priority as there were so many and we needed to have them in stages so time was of the essence. We had to contact a letting agent to come and value the property for renting out, organise someone to look after all the animals, in particular Carolyn's little Birman cats who were the light of her life, and decide what to do with the outside 'Uglies' and the 50,000 goldfish in the pond. But top of the list was to apply for an addition to the mortgage for £15,000 for a new kitchen that we were not ready to have if you get my drift!

With visas in mind, Carolyn opened the atlas borrowed from my Dad. The routes looked pretty straightforward; in fact, there didn't seem to be many options, Europe into Turkey, then Iran or Turkmenistan and Afghanistan. It didn't sound too clever that way so Carolyn retraced her fingered route. 'Well, how about Russia like the Long Way Round, following in the tracks of Charley Boorman and Ewan McGregor,' she said. 'Then drop down into China and on to South-East Asia.' I took a look at where she was planning and decided that we would cover most of the globe in just the one country of Russia and I didn't fancy that. 'Well, the only other option is Iran then,' she continued, 'into Pakistan and India. Bob's your uncle then,' she said. Well, it all sounded pretty simple apart from Iran. I was sure as most places go, the people were great, but it was always on the news so gave us a little bit of doubt. 'Look Carolyn,' I said in a moment of blind confident blagging, 'rightly or wrongly we are going in September, that's only five months away and as long as the house is rented and we have got a carnet, our passports full of visas and loads of dosh, we will be fine', and that was our planning stage over!

***

Carolyn looked fantastic wearing her long black Per Una skirt edged in satin and velvet, which was complemented by her black velvet jacket with crimson satin lining. We were off to the stage show press launch and had our photos ready for exhibition to anyone who asked! I kept the gilt-edged invitation in my breast pocket of my best sartorial suit, compliments of Marks and Spencer, and we made our way to the reception at the Beaulieu National Motor Museum in Hampshire. On arrival we were greeted with champagne and were introduced to the marketing manager for the show, Andrea Sheppard. She was totally wrapped up in the event but said she would catch up with us later. Eon Productions, which were behind all the Bond films made at Pinewood Studios, had lent one of the six versions of Chitty cars made for the film. Still in their care the car was on display, with a barrage of press photographers instigating poses with the all new and recently revealed cast of the Southampton show. Adam Chance, star of the seventies TV soap Crossroads was playing Grandpa Potts with Alvin Stardust posing as the Child Catcher. Chris Balcombe was one of the media multitudes that had covered our story and he made a beeline for us to capture a few photos next to the original car. Why he insisted on this I had no idea but he took a few shots, as did the other photographers, obviously thinking we must be somebody important! While in photo shoot mode, we were introduced to the theatre director and Michael Rose the producer. Mr Rose, despite his importance took the time to say hello and listen to our story. He explained about the photos of our car conducted on his behalf and was delighted to give her a brand-worthy Chitty stamp of approval so that she was suitable to be used for promotional purposes. We both looked at each other feeling so flattered. Mr Rose, to our astonishment, personally introduced us to Lord Montagu of Beaulieu, who was hosting the event. God, did we feel important now, but also fraudulent at the same time as all we had done was build a car on an old Land Rover! Mr Rose outlined the fact that we had built our replica Chitty Chitty Bang Bang and Lord Montagu smiled, raised an eyebrow and said 'What did you go and do that for?' I replied as I pointed to Carolyn, 'Because my wife asked me to!' and both laughed. This was so surreal, hobnobbing and even cracking jokes, I needed to get a grip of myself!

Andrea the marketing manager ran over a few dates and enlisted Chitty at various forthcoming promotional events and in return we were given VIP theatre tickets for the opening night of the show. It really couldn't get any better.

Back in the working world, Carolyn was answering a call from a chap on her beat in Bembridge by the name of Steve Stevens. He had come forward with some information regarding an incident and she turned up on his doorstep totally unaware of what this call would develop into.

Steve was in his fifties and was an ex-customs officer, retired and enjoying the finer things in life. His huge house was on the market and under offer and a large proportion of it was packed up ready for moving on to his next goal in life, which he didn't know what that was! After completing the relevant statement, Steve said, 'You are WPC Pointing aren't you, the one who has built Chitty Chitty Bang Bang and is planning to go off across the world?' Carolyn, trying to maintain a degree of professionalism but struggling as she would far rather talk about Chitty than crime, said, 'Yes, that's me. Has my fame reached even the far corners of Bembridge now then?' Steve grinned, 'I hear you are looking for a support vehicle, have you had any luck yet?' Carolyn then entered into a long discussion about the trip and how we had plans to advertise in one of the Land Rover magazines but time just hadn't allowed it yet. Although support would be a nice thing to have, it was not the number one priority and, to be honest, finding someone who could just up and leave for a year was going to be pretty remote so we didn't hold out much hope. Steve then said, 'I could be interested. My house is sold; I complete the sale the beginning of September. I have got a Land Rover Discovery sitting outside on the drive', and he pointed to a dark green, all singing all dancing new model with personalised plates. 'I have just parted company with my wife and am looking for something to inspire me, would you be interested in me joining you? I will have a chat with my girlfriend about it. I am not sure what she will do as she has got a couple of kids but I am certainly keen.'

Carolyn left his house, somewhat dumbfounded that she had walked in on a potential support vehicle for our trip.

Arriving back home from shift at just after midnight, she came up to bed with her usual cup of tea and true to form climbed into bed freezing cold. 'Guess what,' she said excitedly, 'I think I have just found us a support vehicle.' 'Uh, what?' I said, being disturbed from my warm slumber. I prised open my eyes to see her sitting up in bed wide awake and full of life. 'Listen to this,' she said and proceeded to tell me the story of meeting Steve Stevens. I was pleased, confused and disheartened at the news – pleased because there was potential security and a vehicle to carry spares, confused because I really thought we would never find one and disheartened because I actually wanted to go it alone. I suppose selfishly I thought it was our thing and I didn't want to share it.

A couple of days later, Carolyn was dealing with an incident where a young lad needed speaking to and, because of his age, he needed an adult present. After this was dealt with, Carolyn then found herself chatting to the adult, who unbeknown to Carolyn was the girlfriend of Steve Stevens. Julia Bartlett seemed to know about the trip but Carolyn just thought is was becoming common knowledge around Bembridge so didn't think too much more about it. Later that day, Carolyn called in on Steve, who was somewhat bemused to find that she had been talking to Julia but had no idea that she was connected to him and potentially she was going to be the other half of the support crew!

A meeting was arranged for an opportunity to get to know each other better and the venue was at the Old Gaffers Festival in Yarmouth. We had been asked to go along and take Chitty to put her on display among all the old classic cars, which would also give us a good opportunity to get our fund-raising underway. Steve turned up in his ivory Mk2 Jaguar escorted by Julia and her smiley mum. After formalities, we engaged in the nitty gritty of routes, plans and finance and I explained that we were planning on a budget of £15,000. God only knows where I got that figure from and clearly both parties would be financially independent. We would be responsible for our own vehicle, paperwork and camping equipment; two independent trips going together. It seemed pretty straightforward to me. Julia was about ten years younger than Steve and was the mother of two boys aged about ten and fourteen. It was suggested that they would be going to stay with their father for the duration of the trip to enable her to join Steve and she also had catering experience and offered to concentrate on the cooking of the meals while we were away. As neither of them worked, Julia also took on the task of organising the carnets and visas, which was music to our ears as we were finding time running away with us. We were both still working full time as well as finishing off Chitty. We were booked up with events every weekend on both days , and during the weekday evenings we attended a lot of charity events, country shows and carnivals. We were also visiting primary schools which had agreed to have a 'no uniform day' to fund-raise for us if we took Chitty along to see them. We didn't have a minute to spare.

I was still trying to design a rack to fit on to the back of Chitty to carry our gear and get my head around a roof which was sturdy enough to give us some sort of protection in all weathers but was also in keeping with the car.

Julia, in her early forties with short silver grey hair and dressed in jeans and Lonsdale rugby shirt, was free and more than willing to lend a hand, and for us she couldn't have arrived on the scene at a better time.

Our first encounter with the support crew went well and we all seemed to get on. Both Steve and Julia were keen to get things rolling and we exchanged mobile numbers and agreed to meet on a weekly basis to liaise.

Chitty was getting a lot of attention but it was all good natured and respectful. A list of summer shows and events filled the weekends up to our date of departure, 12 September, and we desperately wanted to generate a bit of cash for our charities to give a purpose for the adventure.

However, as we learnt, fund-raising isn't easy. Both quiet and polite in nature, being pushy just wasn't our game. We displayed the car with various charity tins in the surrounding area and some days we would only collect about £30 in small change after we had put almost that of our own money into the fuel tank getting to and from the show.

I still had genuine concerns about Chitty's mechanical well-being; my grand plans of having a Land Rover mechanic to sort the engine out were running out of time, the funding of a new diesel motor looked right out of the question now with the money spent on work for the MOT test. The medical injections were quoted as costing between £300 and £400 for each of us and we needed them for Japanese encephalitis, rabies, tetanus, polio, meningitis, yellow fever, hepatitis B, cholera, not to mention three months' supply of malaria tablets which added an extra £200 to the bill. If I got knocked down and killed by a bus after this lot I would feel really cheated!

Julia received quotes from a visa company who would action all our visa requirements at a cost of about £500 and I still had to build a rack and a roof.

Chapter 14 **T he start of things to come**

Spare parts for the car – where do I start? I didn't know what to take or what it would cost but today I was hoping for answers as a chap called Neil Watson from Land Rover Owner International magazine had tracked us down and was due to run a story on the modified Landy and take some appropriate photos. Neil turned up on cue and compiled a technically based article. I took the opportunity to pick his brains and explained our impending trip, asking him for his advice on engine modifications. 'Leave it alone,' he said, 'it is a good old Land Rover, it will be fine.' Well, with my time constraints and budget I didn't need to be told that twice, although maybe I should have showed him the oil leaks and asked about the smoke!

The very same day, Steve and Julia requested a practice run on camping. Julia had sourced quick-fold-up tents on the internet, which ironically were an Australian design and aptly named Oz tents. These things were great, excellent quality and fully up in less than thirty seconds. Just what you want if you are going to do it every day for a year. Shame about the price though – another £300 for a basic tent and then it was extras for awnings, ground protectors, etc. We had parted company by now with some serious cash acquiring all our camping equipment and our garden was the location for our first night outside. It seemed only right to test the equipment and further our relationships. As per our agreed guidelines, we erected our own tent and provided our own food. It was a beautiful evening, good humour was in the air, but the alarm bells were ringing. We lit one burner on our Coleman's stove and placed the saucepan of pasta on top. We opened our tin of tuna and buttered a few slices of bread and considered, along with our two bottles of beer as a treat, that we were suitably prepared. Sat on a blanket on the grass we looked over at our support team. Steve sat back in his new Millets' deluxe chair behind a full-length folding dining table showing an array of exotic nibbles including green olives, black olives, spiced anchovies and a large assortment of nuts, crisps and dips, complemented with a bottle of full-bodied red wine and another of chilled Chardonnay. 'Ah this is the life,' he said, gently sipping from a wine glass (as we swigged from a dumpy green bottle with a cheap French label). 'Jooooliaaaaah, what for dinner?'

Julia appeared from behind the tent with a frying pan in her hand. 'I'm cooking steak, of course. Why do you ask?' she said in a questioning manner. I surveyed their opulence and wondered if this was a special pre-trip occasion or whether this evening was the start of things to come!

Chapter 15 **P**ilot's licence

The offers of shows and carnivals came in thick and fast, all with the emphasis on the opportunity to raise cash for our causes, and we really tried to accommodate as many as we possibly could. With some under our belt we were getting the hang of it all and we had sent out a few hundred letters to companies large and small offering advertising space on the vehicle during summer shows and our impending trip in return for a small amount of sponsorship to aid the adventure; all in the name of charity, of course. Sadly, we heard from no one; obviously our marketing skills were crap. Well, I lie slightly. We received one bite of a cash donation, from a newly appointed marketing manager saying maybe they could build a bit for the car, and that was the last we heard. We always planned to finance the trip ourselves but thought it was worth a go to get some sponsorship in addition to fund-raising. We were great at doing things for free but generating cash – no chance!

The Isle of Wight County Show requested the pleasure of our company and, with it being one of the main events on the island, we chose to oblige. Not long after setting Chitty up with wings, a display board and charity tins, a well-to-do kind of a guy in a tweed shirt asked if we could do an arena display. Well, up for anything, we said yes and then asked him what he wanted us to do. 'Oh, just drive the old girl round, that'll do it,' he said. At about 3 p.m., we were summoned to the main arena. The entrance gate opened and one of the officials parted the crowds and handed me a microphone. 'Oh hell,' I said. 'He never said anything about talking!' Carolyn, thinking on her feet, turned on the Chitty CD theme song and held the mic against the speaker while we conducted a few laps. Thinking we had got away with it lightly, the compère dropped a bombshell. 'So I think the audience, especially the boys and girls, need to know why Chitty isn't flying today,' he announced to the world. Well, I could see the game he was playing so off the cuff I said, 'Obviously, you all know Chitty is a flying car. However, I have been in contact with Sandown Airport via air traffic control and have been advised not to fly today because of excessive turbulence at 3,000 feet.' I was on a roll and continued, 'Also aviation fuel is far more expensive than petrol, but most importantly I haven't got my full pilot's licence yet.' Boy, did I feel good about that answer as we left to a round of applause. With the car back in its position on display, a crowd gathered around asking the usual questions; then one man in his forties, well dressed in country attire including Wellingtons, said, 'So, when do you anticipate getting your full pilot's licence?' 'Sorry?' I said, somewhat aghast. 'Yes, I saw your display, very good, so when are you taking the old test then?' Is he for real? I thought. Surely this is a wind-up. I made it up. I'm not capable of taking my pilot's licence and I don't need it because Chitty doesn't really fly; it is a fantasy, doesn't he know that? Obviously he didn't as he was deadly serious. This wasn't helped by the fact that I had spent some time on the computer on the photo shop program creating our Chitty complete with wings and a tail of smoke flying over Culver Downs and it was the shadow which I had made underneath it which was so convincing to so many! I heard one woman say to her husband, 'See I told you, it really does fly, look at the picture!' I thought I had seen and heard it all working in general retail but there is always one who comes along and surprises you. 'Can I ask you how you got it here?' one man said, tucked behind his rimmed glasses and under a tweed flat cap. 'Oh, we drove it here,' I replied convincingly. 'But what is it?' he enquired. 'It is a replica Chitty Chitty Bang Bang, sir' I said. 'A Gritty Gritty Bang Bang, what is that?' he asked. 'It's a car,' I said. 'A car?' he asked. 'Yes a car,' I repeated. 'Well, how did you get it get here?' he asked again. 'We drove it,' I said. 'You drove it?' he went on. 'Yes,' I repeated, 'we drove it.' 'Well I never,' he said. 'Does it run on steam?' he asked. 'No, sir, it is a car,' I said, getting ready to slit my throat. 'Is it electric then?' he asked. 'No, sir,' I said again. 'It is a car, it runs on normal petrol with a normal petrol engine,' I said in a very frustrated voice. I know some people are inquisitive but this was a little excessive. 'So is it taxed then, did you drive it on the normal road in the normal way?' he continued. 'Yes, we drove it here, it has tax, an MOT, insurance just like a normal car and if you hang around for another half an hour, I will be so exhausted you will be able to see me drive it home, nice talking to you, good bye!'

Why was it that people thought that it was us who were mad?

Chapter 16 **W**hat could possibly go wrong

The sixth of August had arrived and we handed the house keys over to the new tenants of our lovely home. We had kept back the garage to house Chitty in for one more month, along with all the equipment we were going to take on the trip. All our worldly belongings were piled high in one corner, and I wasn't sure whether it was just good packing or what but it looked rather disappointing. Stacked up to the rafters and neatly wrapped in an assortment of sheets and blankets, everything we owned and had worked for over the last twenty years was here, this was it. Strangely, among the excitement of it all this was a very sad moment. Today we moved in with Carolyn's mum in Wootton. There was slight relief that the house was now rented and the money would cover the mortgage but there was tension and anxiety as our departure date loomed ever closer. Carolyn and I opted to work right up to the last weekend, saving as much cash as possible – the theory was good but there was so much to do. The weekends were still full with rallies and shows, Chitty still needed a roof but I had designed and commissioned a luggage rack with a local firm. I really felt the old Land Rover engine needed a once-over too and so planned a visit to a local specialist.

Where time went, I had no idea, but late August was upon us and we only had two weeks left with the weekends booked. I spent every evening designing and making a roof, this turned out far more complicated than I had ever imagined. The ash-wood frame was bolted in place with a skin of aluminium to hold off the rain and it could easily be removed, but we had nowhere to store it so it would probably stay on for the duration of the trip. The first day of rain, we took to the roads to test its weatherproofing. What a complete disaster! We were soaked, the rain came in everywhere and some serious thinking and alteration were needed.

Carolyn paid a visit to Jim the Trim on Sandown's industrial estate. As an upholsterer, he had given her some sound advice when she was making the leather seating. Jim had previously worked in upholstery for Rolls Royce and he explained that the whole roof needed a vinyl cover and detachable windows. He inspired confidence and started to measure up. At this late stage it was something we couldn't do without, but the cost was another matter. Every financial surprise was eating into our £15,000 budget. Jim wouldn't need the car for a few days for a fitting so Carolyn took Chitty into John Reynolds, Land Rover specialist. The mechanic kindly whizzed over the car with a few recommendations and paused at the rear prop shaft. He wiggled it for play and delivered a blow below the belt. 'That's knackered ma' darlin',' he said. 'It's not the prop shaft, it's the whole differential.' 'Differential, what's one of those?' Carolyn asked. Chris, the mechanic, looked bemused at a blonde female in a Land Rover workshop dressed up all pretty and asking for clarification on such a long word! 'It's that bloody great big bit there which holds your wheels on and makes them turn!' he said. 'Oh!' was her reply. 'Look,' he said, 'bring it in after the bank holiday on the Tuesday and we can fix it. It won't be cheap, though, and John will have to source the new part.'

I telephoned the firm who had taken on the work to build the rack for Chitty. This was crucial to the trip and I had wanted it made from two-inch diameter aluminium tubing and hadn't a clue on how to weld it on. It was to hold the tent and luggage above the boat tail and needed room for a cage to be fitted holding water and jerrycans. I had also designed a rear plate to home the essential spare wheel, which I had ordered three months ago to allow time to practise packing and to see what we could and couldn't take. With only two weeks to go it was cutting it a bit fine to say the least. 'Hello, it's Mr Pointing here, I wondered if the rack was ready for collection yet,' I said. 'I have rung a few times and now I really need an answer.' 'Ah, yes Mr Pointing, we have been trying to get hold of you.' Have you! I thought. 'The thing is, it won't be back from the paint sprayers on the mainland until next week, hopefully on the Wednesday,' came back the reply. Talk about up the creek without a paddle!

Tuesday after the bank holiday came and Carolyn followed me to Sandown to drop Chitty off at the Land Rover garage at 8 a.m. 'Call in after work,' he said, 'and all should be okay.' Not so. 'Good news and bad news,' Chris said at 5.30 p.m. 'The good news is we have a reconditioned prop from an ex-army Land Rover dealership on the mainland; the bad news is I said the day after the bank holiday to bring it in and you have come in a week early and I won't be able to do it yet.' 'The bank holiday was yesterday,' Carolyn said defensively. 'Are you sure?' questioned Chris. 'Quite sure,' said Carolyn. 'Oh, ah well, sorry folks but I still can't do it until next week, bring it back on Monday and I will fit you in.' 'But that is only a week before we leave,' blurted out Carolyn in total frustration, 'and we are trying to have the roof and rack fitted. Can't you do it before then?' she went on. 'Sorry ma darlin', John won't be picking the part up until Friday when he is on the mainland and I don't work weekends, its against ma religion.' Stuffed again. We were totally helpless. We really did feel under pressure now. Even more so as Chris had advised us not to drive the car as it wouldn't do it any favours and we didn't want to have the expense or embarrassment of being broken down somewhere on the Island when we had told the world to expect us over the next year. We had one more week remaining before we left and Chitty still hadn't got a waterproof roof, a luggage rack and now needed major work done on her undercarriage.

I can safely say that this was now the most stressful part of our lives. Isle of Wight Radio had been broadcasting our departure day, the Isle of Wight County Press was in the know and Carolyn's mother was in the middle of organising a 'bon voyage' party and it just seemed an impossible task ahead. I felt incredibly insecure over Chitty's mechanical bits and quite rightly as I was expecting an awful lot from a 1973 Land Rover which had been around the houses umpteen times. I only wish within the last four years of building Chitty I had done something about the engine and the essentials. The least I could do at this late stage was order some spares.

Fortunately, everything Land Rover is plentiful and cheap and available via next day delivery. Knowing what to take as spares was a logistical nightmare and over the last few months I had picked the brains of anyone I assumed was in the know from Land Rover mechanics to enthusiasts and magazine editors. The suggested list of 'must have' critical spares grew ever longer. It would have been easier to tow a complete car behind us just in case! I heeded the strongest warning and ordered half shafts, which are prone to fail in the rear drive and weigh a ton, universal joints, which have nothing to do with global marijuana, a starter motor, points, plugs, oil filter and fan belt and that was it. I figured Land Rover would be littered across the world so access to parts couldn't be a problem. In Chitty, space was at a premium so only the absolutely essential could come.

It was now Monday and a week after the bank holiday and we were recovering from our last full weekend show at the Havenstreet Steam Railway. As planned, once again we were taking Chitty to the Land Rover specialist for fitment of the second-hand but new to us rear differential. Jim the Trim had also asked us to pop by for a last minute fitting of the roof vinyl and doors. Jim was a tall slim fellow with a slightly foreign accent, which I couldn't place, but very friendly indeed. 'She'll be great mate,' he said as he pulled down tightly the roof sides. 'I just need to fit poppers and Velcro to the doors and, all being well, pick it up Friday.' Finally, I could see it coming together and Friday would be fine. We left Jim's and parked up at John Reynolds, Land Rover specialist. The mechanic said it should be ready on Wednesday.

Still both at work and looking forward to finishing on Friday for twelve months, we both juggled our lunch hours to complete final injections and travel insurance, which was invalid in any country not recommended for travel by the Foreign Office. This was slightly concerning as Iran and Pakistan were both listed and the most likely places you would need travel insurance! We had actually spent hours on the Foreign Office website; it was very detailed and pretty scary. I suppose they have to cover themselves but after reading it you wouldn't go anywhere.

Wednesday came but the spares I had ordered didn't, nor did the luggage rack. I was on tenterhooks, there was so much going on in my head, so much needed chasing up and I am a bloke who can only cope with one task at a time, more than two and I am a total disaster and don't achieve a thing. Carolyn, on the other hand, can juggle a thousand things and concentrate on all of them along with talking on the phone and doing her nails at the same time!

Clearing credit cards and cancelling all our direct debits was her domain although a building society website account with e-mail and links to our travel blog was down to me. Some wise guy recommended I scan copies of all our travel documentation from passports and carnets to log book and licences and e-mail them to myself. Also, print off a few copies of each and for a super-safe foolproof back-up, save them to disc and a memory stick kept on your key ring. Great in theory but it took for ever. This wise guy was an internet intrepid traveller who actually gave some pretty good advice, including presenting a colour copy of your car registration log book on the borders just in case they decided to demand money from you for its return.

Friday afternoon was drawing in. Carolyn and I left work early to collect Chitty from her major operation. Chris the mechanic crawled out from under a car and didn't look too pleased. 'Its done,' he said, 'but it was a hell of a job. Got some more bad news for you, though.' 'Oh no, now what?' I said. 'You know your clutch is going,' he said. 'No, no it can't be,' I said. 'Please tell me you are having a laugh,' I begged, running my hands through my ever decreasing strands of hair. 'Sorry mate, it's on its way out. Have you ever pulled away with the hand brake on?' he asked. 'Uh yeah, probably, I think so, sometime I might have kind have done that,' I replied. 'Well you couldn't do that with a good clutch and the hand brake locks the prop you know.' Carolyn and I were mortified. What else could possibly go wrong? Surely that had to be the last thing. 'I would recommend that you put a new carburettor on it too, this one is well worn and revving too high,' he said, hammering the final nail in the coffin. An unbelievable wave of insecurity enveloped us both. We were entrusting our global plans on Chitty, the whole adventure if not our lives depended upon her. The mechanic looked at us in that usual mechanic sort of way, tipped with a mild dose of sympathy. 'Bring it down Monday, we have ordered a clutch for you. You haven't made it easy, though; the gearbox normally comes out from under the seats, I'm going to have to modify the chassis and remove it from below just like the army vehicles do,' he said with a frown of reluctance. 'Well, it's too late to order a new carburettor now,' I said solemnly to Carolyn, 'that's a tomorrow job.' At 5 p.m. we just had time to pop over to 'Jim the Trim' and collect the roof. True to his word Jim had completed the handmade vinyl cover including roll-down plastic doors which attached by a series of poppers and Velcro. It was a first-class job, fitting snugly over the ash-wood and aluminium frame I had built. Gingerly parting with another £800 we felt relieved we finally had a weatherproof hood. Pulling out on to the main road was our first opportunity to put the new top through its paces. I changed gear into third and with a rush of turbulence both vinyl doors ripped straight off, the poppers gave up their grip with ease leaving flapping plastic hanging by a bungee cord. 'Carolyn, grab the flippin' door,' I shouted. I managed to hang on to my side before pulling over and turning round and heading straight back to Jim's. Gutted and feeling disappointed turned into feeling totally helpless when we realised he had gone home. His mobile went straight to answer phone and we had a car that was as waterproof as a fishnet stocking.

Apart from ordering parts and frantic phone calls to contact Jim, Saturday was dominated by tiptoeing over our now rented-out lawn to the garage to make a cage which would fit on to the new luggage rack when it arrived. A chrome vegetable rack from an old kitchen unit looked a good starting point and amazingly a small wicker basket, two red jerrycans and two ten-litre water containers fitted perfectly.

Chapter 17 **L**oaded to the gunnels

Sunday was completely free and a slight relief from the mayhem. Carolyn's mum had organised and hosted a bon voyage party, hoping that she would eventually meet Steve and Julia who were expected to be with us for the duration of the trip but they had other plans. It was a humbling affair and a focus of attention we felt unworthy of as we hadn't actually done anything yet and the way things were going might not!

After showing off Chitty to family and friends and toasts of good luck and farewell, we darted off late afternoon to Yarmouth to meet Carolyn's twin cousins and their little families from the ferry. They had been unable to attend the earlier function and were keen to see Carolyn before she went away, and likewise she wanted to say her goodbyes. We were killing two birds with one stone as during one show or another, I had agreed to allow a couple of kids to sit in the car for a photo and today was their day too. 'Hi, thank you for meeting us and accommodating us at this short notice. You know we really do get so much stick with our surname, I thought at least if the kids had a photo in the car it would compensate slightly. Look, there you go,' said the man in his thirties standing with two pretty little girls. He handed me his driving licence and sure enough it said Mr Chitty! We were always happy to oblige but time really wasn't on our side. Carolyn's cousins were in awe of the car and congratulated us on the trip we hadn't yet done. 'What if you break down?' Duncan said. 'Well,' as I had just announced during the speeches back at the party, 'if we break down, it's all part of the adventure as long as it's not in England on the way to Dover,' I said and laughed.

Work was now just a memory and Monday and Tuesday were all ours and just as well with leaving on Wednesday.

I was hoping to awaken to a delivery of essential spare parts but sadly they never came. If they didn't come tomorrow, we would have to go without them. With Monday morning and no work, I talked myself into acting with enthusiasm; despite my fears and concerns the show must go on. The first job was to drop Chitty off in Sandown to have her new clutch fitted and then to take the vinyl roof over the road for Jim to have a second crack at making the doors stay on. Carolyn had sold her Toyota Yaris the previous week and the funds were helping us to hold our heads just above the unexpected financial outlays. I still had my silver Mitsubishi Gallant, the old faithful friend who had done me proud over the last twelve years and still going – just. The plan was to take the old Mits to the scrapyard today. When we had dropped Chitty off, we would be down to Ben's 125 cc motorbike for transport for the last few hours in this country. Ben unfortunately had just missed our final days and the bon voyage party as he was leaving for his deployment with the Royal Navy. Carolyn had said her tearful goodbyes to him just over a week ago, which had left her heartbroken not knowing when she would see him again. He was off across the world but via a slightly different route. She had questioned the trip many times wondering if she could actually leave her kids for a year and the whole emotion was quite daunting.

I drove to Cowes and Carolyn planned to pick me up as a pillion on the 125cc bike. It was always on the cards to scrap the two-litre gas guzzling hatchback but I never considered how I would feel. I knew that if it was left in the garden for a year while we were away that would put pay to it through deterioration, but parting with it was stupidly hard to do. The car was weighed and £37 in scrap value was handed over. The old car sat on the weighing platform awaiting its fate and whether it was a combination of the last few days' mayhem or the insecurity of the impending trip but my eyes filled up with tears and I actually cried for the first time in years.

Pulling myself back together, I walked off in the late afternoon golden September sunshine for a few deep breaths. I then returned for one last look. I convinced myself it was the emotion of the whole departure process and focused on getting Chitty back.

Earlier, I had telephoned the engineer regarding the rack and was expecting to see it at home, but that wasn't without a fight. The rather abrupt man on the phone explained the cheque for payment didn't include delivery or fitting. I bounced the fact back that if it wasn't fitted I couldn't get it home. He stood his ground saying fitting was not in the price, so with an assertive moment I said, 'Look, I have been waiting for over four months for this, I leave on Wednesday, you have been paid and I am doing this for charity, I need some bloody help here.' The guy took a deep breath and said it would be dropped off on a gas bottle lorry if they could fit it on. 'Thank you,' I said. In my mind I had mapped out the next few hours and my list of things to do for Tuesday and collecting a rack by some means or another was not on that list.

John Reynolds (or his mechanic) had done a top job on the clutch and we left another £850 in their capable hands. Jim the Trim was on form too and had fitted the twist clips that held fast in all weathers. The roof was complete and competent but another £50 was billed to us for the extra bits. Finally, at home on the lawn was the all new tubed rack. The roof was on and functional, Chitty had a new rear differential and clutch and a slight wave of relief was filling the air. It was slowly coming together but the finances were taking a severe blow and we hadn't started yet.

Tuesday was Chitty's final day in the garage of our tenants' house as tonight she would be sleeping outside Carolyn's mum's home for an early departure in the morning. I spent all day fixing on the rack over Chitty's boat tail. The vegetable cage I had built screwed on top for housing the jerrycans and I fixed the Land Rover spare wheel to the rear plate of the rack. We took hours packing and repacking all our camping bits and bobs and left a pile of non-essentials littering the garage floor with no home to go to. With rucksack and Oz tent onboard, we headed for the open road for a test drive. A test drive that lasted no longer that two minutes! With the sheer weight of the spare wheel on the back, the rack was vibrating and shifting backwards and forwards three to four inches. I pulled over in disappointing confusion and witnessed a hairline crack in the weld already. There was no other option available other than to head home about 10 mph and remove the spare wheel.

I had stupidly designed the rack with the aesthetic look in mind. I had opted for a two-inch tube for strength but excluded any triangulation or brace bars so as not to clutter up the design and hide Chitty's wooden finish. I had gambled and lost. I knew if I continued, the welds would crack and the whole rack would be useless. Cutting our losses, I decided to leave the spare wheel off Chitty and only carry two cans of tyre weld and a tubeless repair kit that I hadn't a clue how to use. At this incredibly late stage and with no time or options, I was taking 'make or break' decisions which could easily creep up and bite me hard on the bum at a later date.

Chitty was loaded to the gunnels, polished to her best and full of new oils and filters. She had four new tyres and a new exhaust, what could possibly go wrong? Tuesday afternoon ran into Tuesday evening and we were still at our old house when a courier delivered a parcel of spare parts. Unfortunately, the new starter motor was broken in transit. However, the new carburettor was intact and took all of ten minutes to fit. I had ordered a Kelly kettle for which I had paid £35 and Carolyn thought I was totally mad. A clever bit of kit, it boils water from a paper fire in only a few minutes. She didn't really have a problem with it. However, she was only allowed to take one spare pair of shoes and I was insistent on taking three kettles! I do like my tea, though!

John and Susan, who were our tenants, came over to Chitty as we were just about to leave from the garden and produced a bottle of champagne and four glasses. It was a very touching gesture and filled us with such optimism that we were leaving our house in the safe hands of a lovely little family. Chitty fired into life and we departed Newchurch for the final time.

Chapter 18 **G**oing POSH

The last couple of months had been the most stressful in our lives; the unbelievable events turning up at every corner just kept coming. Finally, the house was rented, the cats had been temporarily re-homed and the kids at aged sixteen and seventeen farmed out – one courtesy of Her Majesty's Royal Navy and one to pursue a hairdressing apprenticeship and with secret ideas of sofa-surfing with mates for a year! Work had let us loose on a career break and the funds for a new kitchen we hadn't got were in place, if not slightly battered. Chitty was built, prepared and packed and ready to go. Weather-proofed and polished, she really looked the part and with a few new mechanical bits we were away. Having said that, Chitty was thirty-five years old, had well over a hundred thousand miles on the clock and I wondered deep down in my heart whether her condition was enough to get us across the world.

Chitty slept with her new roof on and we reflected on the days past and the days to come. We had done everything we could; if it wasn't done then to hell with it – it never would be. There was a strange feeling of relief; there was no more we could do, we were in effect jobless, homeless and insecure. We had a great adventure ahead, money to go with, each other and a real desire to prove something. There really was no turning back, we had reached the summit of the rickety wooden four-year-building roller coaster and the brakes were off. There aren't many times in your life you have the freedom of no mortgage or bills, no balances of finance and time and feeling the envy of everyone. But it was not without cost, emotional turmoil, hard work and planning. Despite the knock-backs and the fact we didn't even know where we were going to sleep on the first night away, let alone the rest of the trip, we were going to live our dream by driving a home-made Chitty Chitty Bang Bang across the world. God, that sounds like an audition for Pop Idol, but to be honest we were really focused and scared witless!

'Are you awake?' I said to Carolyn at 4.30 a.m. 'Yes,' she replied, 'I haven't slept a wink.' 'Nor have I,' I said. 'Are you nervous?' 'Petrified,' she said. 'Are you?' 'Yeah, want a cup of tea?' I said as I crawled out of my little two foot six single bed with sheets and blankets covered with huge orange chrysanthemums in ma-in-law's granny annexe. Carolyn said it was like sleeping in a compost heap putting her head on the pillow and no doubt we would be sleeping next to a few of those somewhere in the next few months!

We both had butterflies in our stomachs and cereal, toast and tea just wouldn't go down. As the sun rose, the sky above Wootton Creek at the bottom of the garden was crystal clear. The water was like a millpond and reflected everything visible through a gentle mist hovering a few feet above. Chitty was covered in dew and upstairs footsteps could be heard from Carolyn's mum who was fussing over the smallest of things, clearly covering emotion that her only daughter was embarking on an outrageous expedition. We went through the routine of goodbyes, knowing full well they would be coming down to the ferry port to wave us off. In a flood of tears, Carolyn's mum handed her a little box containing a gold St Christopher to wear round her neck to keep her safe. Through a saltwater stream of tears and giving an optimistic smile Carolyn attached it to her chain and gave her mum a big hug. Choked right up, her mum turned to me and said 'Promise me you will look after her.' 'Of course I will,' I said, feeling the emotional responsibility, which I already carried, tighten even more.

We were greeted at Fishbourne car ferry terminal by a fluorescent-coated man saying, 'Wow, Chitty Chitty Bang Bang, you want to travel on the port side, is that right?' 'Yes please,' I said with a cheeky smile. How did he know we wanted to travel port out and starboard home? Carolyn explained that during the week, she had called in at the ferry terminal and spoken with one of the guys on the desk explaining what we were doing and saying that our little theme was POSH as in the song title from the Chitty film. We were ushered into line and Steve and Julia pulled up loaded to the hilt in their Land Rover Discovery which was clad in Chitty decals that I had designed on the computer. We all looked the part, dressed in Chitty sweatshirts and fleeces – it almost looked as if we knew what we were doing! A handful of colleagues, friends and family, full of good cheer and praise, came to wave us off. 'What if you break down?' John from the M&S coffee shop shouted. 'Look, John, if we break down, it is all part of the adventure as long as it's not on the way to Dover,' I said. How many times had I said that? Why were people so concerned that we might break down, it happens all the time. However, I would never live it down if we couldn't even get out of England, I thought. The sun was shining in our faces as the terminal crew waved us forward. We were off, handshakes and waving against a serenade of beeping horns and, as we approached the ferry ramps, a wave of excitement took over. The boat ramp was lined with twenty to thirty people all cheering and waving Union Jacks. 'Bloody hell look at this,' I said to Carolyn. 'There is no turning back now.' I felt the heat of high expectations. I was hoping to sneak on to the boat and maybe ring up in twelve months saying 'We made it' but Isle of Wight Radio had included us in their news stories for the day and we were getting a good old-fashioned 'eccentric Brit' send-off and it was all quite emotional.

After I was put in my place arguing over which was the port side, not realising that the boat turns round after leaving, we texted more goodbyes over a Wightlink cup of tea. Before we had a moment to relax, Chris Balcombe from the Solent News Agency was on the blower after hearing the radio news report. Chris wanted departure photos so before we were going anywhere, we agreed to meet on Southsea Common for a photo shoot. It wasn't that we minded crouching, standing and waving like Mr Bean on heat, it was just that we wanted to get going. Finally, reflective umbrella stands and cameras were put away and we headed towards the A3. Steve followed behind as I put Chitty through her paces on the motorway. Portsmouth to Dover was at least 200 miles so a pit stop at Maidstone was on the agenda for lunch. Chitty will only top fifty miles an hour so the pressure of motorway driving ensured she was running at the maximum.

Chapter 19 **A very nice man**

After a signal of hand waving to the Discovery behind us we pulled off into the service station applying the brakes and reducing speed on the slip road. The confident air of achievement was shattered. Thud thud thud, a rumbling of thunder of mechanical clanging resonated from under the car.

'Blimey what the hell is that?' I said panicking.

Carolyn looked at me with concern in her eyes.

Thud thud thud, in rapid succession. This was a sound I had never heard before and I had no idea what it was, only that it didn't sound good. As we slowed even more into the parking area opposite the café, the rumbling continued in short succession as the wheels turned. I felt utterly sick and I sat holding the steering wheel and gazed at the floor in a state of shock.

Carolyn with no idea of the mechanical situation but fully aware of my concerns, put her hand on my arm and said, 'Don't worry, whatever it is, we will sort it out. At least in this country the mechanics can speak English and let's face it, we have made it to Maidstone! Come on, be positive, let's look underneath.'

I was already racking my brain as to what it could be. Was it the prop shaft? It sounded like a wheel bearing to be honest. I was clutching at straws.

Steve came over as bright as a button saying, 'Fancy a coffee? What's up? You look concerned.' I gave Steve the rundown. After he had pushed and pulled the front wheels looking for a problem, his face wore an expression of crisis. I rang the AA. Fortunately I had taken breakdown membership just to cover Chitty in the UK and this was the time to use it. While we waited for over three hours, I considered all our options. I rang a local Land Rover dealership discussing potential scenarios and tried to locate the nearest campsite with the idea of staying close by while any work was on going.

It really seemed it was over before it began. I felt so deflated and helpless, almost a fraud for claiming to be able to drive across the world and here we were stuck in Maidstone. 'Whatever happens, we are not going home,' I said. The AA man turned up and managed to drive straight past us. He was obviously looking for a Land Rover and strangely he found one the other side of the car park! I ran over to him like a bullet just as the confused guy was losing the will to live. Bob Lacy was an ex-army mechanic and had spent his career working on military Land Rovers which was music to my ears. Once Bob had come to terms with our Land Rover modifications he set about investigating the potential problem. The bloke really did the AA justice. He removed both front wheels, checking wheel bearings, brakes and the transmission. He concluded there was nothing wrong or at least nothing he could find. God, had I imagined this or what? I was starting to feel a right berk and then he said, 'Look, it is possible you need to drive it to heat it up a bit. If you like I will follow you along the motorway to the next service station to see if you still get the problem.' Well, what a great offer and he gave us a tremendous sense of security. We headed off, Bob Lacy in the AA van behind and Steve and Julia following him in the Discovery.

Twenty miles down the road, we pulled into another car park and there were no rumbles at all. I was now really starting to question my sanity! Bob completed the relevant paperwork and then said, 'You know, I have seen some things in my time but never a Chitty Chitty Bang Bang. I am really impressed with what you are doing. Normally, I get the odd tip but on this occasion here is £20 towards your trip and to help you on your way' and he handed me a crisp note. How impressed were we? What a great service, what an even greater guy. He waved us off and by 6 p.m. we had made it to Dover.

Now, despite me griping about negative response to any sponsorship, my brother had managed to blag us a free P&O ferry crossing in return for a photo shoot for the P&O staff magazine. Once on board in fading light I decided to extend the AA membership to include European cover breakdown. Steve did the same and managed a year's cover for £60 extra. My insurance policy, however, for my 35-year-old Land Rover was a bit questionable and I was only allowed four weeks' cover and it would cost me £250! In my panic, I enrolled over a fading mobile phone signal as we sailed further out into the English Channel. This hadn't been my ideal first day, but it is all part of the event I had said. As long as we don't breakdown in England – those words kept ringing through my ears. Finally, the stress of the day turned back into excitement and now with the odd wave of insecurity we approached Calais late into the night and without a clue where we were going to stay or what was in store for us.

The ferry terminal lights faded into the background as we headed off in convoy looking for a campsite for the night. A few kilometres down the road, luck was on our side – before us was a campsite that was barrier operated and closed. Now nearly midnight, an Englishman, running over in a hysterical frenzy at seeing our car, granted us access. 'Bloody hell mate, Chitty Chitty Bang Bang, I can't believe it. I have been living here for six months they won't give my wife a visa,' he twittered on. The bloke was about thirty-five years old, tall, thin and clutching a roll-up fag. He pointed out that his Thai bride called Mali had opted to sit out the immigration process on the border and that was where they were staying. It was quite good having him there to let us in and show us around the site but we didn't want to hear about any immigration problems after the day we had just had.

Chapter 20 **B**avaria bound

It was a chilly start to the day. Making breakfast and packing up for the first time was not dissimilar to building an MFI unit. There is always a bit left over and nowhere for it to go!

Today there was a real sense of relief and for the first time there was no excuse to act like a Jack Russell with a peg stuck on the end of his tail. I soon learnt that Chitty's appetite for fuel was disturbing; Super Fina, Petronas and Shell were just hors d'oeuvres! The buyers' guides found in Land Rover magazines quoted a new series 3 model just like ours was good for sixteen miles per gallon but said nothing about the expected fuel economy thirty-five years later. After expressing my concerns for the next available service station to Steve, he said, 'Don't get fuel in France, it will be far cheaper in Belgium.' Will it? I thought. I really didn't have the luxury of driving across Europe in search of a good deal, but Steve was insistent he wasn't filling up with diesel until it was cheap. 'How does he know these things?' I said to Carolyn after a Belgium goose chase for a low cost litre. It wasn't that it mattered to us; we were resigned to the fact that a huge chunk of the budget was going on refined black gold and that was that. The unofficial secret plan, if ever there was one, was to get to Germany as soon as possible before ringing home. I just didn't want to make contact a week later and still be in France or even Maidstone, God forbid!

Long, slow days took us through Luxembourg and on to southern Germany. It soon became apparent that the communication between the cars via shared hand signals was embarrassingly frustrating. Steve over took and pulled into an electrical retailer with the intention of buying two-way radios. 'It's about a hundred euros which is fifty each,' he said. Well, that was fifty too much for us on our budget. It was a good idea, particularly if we lost sight of each other's car, but it was money we could ill afford and was a tank of fuel. Carolyn was particularly reluctant about wasting money on what she considered a boy's gadget. She said, 'It is not something we will ever use.' I wandered into the shop while Carolyn fended off Chitty tourists, giving them the general story in sign language.

'You know we can't use these in Iran,' I said. 'Why?' Steve asked. 'Because it's deemed as suspicious, I read it on the internet; they think you are spying or something like that.' Steve stopped me in my tracks 'Well, maybe, but we've got a long way to go before that,' he said. He had a point and I succumbed. On the road, Chitty was attracting a good deal of attention – but it was all good humoured and respectful. The majority of Germans didn't have a clue what Chitty Chitty Bang Bang was and had never heard of the film. We were bound for Füssen in Bavaria, bordering the mountains of Austria, and found a campsite en route. In fact, the campsite was very grand, set in the grounds of a huge manor house. I was feeling particularly regal driving Chitty into the grounds, only to have my ideas of grandeur shelved as we entered the residential trailer park camping area. Set among the mature trees and casting dappled shade was a ramshackle collection of permanent, aged and well-weathered caravans set behind flaking painted picket fences enclosing tatty but established postage-stamp gardens containing an array of yapping toy dogs. I always thought there was a fine line between a caravan camper and a new age traveller; if your caravan stays anywhere in the same spot for over a week, you are missing the point! These guys here were more permanent than the Druids at Stonehenge. Reversing into a well-used balding semi-grassy patch we drew along side a fifties period caravan with a huge black skull and cross bones flag flying. I turned to Carolyn and voiced my bemused opinion, 'It looks like we're having tea with Captain Jack Sparrow' then slap me on the back with a string of black pearls, a head complete with authentic eye patch popped round the opened door! ''Allo,' the wannabe black beard said in a German accent. Of all the campsites, we chose to spend the night sleeping next to the village idiot! ''Allo, velcum to uh 'ere,' he said in broken English. 'My name is Andrea, vould yar like dis bottle of red vine?' Well, Carolyn didn't need asking twice and I said, 'Hello, um yes, that is very kind of you' and with that the fortyish, rounded man with long flowing permed hair handed over a fine quality German wine and smiled, saying 'Enjoy your stay here with us' as he turned and disappeared back into his mobile galleon and that was the last we saw of him. 'How wrong can you be, what a nice friendly man,' Carolyn said nudging my arm and looking longingly at her bottle of red!

King Ludwig II of Bavaria had a passion to stamp his mark on the world and he certainly did that in the form of the fairy-tale castle near the small German town of Füssen. Named Neuschwanstein, meaning 'New Swan Stone', because of his obsession with swans, the castle is most perfect in design, straight out of Disneyland – in fact, it was the inspiration for Disney's magic castle. Carolyn and I were on a mission as the castle was used in the 1960s Chitty Chitty Bang Bang and we wanted a photo of the castle and the car.

From some strange misguided view of the world, we assumed that the castle, staff, town and locals – everyone – really would embrace our visit. Surely they would know all about the children's classic film and would welcome a visit from a replica star of the show. We had this grand idea of driving up to the castle, putting Chitty's wings on her and taking a few film-style snaps. As we found out the surrounding area was incredibly beautiful. The castle, whose turrets breached the skyline, was surrounded by pine trees and set against a background of clear blue skies, mountains and tranquil lakes. Perched on its own mountain, the Neuschwanstein is accessed by a well-trodden service road from the tourist village below and that was where we were heading. We made Füssen by 5 p.m. and in fading light. I drove through the Bavarian village and stopped in a queue of shire horse and carriages. The tourist run was taking fare-paying passengers slowly to the summit and I thought I would try to follow. Soon, tourists surrounded the car, every nationality wanted to know the ins and outs and whether they could take a ride to the castle thinking we were just another part of the tourist fraternity. A tall Austrian man, with black straight hair, dressed in bow tie and tails and holding a violin case, leant into the cab and enquired about the car. We told him how Chitty was based on a car that was affiliated to the castle and about our desire to drive to the keep. 'No, that is not possible,' he said with a strong accent, 'no one is allowed to the castle, you must walk.' 'Is there anyone we could ask?' said Carolyn. 'I am playing in the concert in the grand hall tonight and even I have to go by horse and carriage,' he confirmed.

Steve, not privy to the conversation, overtook and boldly drove up the steep narrow lane. The Discovery disappeared behind a wall of trees and we waited and waited to be called up on the walkie-talkie. No such call came so we decided to follow suit, much to a very disapproving look from the violinist. I too disappeared behind a wall of trees and I was confronted with Steve in debate with a police officer. 'Oh dear,' I said and quickly turned round to head back from where I had come. 'See, I told you!' the Austrian man exclaimed, smug at the fact that we had ignored him.

Well, photo or no photo, we did the tourist bit and embarked on a guided tour of the castle. Carolyn was somewhat disappointed as only the outside of the building was used in the film and the guide told her that it was only used as an aerial shot. However, the place was stunning and the location breathtaking and even if no one embraced the opportunity for a photo, we had ticked another box on our wish list.

Since Europe's borders had disappeared, one country ran into another and the hills of Bavaria climbed and dipped into the Austrian Alps, Chitty trundling on like a Noddy car in Toy Town, holding up all the traffic as she went.

Austria was as it should be. Toy Town had turned into a scene from The Sound of Music and the hills were alive with the sound of a pinking engine as the ageing tappets collided internally with other worn mechanical parts. Chitty struggled helplessly over the mountain pass, belching out blue smoke and causing a tailback which snaked into the tiny village below. Light relief was found as Chitty turned off into a gravelled farm driveway against a familiar rumble from under the car just like the first stop at Maidstone. She came to a halt under the eves of a traditional Austrian chalet building. A large blue board, decorated with a white, hand-painted tent, advertising camping facilities was propped up nearby and Carolyn checked in and spent the next twenty minutes getting to know the little tortoiseshell kitten living in a gap between a bunker of winter logs.

Chapter 21 **R**aining cats and dogs

Heidi and Trudy – as we named them – were the two cows roaming the field and woke us up at 4.30 a.m. with the incessant ringing of their neck bells. It should have been a pleasant wake-up call but I was ready to recommend a witness relocation programme for the Austrian rabbits as I was about to commit an off-the-hoof murder!

An early start was normally fine by me but with the torrential wind and rain, a sleepless night was had by all. Chitty had filled with water with the boat tail doing a pretty good job of holding the wet stuff in instead of keeping it out. Among the sodden paraphernalia of guidebooks and maps were my shoes holding enough water to hose down an inferno. In still, cool and misty air Steve emerged first in an effort to make tea; bleary eyed he resorted to matches to light the dual fuel stove. 'This doesn't bleedin' work, crap heap of crap,' he said holding his red gas firelighter. 'I've had this for twenty years and it's never let me down,' he continued grumpily. I can't say that I was too concerned as tea was already made. Carolyn and I were starting to get into a bit of a routine by now with breakfast and packing up. Porridge was the order of the day. .We had brought two huge bags with us in an attempt to save money on food while we were away, along with packets of rice, pasta, soup and dried milk and tins of tuna. This was essentially for roughing it in Iran and India but some of it was easily replaceable throughout Europe at not too bad a price. Steve took charge of the operation and looking a little frustrated he repeated, 'Twenty years I have had this thing, twenty bloody years and it packs up now, it must have got damp or something.' He was still waving it about like a sparkler on firework night and eventually after clicking the thing to death, he threw it in the tent.

We drove off in the rain and headed south towards Innsbruck and I realised that the £800 roof wasn't as waterproof as I had hoped! Chitty's one little windscreen wiper wiped for England and worked so hard whirring from left to right until in the heat of the moment it fell off! If ever I needed to see where I was going it was now, rolling down a mountain pass, a queue of traffic breathing down my neck and with spongy brakes that needed a written request for a week's notice to stop! I stuck my hand out between the vinyl door and the windscreen and grabbed the wiper blade from the bonnet. The rain was thundering down so hard now that anyone called Noah was signing up for a crash course in boat building. All the windows steamed up and the cabin temperature was soaring. 'Carolyn, pass me the chamois,' I shouted. I stuck my arm outside and tried to wipe the windscreen, which turned out to be pretty pathetic, partly because of the fact that as much rain was on the inside of the windscreen as out. The weather had forced its way through every join and seal and was turning Chitty into a mobile paddling pool. Rain streamed over the dashboard, worked its way around the clocks and trickled into the electrics. On Carolyn's side, a whirlpool was forming in the cigarette lighter 'Quick, unplug everything,' I said referring to the mobile phone and camera chargers. By her feet was the CD player and its wiring, now thinking it was on a day trip to the sea side. While I was chamoising anything wet and trying to drive at the same time, Carolyn was tearing up pieces of newspaper and stuffing them in anywhere and everywhere. It worked more like a diversion than a cure but it was okay for a short-term solution. The satnav had just become a sonar and fuses did what they should do – they fused! My attention was strained trying to drive, focus on the terrain and the impatient drivers behind held up at my 20 mph speed, and attempting to manage a flood damage control exercise. The rain continued but we found sanctuary in a service station under the pump canopy. We were in no hurry to move and had learnt a swift lesson. Ever since we completed Chitty, the weather had been fine and I had never considered how detrimental the rain could be to her, especially when the doors are on and it gets unbelievably hot inside. I didn't build any heat-proofing on the firewall between the cab and the engine, as I didn't think it would be a problem. What a berk! I now realised the importance and that when it rained, I was going round the world in a Turkish bath – great!

We both disembarked and squelched over to Steve and Julia in their ever-so-dry Discovery, not that I was bitter or anything! 'You ready then?' Steve said. 'No, I'm not going anywhere until it stops chucking it down,' I said sternly.

When it rains, it pours and today was no exception. A text of bad, irritating news activated both our newly acquired mobile phones. My text alarm tone was somewhat bland compared to Carolyn's vocal message alert, which was a young girl with an East End accent announcing, 'You've got a text you dirty slag.' We had deliberated over various means of communication including satellite phones but opted to buy a worldwide user-friendly SIM card from the Carphone Warehouse called SIM4travel. The text was from the Carphone Warehouse explaining our new SIM4travel cards were void due to a fault and were being replaced. The new cards were being sent to our home address! How useless was that? You buy that type of SIM card because you are travelling, not sitting at home watching Around the World in 80 Days! Carolyn was really concerned as this was her link to the children and her family. This was her outside world. She rang the helpline number on Steve's mobile and was fobbed off with a load of false promises. She tried to stress the fact that we were away for a year, all our mail was being redirected and a credit of £100 was on each SIM card that no longer worked. The useless person at the unhelpful help desk said she would look into it.

Finally, a ray of sunshine filtered through the parting clouds and we made northern Italy for a cool beer in a campsite on the banks of Lake Garda. Still with soggy socks, Carolyn and I squelched over to admire the view. It was really impressive and not what we had expected at all. The thought of Lake Garda conjured up images of stretches of grey, deep water set against a bland, nondescript background. How wrong I was. Beautiful sharp-edged mountains enveloped crystal clear water fringed with palms and charismatic villages. The sun had now broken through completely and the surroundings were mirrored on Chitty's bonnet. Before I could savour the moment too much, I was playing host to a mixture of interested tourists and locals intrigued with Chitty. I really enjoyed giving our story to a coach of tourists partly from the north-east of England. They all listened intently, asking questions now and then, in a broad Geordie accent.

Steve and Julia offered to babysit Chitty while Carolyn and I went for a water's edge walk. It was truly stunning. 'I've got a confession to make,' Carolyn said with a cheeky giggle to her voice as we strolled along, 'Go on,' I said with anticipation, wondering what she was about to come out with. 'Well, you know Steve's red gas firelighter thing that wouldn't spark and he got cross with?' 'Yeah?' I replied questioningly. 'Well, you know he said that it had probably got damp with all the rain,' 'Yeah,' I continued. 'Well, it probably was damp because I washed it up with the dishes last night as I didn't know what it was and thought that it was a steak prodder or something,' she went on in fits of laughter. I laughed as well, the dozy article, how could she not know what one of those was?

During dinner, against a backdrop of a setting sun over a lake that looked big enough to be the sea, Julia poured a glass of red wine and said, 'So what do you think about the "kitty" idea then?'

Julia had made a great effort to get involved with the planning and had been a godsend when it came to organising the trip visas. Now that we were on the road, she was putting into use her catering skills and forging a role as camp cook. I was reasonably comfortable with somebody making tea but I could see a clash of personalities coming. We had bought our own cooker, our own plates and utensils and some of our own food so logically we would be preparing our own meals. Our budget only allowed for practical and nutritious food with no frills and that was the reasoning behind two independent vehicles travelling together. Over the last few days a subtle and courteous sharing of provisions had taken place and now we were sitting down to a shared meal together. Steve, forever obliging, would offer around his red wine and assortment of anchovies, olives, crisps and pre-dinner nuts and on most occasions Carolyn and I would politely refrain, as we had nothing in return to offer.

'Kitty, ah well, so what's the kitty for then?' I said. Julia replied, 'Oh, just bread, milk and butter bits, the daily stuff that we all use.' After a brief consideration, we agreed to get a kitty together for just those provisions and both parties put in fifty euros in a plastic tub, which Carolyn initially kept hold of.

The morning started with my usual pre-flight checks, so to speak. I checked the engine oil and topped up about half a litre, which seemed to be a daily occurrence. I had a general look over the engine and alarmingly there was more than the normal oil dripping from the sump and a pool of clean oil was on the ground directly under the gearbox.

'Carolyn and I are going shopping when you are ready,' Julia called out. 'We ain't going anywhere until I've finished with the oil,' I replied in a slightly concerned way. 'And if you come back with one of those Italian leather handbags which you fell in love with yesterday, you will have to throw something out to make room,' I continued, tongue in cheek, to Carolyn. Climbing under the car, I managed to get oil on my shirt and trousers and I knew I would be for the high jump when Carolyn returned. Before we left on our trip, she had gone on and on about me taking my overalls but due to space, I decided they were not an essential item. Wrong! Nevertheless, the gearbox needed topping up and this was a pretty straightforward job, although I was disturbed to find it took a complete litre of EP90 oil and it only holds one and a half litres. God only knows how long I had been running on that small amount, I said to myself.

Chapter 22 **V**enetian whirlwind

In the car, Carolyn set the satnav for Lido di Jesolo, which, according to Steve, had a great campsite and was a ferry ride away from Venice. Feeling relatively confident, Chitty was suitably topped up in all areas and we headed south. The plan was quite simple: as we could never leave Chitty, we would watch her and stay on the campsite for a day while Steve and Julia did Venice; the following day we would go and they would babysit our old girl.

Having a few days in one place was a novelty so Carolyn rang the ever so unhelpful helpline for SIM4travel to arrange the swift dispatch of new SIM cards to this campsite. After World War III on the phone, they finally agreed to send them swift air and we should receive them in three days – by Friday.

Rain was now a thing of the past as the Italian sun baked down on the tarmac highway. Listening sadly to one of our only two CDs that we had brought from home, Carolyn was interrupted by my mobile ringing (I had brought with me my original Orange SIM card so was able to receive calls). 'Hello,' said the enthusiastic voice, 'Michael Coombes from Isle of Wight Radio here; is it convenient to talk?' 'Hello Michael, how are you?' I heard her say not having the foggiest to whom she was talking and unable to think of anyone called Michael. 'We would like to follow your trip live on air if that is okay with you. Can you give us a brief run down of where you are at the moment and what it has been like so far for you?' Carolyn indicated that it was Isle of Wight Radio and I pulled in pretty sharpish so she could hear above the noise of the wind in the cab. Steve pulled in hard behind us thinking something serious was up until I explained full of excitement that we were live on air on the Island. Carolyn spoke for a good five minutes and gave a great run down of the journey so far. It was the first wave of slight homesickness we experienced and it was quite emotional to think that all our friends and family at home might be listening in.

On the road, it was coming clear we were attracting a lot of attention and, instead of admiring the view, I had to concentrate on wayward mobile phone photographers. Today, we had been filmed by a lorry driver passing us on the hard shoulder, a busload of tourists almost tipping the bus as all the passengers darted to the offside to look out the window at us and over fifty cars and bikes taking photos with their mobile phones. Driving on the right I hugged the slow lane and cars would manoeuvre into position for a snap while others waited behind for their turn. A white van pulled alongside and smiling back at us was a well-built voluptuous Italian Mama Mia. She had a big round face, a huge grin and dimples in her cheeks. Her curly black hair framed her olive face and she waved frantically, her other hand holding the camera. The wave turned into a beckon as she ordered her husband to move closer. I held my position as the white Italian job moved in but our reciprocal waving and smiles soon waned on their third attempt at a close encounter with my facial stubble. The gap narrowed between us and I could almost smell Dolmio and garlic on her breath. She beckoned again and her obliging husband swerved right across our path. 'Bloody hell,' I shouted and whipped the steering wheel over to the right. How they didn't rip the front wing off Chitty I shall never know. I swerved on to the hard shoulder into the path of an Audi sneaking up for a photo on the other side. 'Beeeeeeeeb.' The horn made me jump so much I swerved back left again and nearly into Olivio as I called her. 'Christ, get out of the bloody way for God's sake,' I shouted. The road rumble was over. I straightened up, huffed and puffed a bit and then patted myself on the back for managing to avoid a collision. Just as I caught my emotional breath, a presidential-looking police officer stepped into the road. We were now chugging up a steep hill, cars were overtaking us left and right, but clearly this officer had us in his sights. He waved a reflective baton and ushered us off the road. There were two other uniformed officers hidden under intimidating police hats and wearing dark sunglasses. The first thing we noticed was the revolvers secured to their belts as this was an unusual sight for a Brit abroad. Very formally, the first police officer said in broken English, 'Passports and papers please.' I swiftly handed over my passport; he looked at it with no expression at all and said, 'Car papers, I need your car papers.' Hell, they were under the seat. We both leapt out of the car and lifted Chitty's chesterfield button-back bench seat. The two other officers stood like bodyguards in total silence. Searching for the logbook seemed to take for ages but finally among the tool bag, jump leads and first aid kit, I found the document folder and handed it over. I wondered if he knew what he was looking at and clearly he did. 'The car is not for you, different name, I need correct papers,' he said. Crap, what was he going on about I thought. Then Carolyn piped up, 'The car's in my name, I am the owner so he wants my stuff.' 'Give me your passport,' the policeman said, losing patience. Carolyn opened up her black rucksack and started to remove her soft toys. First out was 'Bear', which I had given her years ago and which has travelled the world with her, never spending a single night apart, and he was quickly followed by another six. Space was a premium and I had had to leave behind essentials including a spare wheel and a water pump for Chitty knowing that these seven incredibly useful items such as Piggy Wig, Cotton Tot and Monkey were in their place. Carolyn pulled out the first furry friend and sat him on the front wing but by the time she had got to soft toy number five in search of her passport, the mood had lifted and the officer said, 'Ah, bambinos, bambinos, it's okay, no problem, you go.' He was clearly no longer interested so I pulled out a photo card of Chitty, complete with wings out, which we had taken in the garden before we left and gave this to him as our souvenir. This was a perfect move as we were now acting like we had forged a long lost friendship and Carolyn explained that she was a police officer in England and we all posed for reciprocal photos.

The campsite at Lido di Jesolo was a well laid out and accommodated mostly Germans, but more to the point it was an excellent stopping off place for Venice. Still waiting in anticipation for our SIM4travel cards, Carolyn and I stayed home while Steve and Julia embarked on a romantic voyage of discovery into Venice. Well, that's how Julia saw it while Steve on the other hand was in search of fine wine, a good nosh-up and a postcard!

The reception on site confirmed to us again that no mail had been received for us so Carolyn – now close to boiling point – rang the unhelpful helpline only to be told they had no recollection of the previous conversations. After a few choice words, a guaranteed delivery was granted and we had to wait a few more days for them to supposedly honour this, although it was without much trust based on the service so far.

I took Steve's Discovery down to the harbour nearby to collect the pair after their Venetian experience and I was looking forward to the tales of the day. They both clambered on board with faces like they had been licking battery acid off a porcupine, and intuition told me that all had not gone according to plan. 'Had a good day?' I asked cheerily. Julia looked solemn and said nothing. Steve said, 'Not really, it's just a load of commercial rubbish, everything's overpriced, everywhere is crowded, and they wanted a hundred euros for a ride on a bloody gondola. I wasn't paying that. I've been here and done it before.' 'Oh,' I said. 'What about you Julia, did you enjoy it?' 'It was okay, but not what I expected,' she replied, unimpressed.

Undeterred, the next day Carolyn and I left Chitty in Steve and Julia's capable hands and set sail over the the lagoon to Venice in an Italian version of the African Queen packed to the gunnels with eager, hot, sweaty and overweight tourists. Yes, maybe it was an overpriced and commercial racket, but come on it's a tourist attraction so who cares? The Italian sunshine and hospitality ensured we had a great day doing all the silly things tourists do, photos in St Mark's Square, an alfresco cappuccino, which we almost had to take out a loan to buy, and then mastering the art of feeding pigeons all of which delighted in trying to sit on your head! Carolyn, with her fear of fluttery things, hid in handbag shops while I dodged every descending squirt of poop from above.

It became a real challenge to barter for a gondola ride at less than a hundred euros and at every canal, bridge and waterway we allowed the boatmen to haggle and hassle us, saying to them, 'No, that is too much.' Finally, we bargained so hard with a young gondolier dressed in a red and white stripy shirt and boater hat that he said, 'You give me forty euros then, my final price' in his distinguished Italian accent. Wow, that was less than half price for a romantic tour of the Grand Canal. 'No, no thanks,' I said; although it was cheap, it was still half a tank of fuel for Chitty but it was fun bartering!

Venice is very much a tourist destination for couples in love and many a proposal has been put forward aboard the gondolas. Classy boutiques of Gucci and Prada lined the cobbled streets and although a trifle smelly in some areas, it was beautiful, busy and yet majestic, manic and romantic with not a Cornetto in sight! What was made very apparent were the Do's and Don'ts of the city, which were signposted for all to see:

Don't sit on the ground
Don't eat while walking
Do not swim
No bathing costumes to be worn ....

So, sitting on the kerb in your bikini would land you in serious trouble!

Chapter 23 **M**aximus Guideus

We had a long day ahead so an early start was in order.

The route through Florence and Tuscany was on the agenda so I gave Chitty a good once-over, one that seemed to raise as many concerning questions as it solved. The oil was dripping from the sump and was leaving its mark below. This I was half expecting but not in such volume. Once under Chitty telltale signs of failing seals over the last three decades or so were emitting droplets of black gold from the gearbox, the transfer box, the engine and both the front and rear axles. I was making a fuss about the new rear axle now leaking oil and Carolyn was making a fuss about the SIM4travel unhelpful helpline which hadn't rung back as promised. With the summer season coming to an end and as it was a Saturday, we were not the only departures. As we packed up, so did the rest of the campsite. With a mixed bag of nationalities the whole event was an eye-opener to say the least. The Germans directly opposite were incredibly efficient, the tents and awning were dropped by numbers, cleaned, folded and packed away. However, the extended families of Italians just to our right were as flamboyant as only Italians can be! It was hilarious. Dad delegating, Mum ignoring him, kids fighting over how to fold the tarpaulin and the rest of the in-laws creating enough noise and bravado to drown out the Manchester United football team playing at home. Well, as for us conservative English folk, we packed up and prepared for the road over a nice cup of tea.

Curiously, before the trip, I was guilty as with so many Brits of taking for granted the fruits of the world while having a complete lack of understanding of it. I had been to Little Venice before I went to Venice, I had drunk at the Tyrol wine bar before going to Austria, partied on Belgian beer in an Irish pub before we passed through Brussels, driven a German car to work not knowing one day I would be passing through Bavaria. Turkey was not a 'must see' country when I devoured my Turkish kebab after time was called for last orders at the bar and the now national dish of curry burnt my lips on many a night of celebration without a thought of India. I planned the adventure on an American program running on my

Japanese computer, sat on our Swedish furniture and, most importantly before I left Britain, I was incredibly suspicious of anything foreign. How the world enlightens you.

At the campsite gates, Carolyn arranged for her hopefully impending mail of international SIM cards to be forwarded on to Rome as we couldn't wait any longer for them. Now with blood boiling into vapour and becoming emotionally distressed over the shop that had recommended the SIM4travel card were on her hit list..

The drive through the Tuscan hills was stunning but sadly the mobile madness was dominating the day. We should have been singing out of the window as the world went by but Carolyn was drafting a speech to the managing director. Steve was disillusioned at the motorway services incompetence to produce a decent Italian cappuccino and I was now stuck in the front of a six-car queue at a motorway toll that only accepted a telepass that I had never heard of. Playing the dumb English tourist fool (not having to try too hard), we negotiated a hazardous reversing exercise to the tone of choice Italian words. And if that wasn't enough, the only site available on the Tiber campsite in the heart of Rome stank of dog poo. We were all a little bit tired and ungrateful but at least the city had a few treats in store. When in Rome, do as the Romans do, so we opted for a spaghetti tea and planned Chitty's babysitters. Steve and Julia would go first and contemplate what the Romans actually did for us and we could stay home and entertain the Dutch couple that had just cycled from the Netherlands. Telling Chitty tales was all I was capable of as during the unloading of our tent, my back decided to give out. Now surely with the Colosseum, aqueducts and nearly 3,000 years of history, Rome would return our support crew from a better day than Venice did.

'I am at the main gate, have you got twenty euros for the taxi,' the text message came through from Steve. After settling his bill, Steve and Julia relayed their day of contrasts; embroiled in history they were unaware of the calculating group of bambinos relieving 'ice-cream eating tourists' of their wallets and Steve and Julia were now a grumpy statistic. Steve had parted company with his credit cards and Julia's total expedition cash supply of £600 just happened to be with them.

There was a sombre mood in the camp now and Carolyn and I were feeling guilty for looking forward to our Roman excursion tomorrow. We heeded the warning and separated our cash and credit cards and entered a hot line number to Barclaycard into our mobiles.

I awoke next morning to what felt like a slipped disc as the bits in my back were clearly having a disagreement with my nervous system and I was as enthusiastic to walk around aqueducts and vaults as I was to agree to a manual handling exercise in a pit full of vipers. But not only was I hoping to imagine Russell Crowe as a gladiator on the main stage but the Roman streets offered an endless supply of tempting high fashion and leather wear boasting the names of Gucci and Prada and without my financial control Carolyn would run away on a credit card frenzy! Although I could hardly sit or lie or walk or stand, I managed to do a bit of each, whinging my way through 3,000 years of history. Shopping was on Carolyn's agenda, however we had no money to spend, and so while I was focused on culture and visiting the Colosseum, Carolyn decided to people watch instead and sat on a grassy patch outside the ruins, giving her bemused attention on the overweight American tourists. I joined the thirty-minute queue to enter the site in anticipation of enjoying the marvels of history.. Afterwards, all my enlightened and amazed ancient architectural comments were wasted on my wife with the general response being, 'It's a ruin for God's sake, take a bulldozer to it and put it out of its collapsed misery and do something decent with the land and build a shopping mall or something.'

The sites of historical Rome bring every film you have ever watched into life and the grand scale of things is really thought provoking. Tourism is the new heart of the Roman Empire and the control of the masses is no different. Carolyn had the right idea by sitting in the sunshine amused by a group of thirty guide-following, earplug-listening porky friends from the USA intent on hearing the recorded tour and all looking down at their feet as they shuffled along – a collision of bodily parts rippled through the line when the group leader decided to stop. Touts for a personal tour hovered about advertising a price of twenty euros instead of the normal entrance fee of nine euros with a tempting reward of queue jumping and instant access. Sod that I thought, I've got a year off, I'm in no hurry! Strangely enough, the enrolled victims after parting with the extra euros then joined another queue, which was moving no faster because of overzealous touting success, which tickled me!

Times may have moved on but the Colosseum is playing out a daily tournament. The ticket staff take the role of gladiators doing daily battle with tourists – the would be Christian slaves. Maximus Guideus, the tour leader takes them into battle, weapons of Pentax, Canon and Nikon jostle for higher ground; the Romans take the lead with the twenty euro entrance fee. Points are awarded for the tourist paying only nine euros and for skipping the guidebook. Sweat and tears take their toll; three flights of weathered steps and the tourists puffing and panting like a fat club on a day out are waning with the final blow bringing the sweaty day trippers to their knees and having to exit via the gift shop fast! If carting Carolyn around a dusty monument wasn't enough, we then walked along the River Tiber to the Vatican City. It is what it is but I never expected to see so many men of the cloth. Carolyn's convent education had prepared her well, pointing out various ranks and hierarchy. 'Oh look, she's missing her habit head scarf,' Carolyn said as a half-dressed nun walked by. I just couldn't resist: 'It must be in the wash, she's got a dirty habit.' We both laughed so loud it was embarrassing and I then started to feel guilty for making fun in such a religious place.

Rome really was full of Romans, that is period-dressed, authentic-looking, full-on centurions. I mean if you're going to milk the tourists a bit of theatre does the trick. Groups of centurions posed with Hank and Chuck for a few shekels, normally five euros; it made for a great photo apart from a smoke-filled exposure as Marcus Maximus dragged on his MS Filtro cigarette.

We left Rome early the next morning after what we thought was a thoroughly good time. Steve and Julia didn't quite see it that way and reminded us of their disappointment every time we stopped for fuel or a cup of tea. Understandably the frustrations of losing your wallet do taint a place a bit, 'But hey it's all part of the adventure,' I said in a way that obviously wasn't helping. Two-thirds down the bootleg of Italy our fuel stop resembled a scene from the film Gandhi. There were so many people milling around us, while among a chorus of beeping horns a flotilla of Italian police cars descended on us blocking the pumps, and what for?

Yes, you've guessed it, a photo shoot Kate Moss would have been proud of. We were both very obliging partly because they were the police and partly because they looked capable of ensuring we woke up with a horse's head in the bed if we didn't play ball. We had been driving for three hours so this unofficial policemen's ball with potbellied Carlos sitting behind Chitty's steering wheel was a welcome break. At this point a Mini would have been more fitting to the wail of 'You were only supposed to blow the bloody doors off.' Steve and Julia sat patiently while we stole the forecourt limelight. I was engaged in Fingerbob sign language and Carolyn was under scrutiny from a well-healed businessman in a Range Rover Vogue. After relenting to the queue of persistent horn honkers eagerly waiting for benzene I parked up in an area of no man's land. Carolyn ran over to Steve in the Discovery explaining that the very nice man in the new shiny 4x4 was so impressed with Chitty he had invited us all to stay at his home on the Amalfi coast. Steve looked slightly unimpressed, dropping a bombshell of a statement: 'I've left my bloody passport in the campsite reception back in Rome.' 'Oh dear,' said Carolyn, more intent on sharing her enthusiastic story of how the guy would be home to entertain us once he had delivered a Ferrari to London. Promises of grand views over the Amalfi coast and the best pasta this side of Rome. This all sounded so exciting and incredibly tempting, unless you had just had your wallet stolen and lost your passport, that is.

Chapter 24 **S**pinning plates on Amalfi

Steve had the benefit of speed unlike the 45 mph he was usually limited to behind us, so headed north and agreed to meet at dusk at a campsite we hadn't yet found.

'I feel a bit guilty about heading off, don't you?' I said

'No, it won't take them long sitting in comfort with air conditioning, an automatic gearbox and cruise control,' Carolyn replied in defiance at the negative response received on her Italian dinner date. The old series 3 Land Rover's hardware was tucked under Chitty's outward persona and had a turning circle of a tanker, which was made even harder without power steering not to mention the coach load of tourists disembarking behind me. Satnav was really now just a 'satnag' pointing out the obvious and highlighting how many thousands of kilometres we still had to cover, with a real chance Steve and Julia would arrive before us, despite having a 500-kilometre excursion. Before we could make a hasty exit from Patronas oils the happy holidaymakers decided to forgo an espresso and talk to us. The novelty was waning a bit now and we needed to hit the road. 'G'day mate, she's a beauty, what a ripper, what is it?' 'Er it's a Chitty Chitty Bang Bang replica,' I said trying to move the conversation on. 'Fair dinkum, where are you heading?' the flamboyant Hawaiian shirt-wearing man said, tucked behind Polaroids and a Aussie rules football cap. 'Er, well, trying to make our way to Australia,' I said as I edged Chitty backwards. 'Strewth mate I'm from Australia.' No kidding, I whispered under my breath.

Finally, we hit the road and found max on the volume of the only CD we brought with us apart from the Chitty film sound track, of course. Mika blasted out over the Italian hills and Carolyn's mobile vibrated for attention. 'Stop, pullover,' Carolyn shouted. We had only managed a few kilometres down the road but this call was worth taking. 'Hi, I am Michael Coombes from Isle of Wight Radio. We would like to do a live link up, where are you,' the crackly voice said. How flattered we felt. The local station was still interested in following us across the globe. Everyone would hear back home, which should save on a few postcards. Michael's enthusiasm gave us a real sense of achievement which we really didn't feel worthy of. However, with the world listening, well the Isle of Wight then, we felt a moral obligation to keep going. On air, we were full on, although we still painted a genuine picture. It sounded wonderful, but then it was. The Mediterranean sun was living up to its reputation and the sights of Rome, the Tuscan countryside and transcending the Alps made it all so easy to sound positive.

On arrival in Marina del Cantone near Amalfi the broadcast would have been so different. Our partners in crime turned up close to 9 p.m. wearing an expression of sucked lemons. It was pitch black, the heavens now opened to a downpour equivalent to that of a bank holiday and our pitch was a Glastonbury mud bath. True to form, Carolyn didn't help matters by encouraging the little tortoiseshell kitten (intent on adopting us) stinking of rotting fish. Carolyn and I wrestled the tent to its feet, soaked to the skin, covered in mud and fighting a storm force gale. We were both starving but cooking was out of the question; the hillside campsite funnelled the entire washout to our bottom corner and we were on bailing duty.

Whenever there is a terrific thunderstorm in a film, the next day everybody wakes to a perfect day. It must be true, because the next morning was cracking. 'Fishy' the smelly kitten had found a bed on Steve's rucksack last night and my only shoes tucked under Chitty were full of water. Carolyn did real justice to her cooking skills on one burner and provided a feast to make up for no supper. By ten we were on a mission to tackle the Amalfi coastal drive and seek out the location of the Italian offer of hospitality.

'It's Italian not Greek and you should concentrate more on the road,' advised Carolyn. 'Well, I can't make head or tail of it, at this rate were going to miss it,' I replied somewhat frustrated at not being able to find the address of our Ferrari delivering would-be host. 'Well, stop then.' 'I can't stop, there's nowhere to bloody stop,' I said, hugging the cliff-hanging corners of the Amalfi road.

We had received a kind invitation from an Italian car dealer to stay at his house and stupidly we couldn't find it. He was so keen to see Chitty but we were stuck on one of the world's most scenic drives locked in until the end. The Amalfi coastline surpassed my Judith Chalmers's Wish You Were Here recollection. The drive along it was breathtakingly beautiful, but challenging to say the least. We covered about fifty kilometres, which took us most of the day. The cliff edge was all too close and the Italian drivers made the whole experience like a game of roulette with a team of risk-taking Russians. My concentration was on overtime keeping Chitty on the tarmac. With a whisker's clearance, the chances of careering into a granite cliff face or plummeting thousands of feet into the sea below was as likely as pulling the short straw when there is only one left. No power steering and huge amounts of play in the steering wheel reminiscent of driving a boat, it was like spinning plates while juggling three chainsaws. My mind was drifting, recalling the notes I had made from the Lonely Planet guide. Naples, with its sprawling, overcrowded suburbs, was not a place to stay; great for a view of Mount Vesuvius, but one year the Mafia was reported to have been involved in 400 murders. I also read there was a bit of a drug problem only to be confirmed when we passed a young woman with a needle still hanging out of her arm.

I snapped back to reality: an oncoming coach had just emerged from a tight corner on my side of the road. 'Jesus,' I said, 'it's over the side or a full frontal.' I had never pumped Chitty's brakes so hard. The coach driver did a far better job of avoiding a head on than me and just as a gap appeared between my front bumper and his, a Lycra-clad racing cyclist overtook me and disappeared through it. Fighting every corner, pumping the brakes and a thousand gear changes later, we were on the downward stretch and had made ground on pedalling Peppe with the yellow jersey. Afterwards, struggling uphill in second gear Chitty was overtaken by a cyclist. How embarrassing, a cyclist and we couldn't catch him. If only I could get Chitty's wings out, even if we couldn't fly away I could have knocked him off with one!

My oil stops seemed to be overtaking my fuel stops by now. Chitty had acquired an oil problem and her consumption needed an Occupational Health referral to Oil Anonymous. Despite frequent stops, we were now bound for a campsite in Gallipoli and had made contact with the site manager to enable us to have Carolyn's SIM4travel card delivered there from the UK along with Steve's new credit cards. We planned to hang around for as long as it took as clearly Steve wasn't going anywhere without plastic and Carolyn was at her wits' end over the lack of service and no contact with the kids.

Southern Italian roads are really long, hot and dusty and finding a pitch for the night was like discovering an oasis. 'Gallipoli, that's where the Australians had a major war campaign,' I confidently remarked, using my limited knowledge of history. We debated the events of the war over setting up camp and I considered the options of fitting a new engine sump gasket as time was on our side.

A morning liaison with the campsite staff confirmed no mail had been received and we would have to make for the post office in town. Steve whinged about Italy's lack of postal competence and Carolyn moaned about SIM4travel's incompetence, while I just moaned about them moaning. I expected to see a grand wartime memorial to the Australian conflict until a friendly local pointed out there were two Gallipolis and the one we were looking for was in Turkey. I quickly decided to stop harping on about historical knowledge. In haste, I bought eight litres of engine oil costing £80, with a plan to refill once I had changed the sump gasket. Carolyn lightened the mood by saying, 'I don't know about you but I'm off to the beach.' The nearest taste of the salty Med was about a kilometre away so Carolyn and I walked the dusty sun-baked road and Steve and Julia drove.

By 4 p.m. it was just Wiggy and I, as I call her (don't ask), on a deserted stretch of rugged beach. The sea was cooling in the autumn sun, but still comfortable for a dip. It was idyllic apart from the graffiti and unlovely surroundings of litter and a lone ownerless dog that kept cocking his leg on everything. We were in for a romantic seashore evening watching the sun tuck below the horizon, or so we thought. First to shatter the silence were two transit vans driving on to the beach. A team of uniformed men erected a temporary barrier of railings in a huge square open to the sea. We sat cleanly in the middle, looking on. The men said nothing. Then three police cars drove on to the beach and lots of officers got out including a cop in motorbike gear. They all milled around the railings looking at us, but saying nothing. 'Do you think we better move?' I said to Wigs,. 'No, we were here first; anyway, I want to know what's going on.' To a loud din of voices a platoon of Italian soldiers rambled down the sandbank and joined the audience looking at us; all now talking but not to us. 'I really think we need to move,' I said.

With that a coastguard patrol boat escorted by two rigid inflatable boats cut across the bay; they anchored off shore and a diver complete with underwater TV camera took to the water.

The TV theme carried on with the arrival of a complete location set-up. The beach was now packed with families, kids and tourists and all heads turned towards the arrival of what looked like 'Il Presidente' with a never-ending entourage of military generals, dignitaries and admirals hiding behind seventies-style sunglasses and hosting more brass than Chitty. 'Right that's it, I'm out of here. I need to ask somebody,' I said, leaping to my feet. Well, communication was hopeless so we waited with anticipation. The TV crew on full alert commenced filming a large container being manhandled out of a van labelled 'Istituto Marino' The container was placed in the centre on our old seating area and a huge turtle was released back into the wild. It was lovely to see but I was expecting so much more.

Chapter 25 **M**ore oil and ferry boats

The first of October brought a sense of achievement but was the first time the topic of sharing finances became an issue. I had outlined the importance of two separate trips going together right from the start;, this would mean own gear, own car and own money. Initially it made sense to start a kitty for teabags and milk because we were all sharing these. However, this soon evolved into full scale shopping, throwing in fifty euros here and there.

I'm not really sure who was at fault, us for not making clear our limited budget and our consequent need to eat, frugally or Steve and Julia for lack of awareness of our limited money and their flamboyant eating habits. Our ideas of provisions were fruit, vegetables, pasta and rice with the odd bottle of wine, while theirs were all of these enhanced with a selection of cheeses including Stilton, Camembert and mature Cheddar topped off with a variety pre-dinner nibbles: crackers, jars of anchovies, green and black olives, celery sticks, peanuts, walnuts and cashews. The shopping list grew to accommodate Parma ham and pastrami..All these were always offered round. The thing is, we didn't eat like this at home, so we certainly couldn't afford to now, and we were both too polite to say something. The arrival of new SIM and credit cards gave us the licence to head for the Brindisi ferry bound for Patras in Greece. Packing away took longer than usual because of protracted goodbyes from the campsite staff. The site was eerily empty at the end of the season so they were glad of someone to talk to, especially as we were leaving. Now without time to change the oil I conducted my normal routine of topping up the engine oil, the gearbox, the transfer box, the front differential, the rear axle, the clutch fluid and the brake fluid as they had all started to leak. In fact, anywhere that held oil on Chitty was leaking and my anxieties and concerns over the state of the mechanics were growing. We had only covered a bit of Europe and the thought of conquering Australia seemed a joke. Every 200 or so kilometres I was having to top up with a litre of Castrol's finest. At this rate we would be spending more on oil than we did on fuel and that was only good for sixteen miles to the gallon.

I reached into the back of Steve's Discovery and packed under their assortment of goodies, bags and holdalls was my reserve supply of engine oil. As I lifted the litre container by the lid, it came free and in the slowest of slow motions the bottle of thick black stuff glugged into their opened clothing bags. 'Oh bloody hell, Carolyn,' I yelled. I was swearing and leaping around like I had electrodes attached to my gonads. I fumbled with the slippery container making the whole thing worse and finally the oil dropped down my shirt front and my only pair of long trousers. I legged it over to Carolyn. 'Kitchen roll, quick, have you got the kitchen roll?' 'What?' 'Bog roll, I need bog roll.' Time just wasn't on my side; the oil had leaked into everything, stained the lot and stank awfully. 'God what am I going to do? I'll have to tell 'em. God I can't tell 'em, no I'll have to tell 'em. God what shall I do?' I rambled frantically. 'Like you say you will have to tell them,' confirmed Carolyn. I could see they were not impressed but credit to them they said nothing and got on with it.

For some reason travelling to Greece from Brindisi in Italy was a passion of mine. Gazing out of the window during a mind-numbing English lesson at Ventnor middle school, I imagined the adventure and excitement of an overheard story of a couple touring Europe. It was the sixties done thing I was told and Brindisi stuck in my mind from the age of eleven. No one really had an opinion on the route, so this was why we were here, in not the most scenic part of Italy. It was a busy port,, functional and not very attractive.

A good night's sleep was in order and so it was a pretty good idea to book a cabin The price difference beween a cabin or none in broken and misleading English from the Italian ticket seller appeared insignificant. Steve and Julia booked an outside top-of-the-range-suite complete with four bunks and bathroom for 260 euros, while we debated saving a bit of money by opting to sleep on the car deck. Before the idea of sharing the cabin had entered my head the cashier said, 'You have to book own room, no four people.' Oh how unsporting. 'Okay, we book own room,' I said, stupidly adopting broken Italian.

The police were everywhere; I could see a pattern forming. There were only two cars waiting to board, parked on the runway-sized holding area, and one of them was us. Policemen swarmed up to us and then three police cars pulled up alongside and disgorged a collection of fat, short, tall and skinny officers. They were all incredibly enthusiastic and friendly, and e-mail addresses were exchanged, Chitty photo cards given out and another blue light photo shoot took place just as we were summoned to embark.

Chitty chocked and secured for an overnight crossing and the complement of truck drivers scrutinising her vital statistics, we found our cabin. Comfortable and pleased with it, my illusions were soon shattered finding out my fare was no bargain. Reading an onboard brochure showed the broken and misleading English accent was obviously only serving the company share price and I could have saved 100 euros if we had slept with Steve and Julia!

My parents took turns in sharing their compliments for our achievements and concerns for our wellbeing via mobile phone and it made us both feel very proud, well loved, missed and really insecure, questioning what the hell we were up to. It was moments like this the pressure of fulfilling everybody's expectations came to bear. The ferry ride was a sanctuary away from the weight of vehicle reliability, questionable overland routes and the never ending searching for a suitable camping spot and a bed for the night.

Carolyn was out like a light but my mind was racing; the engine-room vibrations resonated throughout the cabin, sending shudders down my spine and as I breathed out I did a pretty good impression of a Red Indian. Then Greek ferry disaster awareness took hold. I was reliving the news stories of sinking burnt-out ships where the tourists launched the lifeboats while the crew legged it. Where's the exit, the fire hose, quickest way to the upper deck? 'Carolyn, are you awake?' There was silence. Oh stop whinging and go to sleep I told myself.

Chapter 26 **In search of the Golden fleece**

Carolyn lay back in a white plastic garden chair normally found in B&Q and not on the top deck of a Greek ferry. Leaning back with two legs resting against the railing, shorts hoisted uppermost and sunglasses perched like a tiara, she was in optimum position to absorb the morning rays.

Sailing past Corfu, Zakynthos and Cephalonia, we gazed of the heat-hazed view. The two blues of sea and sky joined seamlessly on the horizon, interrupted only by a trailing distant wake from the ship. We could have cruised all day, island hoping the Ionian Sea. Arriving early was somewhat disappointing. Our eyes heavy from an uneasy sleep anticipating the next chapter of our journey and the relentless thunder of five Italian children and their mother in the cabin next door, gave good reason to linger.

The main mover and shaker conducting the embarkation process was supporting stripes of gold on his lapels and carried an air of authority, which was wasted on us. Signalling us to start the engine, the thick moustached man, who wore an open shirt and medallion, flicked back his wavy hair and raised his hand. Now with an exposed rug of curly chest hair, the seventies porn star lookalike took charge of our safe arrival in Patras. Chitty under his watchful gaze rolled on to Greek soil to a camp wiggle and a wink to Carolyn. His ego boosted and Carolyn flattered, we joined the flow of traffic out of the city towards Athens.

Today making miles was top priority as the Greek capital not only housed the Acropolis but also according to our dog-eared map was positioned close to a little green triangle which I was hoping was a campsite.

Negotiating the highways of the Med was becoming a hot and bothered affair. Chitty's cabin temperature was rising and the gauge needle, which I had thought broken, had finally moved off cold. Hugging a mountainside motorway the scenic display unfolded around every corner and a constant chatter of 'Oh look at that' and 'Isn't it stunning' bounced between the hand-held radios. 'Find a place to stop for a brew up,' came the call from behind. 'I'm looking, I've been looking for the last hour, don't you know,' I mouthed impatiently. Trying to find somewhere to park up was proving a challenge; a mini heatwave twister, full of dust and debris, whistled across the road into our path. I braked; no, it was still coming. I swerved hard into the fast lane into the path of a distressed local with a compulsive horn-pushing disorder and bang … No, he missed us but the twister didn't. 'Grab the bloody roof,' I shouted; the vortex exploded in a supersonic sound bomb, shaking Chitty sideways and lifting the roof off its mounts. Both gripping the aluminium and heavy ash wood roof frame, pulling down hard with one arm each, I pulled over into the nearest lay-by. 'That was close … put the kettle on,' I said. We had just managed to save Chitty from a mini tornado and found the only view point had been used as a truckers' toilet. I wasn't surprised given the lack of stopping facilities but the overwhelming natural beauty of sun-drenched cliff face and turquoise Med below was being spoilt by human excrement and a bad smell of urine. The thought of a sandwich and a mug of tea had lost its appeal.

I had just come to terms with Italy's obsession with full-sized religious icons but at least they were static. Searching for leaded fuel was made so much more entertaining when the forecourt had a gigantic white marble Jesus Christ welcoming you with open arms. It was not just with petrol, the Son of God could be purchased in various sizes from what looked like a never ending chain of garden centres. Greece added a new dimension: mobile churches. Displayed pn the roadside, these temples on wheels come in all shapes and sizes from a moderate Halfords' trailer option to the light haulage, carnival-float type. I'm all for religious freedom of expression but if anyone needed saving it was the driver towing a mini Vatican city like it was sponsored by Red Bull as a new extreme sport. The sprawling suburbs rolled into city claustrophobia and congestion.

Athens is full of three things, Garages, garages, oh and garages. I have never seen so many car dealerships in my life: main dealer for Mazda followed by another main dealer for Mazda, then a shop, and then a main dealer for Citroen; a bit further down the road another main dealer for Mazda. I could go on about all the other car makers filling any amount of Greek soil and all I wanted was a pint of milk! Well, to be truthful, it wasn't all about cars; there were lots of garden centres too, not that that helped in the way of a cup of tea.

Twenty-six miles later the smog of Athens had spat us out on to the campsites of Marathon, with cartons of milk stocking the reception shelves.

Chitty was quickly becoming a local celebrity. I pulled into the reception car park and. while Carolyn darted of to find a pitch, I entertained the world. From the cleaners upwards everybody wanted to talk, touch and shake my hand. Chitty Chitty Bang Bang, they had never heard of it.I could have said Choppy Choppy Boing Boing and, in fact, sadly for no reason on some occasions I did!

We pitched the tent, put the table up, Millets' self-inflated beds struggled to inflate past the limp lettuce stage and the sleeping bags were unravelled. Carolyn was in heaven, the tent had found a home literally on the beach; it was pitched on golden sand with the water lapping at our feet. I rambled on how an ancient overenergetic local chap ran twenty-six miles to inform the Greek big cheese of an invading army. To save the day he ran his heart out, passed on the bad news and then dropped dead just up the road. 'So this is where it all started, all those epic charity runs with Hello magazine celebrities were all down to this place,' I said full of wisdom and knowledge. Carolyn far more concerned with manoeuvring her chair towards the late afternoon sun replied, 'Um that's nice dear, pass the lotion.' After the 'pull it down and build a shopping mall' Roman Colosseum comment from Carolyn I knew my visit to the Acropolis tomorrow would be a one-man affair. Every thought around anything mildly Greek captured in classic films and Christmas afternoon blockbusters came flooding back. I was reliving Jason and the Argonauts, battling with Spartacus wherever he came from and climbing Mount Olympus in a vivid mind journey in anticipation. Tomorrow Carolyn was in search of the golden sunshine while I was in search of the Golden Fleece.

As I climbed to the Acropolis, looking like a pale English tourist who had actually gone mad in the midday sun, I found myself going over and over my insecurities with oil leaks and the fact I still didn't feel we had achieved anything yet. Finally, taking the last step to the summit, sweat pouring from my forehead, I surveyed the smog-filled skyline. The search for the Golden Fleece was out of the question; all I was capable of searching for was a seat in the shade with a disappointing view of tourists and scaffolding. Trying to make out the ancient Acropolis through a renovation site and steel tubing, my mind wandered to my reservation about Iran. All summer I had joked and played down the fact we were planning to pass through a strict Muslim country which had only just released a group of sailors from the British Royal Navy, which not so long a go I was part of. Somehow whether I was ambitious, brave or just plain stupid, tackling Iran was meaningful to me. Touring Europe was no great feat and until we had crossed the Bosphorus and Golden Horn into Asia and were knocking on the Iranian door I had proved nothing. I knew deep down Carolyn was hiding concerns over our impending route and it was certainly based around her worries for the kids; she would deal with danger but they still needed a mum. Despite being camped near the lapping waves on a sandy beach, neither of us could sleep knowing that so far this was just a holiday in the Med, the lull before the storm.

The morning brought a sand-filled wind whistling round Chitty so the plan to try to replace the sump gasket I had tucked away in the spares box looked futile. Now burning and leaking a litre of oil every 500 kilometres a replacement was in order. Oily engine parts and sand do not mix well so the leak would have to wait. This was just as well because my overpriced Italian oil had a recently noticed label on it saying 'Sintetico' and I needed mineral, I thought. Not only had I wasted 80 euros on the wrong black oily stuff but also I had to think of a way of telling Carolyn. The sump gasket set now found a new home above our heads in Chitty's roof netting for easy access along with an encyclopaedia of internet articles I downloaded just before we left. It really wasn't the time to start going through this stuff because among the Foreign Office warnings advising strictly against travelling through Iran and Pakistan I came across an article where a well-travelled overlander had recommended photocopying the vehicle registration documents and just about any other important paperwork in case the border guards demanded a bribe for their return. But more to the point I found the note on the location of an ex-Camel trophy rally

Land Rover mechanic working out of a back-street garage in Istanbul, so maybe I'd wait until then to replace the sump gasket, I thought.

The day was becoming somewhat overcast and getting wet looked probable. Packing up before the heavens opened, I realised our obsession with tea. Apart from the 2,000 PG tips tea bags on board, we had three kettles, one for on the move with a cigarette lighter adapter, a standard kettle and a bushman's Kelly kettle from Ireland. The Kelly kettle heats with just paper and I figured it would be great for emergencies in the desert somewhere, although we hadn't used it yet and I never figured on the grief I would get from Carolyn for its sheer impractical size.

The Ramnus campsite run by a young slim-built Indian lad had provided us with a great base but it was now time to leave. He spoke great English but was far more interested in entertaining the pretty girl sitting wrapped in a duvet in his front room. She appeared younger and from Greek stock and was waking from a sleepover. Charging us the correct pitch fee as advertised on the board behind him was just too unimportant with a beckoning female within. 'You stayed two nights,' he said hastily. 'No three,' I said. 'Um that's, um let's see, er 30 euros, yes 30 euros please,' he said looking towards his duvet date. Well, that was fine by me, the cheapest so far.

It was 8 October and four days from completing our first full month away from home. Apart from oli guzzling, all was well. The 'satnag' had decided to take us the scenic route on a coastal road reminiscent of intestines. I normally was up for a scenic drive but not this time. Thunder and lighting accompanied the downpour of Grecian cats and dogs, and just like before, the rain was as prevalent on the inside of the windscreen as on the out, working its way through dashboard electrics and filling my recently removed shoes with water again.

Negotiating bendy wet roads with a view similar to looking through damp tracing paper, my greatest fear became a reality. The oil light was on. 'Oh God, no, no, no, no, no, the flippin' light's on Wigs, the oil light's on,' I mumbled in a pathetic and distressed way. There was silence. Carolyn knew by the tone of my voice this was serious and not knowing anything at all about oil lights said nothing. 'How long's the light been on,' I said in a unfairly accusatory way. Still silence. 'Oh bloody hell we'll have to stop. I can't stop,' I answered my own question.

We were travelling uphill on a single-carriage road with a queue behind longer than the Great Wall of China.. I knew the first thing to do was stop, but I couldn't because the time it took to screw the engine was unreassuringly short, so in a frozen state of panic I carried on driving,

Chitty kept going, the rain continued to pour and the queue behind grew longer. Finally, the road became a duel carriageway and the impatient drivers behind were able to overtake. At the first sight of a service station we careered off the road for advice. Now when I say service station I was hoping for a garage. Carolyn sat with Chitty and I ran into the café. 'Excuse me, do you have a garage, a mechanic. Me-chan-ic.' The blank look from the Greek serving ladies from hell didn't fill me with much confidence.

'I need a me-chan-ic, car, auto me-chan-ic,' I tried to explain to a suited lady of visual authority. The lady kindly acknowledged my request and asked me to follow her. Her positive body language brought a glimmer of hope until we arrived at the ATM. This really was hopeless; however, across the road was a tyre fitter.

A coachload of Russian tourists had now gathered around the car and my short but polite answers were giving the hint I needed to move on.As I explained that Chitty couldn't really fly to a large man in a singlet and his fake-boobed girlfriend, I started the engine. It was like the paparazzi with foreign lunatics throwing themselves in front of the bonnet. Mobile on full alert, a desperate man ran alongside and videoed as we entered the slip road; flattering but how annoying.

The tyre-fitting centre was just that with not a glimpse of an oiled-up grease monkey. With overalls turned down to the waist the attendant leapt to his feet and rushed over, ran his hand along the bonnet and then kicked the front tyres. 'Good … Good' he said pointing to my new Nexen tyres. My Greek was non-existent and his English included one word only, 'good'. I pointed to the oil light and then indicated the Land Rover chassis plate; he clearly could see my concern and made a call from his mobile. I smiled, he smiled; I had no idea what was happening so we waited, and waited. Steve and Julia went to the café for more coffee and before long two guys pulled up in a rather swish BMW. 'Hello my friend my name is Yanis.. You have a very nice Series 3 Land Rover,' the portly well-dressed Greek-looking businessman said. 'Hi, yes, thanks my name's Nick, the oil light came on and, oh, yes, this is my wife Carolyn, I am really worried about the pump,' I rambled on.. 'I have three Series 3 Land Rovers, I will help, you park on road, must always park on grass, that's the joke eh,' Yanis said. 'Sorry?' I questioned. 'Land Rovers always leak oil, you must park on grass ha ha,' he said, head under the bonnet. After disappearing for a few hours, amazingly he returned with an oil pressure switch to swap for mine. He checked the oil was being pumped around the engine by removing a feeder pipe and then concluded nothing was wrong. I still wasn't convinced but eternally grateful for out of the blue genuine help and friendship. Yanis recommended a Land Rover dealership in Volos and gave me his card. Just as we said our goodbyes he touched the dial on the dashboard and guess what, the light went out. He pushed again and on it went,.Oh dear, I thought, all that worry and it's down to my dodgy wiring.

Both Carolyn and I were touched by the free support we were given. I wasn't sure if it was because we were lost travellers in need or it was just the charisma of Chitty.

Chapter 27 **P**ainful eye for detail

Volos came into view and the plan was to find the Land Rover dealership first. The business card from Yanis was written in Greek so finding the address was as likely as picking out a four-leaf clover at hay-making.

Chitty came to a halt outside a local fish market. It was impressive, fish, ice and hundreds of people, who were now abandoning their fish duties and were gathering round us clutching smelly gutting knives. Chitty had brought Volos and the central fish market to a standstill. Photo cards and photo shoots were exchanged for a translator. I rang the garage number and handed my phone to the translator, who had reasonable English. I was hoping for directions but to my surprise I was informed the garage had sent a boy out on a scooter to find us and we could follow him back. An appointment was booked.However, we were lucky; a fully booked week of servicing allowed only for an unofficial slot at 8 a.m. Chitty's charm had won favour with the mechanics.

Now en route for a bed for the night we parked up in the town centre in search of a cash point. Carolyn was on the money run while I was chatted up by the locals. A crowd soon gathered round including a delightful, frail old gentleman aged 83 who gabbled on the ins and outs of his 1965 Morris 1100 parked over the road, a parking attendant who via a translator pointed out I was parked illegally but could stay because she liked the car, and a news reporter who could only speak Greek. A young student passing by translated our talk; by insisting on the fact I had built the car for my wife she made it a love story. She relayed it to the press and gave an off-the-cuff talk to the group of bystanders, who in turn oooed and ahhhed and then gave a round of applause. This really was becoming quite surreal. Carolyn was taking her time, maybe she had asked for an ATM and somebody had taken her to find a mechanic! The wait was forcing me to listen to the war stories of the old boy, his time in Piccadilly and a guided tour of his now sorry looking Morris motor. I wasn't paying too much attention until the slim built, white-haired old man dressed in a smart formal shirt explained how he missed his late wife and how much she loved the little car. His heart was well and truly wrapped up in the old

1100 now sprouting grass from its undercarriage. His voice quivered and a tear came to his eye as he tried to tell more of his fond memories.

After the town of Volos, 300 kilometres from Marathon via wiggly roads, service stations, tyre fitters, a fish market and another litre of oil consumed, we found a great little campsite. Not exactly on the beach but pitched very near the gentle evening ripples of the Med. Tomorrow was oil repair D-day and an early start was on the agenda. The rain returned in force and we both soon realised why the lower camping area was free. The rain became streams, which in turn decided to forge a river and funnel it down the weathered ruts in the soil caused by previous downpours. The gentle Med was now blowing a gale and our tent was tossing wet and wild.

Anxious to make the garage early and hoping to hit the road once the sump gasket was replaced, we woke to my watch alarm in the pitch black. The morning was still and there was an air of anticipation. Carolyn and I tiptoed round packing up the tent trying not to wake Steve and Julia, who we would be meeting later. With daybreak the dawn light allowed making Chitty road ready easier. Carolyn secured the roll-down plastic doors in the roof netting behind our heads and I lashed the tent to the rack. We had taken to covering all our luggage with an old motor cycle cover after having experienced the delights of wet bedding and damp clothes. This was the final stage of the now well-rehearsed packing-up process. Carolyn and I had never discussed who would do what but we had found a perfectly synchronised routine for quietly making and unmaking camp. I stood on Chitty's rear wheel reaching across the luggage on the rear. I grabbed the bungee and pulled it tight over the tent looking for a secure point when bang, and I mean bang, the bungee snapped. My whole life, the trip and just about anything of any importance had just flashed before me; the thick corded bungee on full stretch had just snapped clean into my eye, my left eye, the eye I was blinded in for a few months when I was aged 10. Pain, I can't tell you about the pain, it was unbelievable. My brother shot a sucker dart from a bow and arrow hitting me clean in my left eye and I collapsed in pain, rolling over and over in the road. Today's horror was too reminiscent of my childhood. I covered my eye and collapsed, falling off the back of the car. I yelled out in agony, waking Steve and Julia and bringing the assistance of my wife. Blood poured through my hands and I rolled over and over in the campsite dust. Grunting and groaning, I managed to raise myself on all fours. Panting heavily and sweating profusely, I opened my eyes. A red-stained world of blurred images came into view. Thank the Lord, I could see. A wave of shock-related nausea engulfed me and I fell into Carolyn's arms. 'You'll be okay, you'll be fine, don't worry,' Carolyn whispered gently, wiping my brow..

With deep breaths and among shooting pains through the side of my head, my mind went into overdrive. That's it I thought, it's all over, the trip, it's all over. We have made it only to Greece. Four years to build the car, a year in the planning, everybody expecting so much and it was over. 'Let me see, come on lift up, sweetheart,' Carolyn whispered to me. 'You need an ambulance; you have to go to hospital,' Steve stated. Carolyn gently lifted my head, coaxing me to open my eye, saying, 'Come on, let's have a look.' I opened my eye and I could instantly see the concern on Carolyn's face. A small chunk from the white of my eye was missing; the bungee had fortunately managed to miss my pupil and whipped out a small chunk of my eyeball, which was now resting on the side of my nose. Carolyn went into first aid mode, flushing out my eye with eyewash and dressing it to the standard of clinical pirate. The shooting pains developed into a deep throb but at least the immediate panic was over. Steve piped up again 'You have to go to hospital.'

Carolyn drove Chitty to the garage for 7 a.m. just before I was dropped off at the hospital. Slightly panicking a bit about travel insurance, I was greeted by an extremely enthusiastic doctor, who in a wave of animated hand gestures, recognised me from that day's Greek newspaper. After signing me in, he told me our overland love story was headlines, and, oh, not to worry about the insurance paperwork. He then reappeared from behind the counter with Chitty, Carolyn and I adorning the front page of the daily rag. I was flattered but had more on my mind than revelling in our fifteen minutes of fame. Not that I could see the picture with one eye patched up and the other blurred with fluid. I was nervous, feeling sick, worried about the entire trip, and Doctor Ziverge wanted to know the whereabouts of the car and was acting like a PR agent passing the article around the reception.

I was lucky, an ultraviolet scan proved the pupil was still intact and it was all repairable. After a good patch up and fulfilling my prescription, Carolyn and I walked through the town's shopping centre to towards the garage where Chitty was also undergoing minor surgery.

Searching for eyelets and an eyelet-making tool to help secure the tarpaulin in wind and rain, we were in and out of just about every shop Volos had to offer. We couldn't find what we wanted, but we were compensated with an overwhelming warm welcome and good luck on our journey by the Volos newspaper-reading community.

It was only 11 a.m. and so much had happened. The garage was small, located down a dusty back street, and the entrance was obscured by interested front-page readers milling around hoping for a glimpse of Chitty. The word had got around fast and the gathering crowd included a butcher. The man was as a butcher should be: round, fat and with a huge grin supporting his double chin. His chef's chequered trousers and white T-shirt stretched over his flab. Clearly he was keen to see Chitty as his hands were covered in freshly butchered blood and his not so white top looked like he had just taken part in mass murder.

Chitty was the proud owner of a new sump gasket but the ever so helpful mechanic pointed out more leaks than the Titanic. The engine had a few small trails of oil from most joints and seals; the gearbox was leaking like a sailor on his first run ashore after consuming fifteen pints. The transfer box didn't look too clever and the front and rear differentials were leaving pools of black sticky stuff wherever we parked. But hey, it's a Land Rover, I kept being told.

Handshakes, photos and a big thank you as the motor sparked in to life and the crowd parted to allow us through. A huge BMW pulled up alongside as we entered the road. A man of authority leant out the window and shouted, 'Rolls Royce? Daimler? Bentley?' I was flattered but replied, 'No, sorry, Land Rover.'

We made Olympus Beach by nightfall in the hardest downpour yet. All the bedding was soaked.

Carolyn woke to the cries of kittens. The campsite was full of pregnant cats and kittens. It wasn't long before milk was being dished out, tuna tins reserved for the Iranian desert were opened and an eager queue of wiggly tails filled the pitch. I did the normal one-stop all-round oil top-up; Carolyn wasted no time playing mum to a grey little kitten on his last legs while Steve munched on a bag of peanuts and made faces.

Our last night in Greece was in the northern town of Alexandropoli, close to the Turkish border. The beach campground was empty; the end of the season had left the site unloved and quite frankly depressing. It was still raining which didn't help but there was underlying optimism.

Greece had opened our eyes to the potential maintenance of Chitty and her demanding fuel and oil consumption and our own vulnerabilities. Physically we had to be careful and emotionally we had to manage the relationship with Steve and Julia. Leaving Europe at the Turkish border would bring a sense of achievement and we would be well and truly on our way across the globe into Asia, with this leg confirming the point of no return.

'How are you feeling,' I whispered in the still dark night, lying alongside Carolyn. 'I miss the kids,' she said in a tearful voice, 'night night.'

Chapter 28 **T**urkey trials

Bold and confident we join the queue of lorries waiting to cross the Turkish border at Ipsala. So far in Europe we had seen no political boundaries so this was the first. Paperwork in hand I brazenly walk up to the check point booth. The stern-faced suited gentleman looks up and says 'Wait' so I do for about twenty minutes. This was starting to grate a bit as various lorries and cars pulled up behind us, pushed in, were processed and sent on their way. Finally the guy who looked as if he was about to hang someone said 'Passport'. Gingerly Steve and I handed over four passports. 'Visa, no Visa,' Grumpy said slamming the passports on the counter and pointing to a grey official-type building.

Before even getting back to the car a uniformed border guard, a machine gun slung over one shoulder, pointed to Chitty, flicking his hand in a move your car gesture. Now with us parked in front of the bureaucracy building, Carolyn and I joined the visa queue. That wasn't too painful apart from being relieved of 15 euros for the pleasure. Returning to the booth without the car this time, again I offered the four passports, now in my schoolboy best behaviour mode. Flicking through the first book, Grumpy, whose face looked as if he had been sucking a grapefruit, looked me in the eye and said, 'Insurance, give me your car insurance,' Before I could ask why, he slung the passports my way and pointed to the grey building again. This wasn't going well; back we trotted, queued again and parted with 48 euros for the obligatory one month's third party car insurance. At our third attempt we queued while Mr Grumpy was putting an Iranian truck driver through a hoop-jumping exercise unloading the entire contents of his juggernaut and trailer. He then returned to the booth so I passed over the passports complete with visas, my car insurance certificate which I couldn't understand and Chitty's registration documents. Immediately he picked up the registration documents, which naively I thought he wouldn't recognise, and then with fire in his eyes slung them back saying, 'This is fake, you cheat me, origin-nal origin-nal.' This was serious stuff. I was at our first major border having just presented copied documents and the border official just wasn't happy. He turned to a border guard and ranted on in Turkish, pointing to me and the car and waving his hands around like we had just been caught smuggling drugs. Hell, maybe that's what he thinks. All of a sudden am I thinking of the film Midnight Express. I was speechless, I felt awful, this was not the kind of start I wanted. Mr Grumpy was now Mr Very Angry and his voice was full of 'don't hack me off any more or I'll lock you up'. Not a good start.

'Carolyn get out quick, I need the car documents,' I panicked. 'What?' she replied. 'I need the originals, matey's going berserk,' I said, fearing for my life. Lifting the front seat I pulled out the waterproof document folder squashed between jump leads, towrope and a first aid kit. I rifled frantically through it.. 'Bloody internet, see you listen to that lot, this is what happens,' I said blaming anybody but me. Fourth attempt and four hours later I handed over all original and visa ready, insurance-stamped legal paperwork. Everything was scrutinised, signed and shuffled around. Carolyn drove Chitty towards the booth and Mr Very Angry shuffled my paperwork, handed it over and escorted me to the car. 'Whisky, drugs, smokes, what is this,' he said pointing to our sausage-shaped roll mats. 'Sleep Sleep,' Carolyn said, making a sleeping gesture with her two hands against her head. 'Okay you go,' he told us. However, before we moved he said, 'No stop there', waving us over to a parking space the other side of the booth, 'I want photo.' Mr Very Angry now had a grin from ear to ear; his cigarette had a long, teetering tower of ash as he climbed into the driving seat. Both hands on the steering wheel, he bantered in Turkish to the group of surrounding guards. I moved to the middle of the front bench seat just as an armed guard took it upon himself to climb into the passenger side. I didn't really mind considering the circumstances, apart from the fact he was over six foot tall and his boots were scuffing all the woodwork, and to top it all the barrel of his machine gun was sticking into my ribs. I just hope that thing's not bloody loaded, I thought, of course it's loaded. Mr Very Angry is now my best friend. There isn't much English spoken but with the aid of a Chitty photo card and a lot of handshaking between us and the guards the mood lifts. With the guards' arms around my shoulders a group photo concluded the exercise. Boy, that was hard work. This was something I had to get used to: the men dealt only with me, and Carolyn didn't get a look in. I could handle that. Putting their arms around me and holding my hand, all that male bonding stuff, was quite normal as we moved east, but not for me. I had left that behind in childhood

We entered Turkey with a sigh of relief, stocked up on cheap duty free fags and biro pens to offer as bribes across the world and made for Istanbul.

Rain, more bloody rain, I probably wouldn't have noticed in a standard car but in Chitty it was a constant battle to keep our luggage dry. The rain was unrelenting, we both held tightly to the roll-down doors forcing them close to the windscreen, trying to prevent rain soaking our legs and feet. Driving like this with just one hand, as well as periodically wiping the inside of the windscreen to see where we were going, was taxing to say the least. Signs to Istanbul directed us to the wet city centre. I had read on the internet about the Londra campsite in the heart of town but I did not hold out much hope after our last online advice. The Shell petrol station came into view as per the directions; so far so good. We entered the forecourt and passed into the camping area behind. 'Oh dear it's a car park next to a go-kart track,,surely this can't be it,' Carolyn said, looking for something that slightly resembled a tent. Now if there was a day to feel homesick and insecure then today was the day, our bedding was still damp and the temperature had plummeted to 11° Centigrade. Carolyn found reception and confirmed this was it; how disappointing. It was still bucketing down and not a sight of grass to pitch the tent. The mood was sombre to say the least. Steve piped up, 'Well, I'm not staying here.' I engaged in a battle of words outlining the lack of alternatives, while Julia compromised with campsite owner on camping in a carport. He allowed us to park undercover in the corrugated tin building. Damp, depressing and disillusioned were a few random thoughts but at least we had a bed for the windy, wet night ahead.

We sat in the car drinking tea dressed in our fleeces and with full waterproofs complete with hat. The best way to describe this place is as follows: the campsite was a car park, behind a Shell petrol station located next to a motorway passing through Istanbul. The car park, sorry campsite, was surrounded on all sides by tall buildings. On one side was a university with a manned barrier five metres from our tent; this opened every five minutes to frantic loud horn beeping by the awaiting cars, which seemed mostly to be police. This went on all night, preventing sleep. On the other side there were three five-a-side semi-covered football pitches, floodlit and entertaining teams until midnight. We were kept company by six or seven stray dogs that barked every time the ball was kicked and carried on through the night to the sound of the beeping cars. The third side was a covered go-kart track packed with enthusiastic kids and F1 wannabes. At least they wrapped it up at 10 p.m.

Now we come to the wind and rain. Luckily we had been allowed to park under a corrugated tin-roofed carport. However, it did have a concrete base so the torrential rain formed Lake Windermere around the tent. The noise was deafening and as rain turned to hail and forked lightning crackled we had to shout to each other to communicate our gripes. In between the dogs, beeps, rain and thunder a huge go-kart advertising banner some fifteen feet across had ripped free in the wind and was flapping about above are heads to the sound of a motor boat. Funny really, we came here because the internet said, 'Nice relaxing place with good connections to the centre of Istanbul.'

It was a Sunday morning and the usual routine took place. Steve and Julia took to the city highlights first thing and Carolyn and I polished Chitty's brass for eight hours as the following day it would be our turn to sightsee.

We didn't know much about the city sitting on the Bosphorus, or the Golden Horn, whatever that was. I had seen a photo of the Blue Mosque so we figured that was as good a place to get ripped off as any. 'Where are you from my friend' said a very smart and softly spoken man. 'Oh, the Isle of Wight', I said, hoping to catch them out with that one. 'Ah yes Jimi Hendrix 1960s pop festival.' See, you can't take anything for granted. 'Would you like a short story about the Blue Mosque my friend,' he said, ushering us along. 'Um no we are fine, we are okay thanks.' ' Good, you see the Blue Mosque was built in …' What part of no didn't he understand. We were both completely ignoring him and he was following us around like a friendly puppy. I had made the fatal mistake of making eye contact and with tour over he said, 'You must give me 25 euros my friend. I will accept dollars or pounds sterling my friend.' I bet you will I thought as I succumbed to parting with 10 Turkish lira and then moaned about it.

The old spice market, which really should be renamed the old tourist tat market, gave us a feeling of being foreign. This was the first time so far we really felt abroad, Asia was eagerly anticipated and we loved it.

We caught the number 82 bus back to the campsite after buying walnuts, pistachios and hot chestnuts, and a car cover from B&Q. The day ended with a camping bill of 123 euros, which nearly made me choke on my pistachio, and an ear bending on how shit the site was from Steve.. Sadly enough, though, because it was so bad, it has left a lasting memory with us, one to reflect on over and over again and laugh about!

We woke the next morning to the Islamic call to prayer, which was now becoming a familiar sound, and left the city at dawn. The approach road to the Golden Horn and Bosphorus waterway gave a splendid smog-filled view of Istanbul lit up in an orange glow of early morning sun. The day felt positive, bright and full of optimism as we pulled up at the tollgate booth. Crossing the huge suspension bridge would bring credibility to our adventure as we moved on from Europe, if only we could get past the barrier. The booths were all automatic and the barrier wouldn't lift unless you had a bridge card, so I was told by a friendly motorcyclist who recommended we reverse up and buy one. This card needed to be purchased from the building behind us, which was closed because of a strike. So here we were on the verge of traversing the globe and I hadn't got a ticket. The queues of cars having to reverse back to allow us out weren't too pleased and the motorcycle cop with his beady eye on us looked concerned. 'Sod this, I'm off,' I said in defiance as a black Mercedes drove round the barrier. I followed suit, then wished I hadn't, because negotiating the barrier triggered a loud alarm,complete with flashing lights. 'Stop, no go, crap, the policeman,' Carolyn hollered. I slammed on the brakes and looked back, as indecisive as my four-times married sister's wedding vows. Oh, he is waving me on, 'Thank God.'

The bridge offered a cracking view and as the 'Welcome to Asia' sign came into sight a big smile filled our faces. I looked at Carolyn and said, 'This is where it really starts.'

Chapter 29 **L**ast King of the Hittites

Vaguely heading east, the road to the Turkish capital, Ankara, passed by Izmir where getting petrol has now become a very civilised affair. A larger than life character, just stumbled out of Texas it appeared by his tall Stetson hat complemented with dark glasses and cow boyboots, greeted us. 'Magnifico, bella, super,' the big Turk said making kissing-hand gestures; then he took my hand, slung his arm round my shoulder and escorted me in for a cup of tea. The tea I liked but I was still getting used to this male hand-holding lark. An interpreter conveyed my best wishes and thanked the big fellow for the two cups of hot sweet black tea served in sherry glasses. The big fellow nodded and insisted on giving me a loaf of bread. I have to say the hospitality was exceptional even if we were sitting in a forecourt alongside a butcher's shop with fly-infested carcases hanging from the ceiling. The smell was unbelievable.

On this occasion, for Carolyn, taking a back seat for being female was a lucky escape. 'God, how long does it take to pay for petrol,' Carolyn said. That was when the bread came in handy.

'What about any water, did you get water.'

'Um, well, you see …' Luckily for me, just as I was about to relay the whole story a guy from nowhere brought us six bottles of sparkling water. He shook my hand, smiled and walked off. At this rate we were going to save a fortune on food.

With warm sunshine constantly on my right side, heading east we drove and drove and drove into the Turkish mountains. I'll be honest, we had no real idea where we were going and no idea how high and beautiful the mountains were. Chitty struggled up hill at a snail's pace. In Italy we had been overtaken by cyclist but today was potentially humiliating as goat herders looked as if they had the edge. The summit was welcomed with fresh snow and a postcard view. Camping was now a concern, and an hour or so from sunset we found a hillside farm. Carolyn and I left Chitty running, keeping the cab lukewarm, which was the best we were ever going to get at minus 3° Centigrade. At breakneck speed the tent was up, two sleeping bags each were laid out and we donned the look of 'I don't want a suit case so I'm wearing everything.' Hot porridge bubbled away in the pan and Steve and I debated the route to Iran. 'North and follow the coast of the Black Sea,' said Steve, 'sounds good to me.' Carolyn snuggled up to me, puffing out steam as she whispered in the cold air. We each looked idiotic under two sleeping bags, a tartan blanket, leather flying jacket open wool side out to give extra weight and a Noddy hat and gloves on,

Why now, in the middle of nowhere up in the Turkish mountains, with not one bar of mobile signal at all and miles from the glimmer of civilisation, did I get toothache? I thought the Londra campsite was a low ebb but tonight my mind was full of insecure what ifs, what if it's a root filling thing, you know an abscess, we have got antibiotic I told myself, what if we can't find a dentist, and what if, what if I just shut up and go to sleep.

The next morning, water although free was now frozen. Ice was popping the tops of the six bottles. Snow and a solid ice sheet capped a grand natural pond, with reeds standing like frozen statues reflecting in the snowy crystal surface. Strong sunlight streamed between the leafless trees and evergreen pines creating a diamond-bright light. Optimism had returned with the dawn and amazingly my toothache hadn't.

The road ahead was confirmed by a local walking atlas. This man took it on himself to offer his local knowledge on routes, the weather, how my car was a Rolls Royce and where to get the best goats' cheese. He advised heading north to the Black Sea as at this time of the year, 17 October, it was the only option because the mountains to the east were very high, full of snow and would be impassable. It seems every country has a Harry Enfield character offering tips, 'you don't want to be doing that do you', and this was the Turkish version. But to be fair he had a point. Dropping down into the lower mountain valleys the air temperature rose a degree or so but Carolyn looked like she was about to reach the Himalayas.

. I had heard of the Hittites, but I hadn't a clue who they were and didn't know they lived in Turkey. . The little village where we were to spend the night had a restaurant and a small museum and gift shop. Only when I read the local notice board did I realise the village's importance.

Nestled in the hill were the remains of Hattusha, ancient capital of the Hittites. These formidable warriors apparently saw off the Egyptians and still boasted a living legacy. The archaeological remains, including the Lions' Gate up the road, were impressive. There was obviously a small tourist industry but the site was closed.

A white-haired, tubby old man, who would make a great Father Christmas if he lived in the West, was our host for the night. The man, who spoke so fast I thought he said his name was Diarrhoea, led us literally down the garden path to an orchard full of windfall apples. Cold and hungry, once camp was made we took up the old boy's offer to dine in his restaurant over the road. A beautiful roaring fire took centre stage and filled the small timber-beamed restaurant with a deep glow. The old boy found us seats in hand-warming distance and offered to bring us wine and a menu. We had only been on the road for a couple of months but we quickly missed home comforts. I couldn't believe it, for here they were. Carolyn loved the wine, warm fire and the thought of a hot meal. 'I think this is a bit of a cop out, don't you. Here we are roughing it across the world and suddenly we are on an upgrade to first class,' she exclaimed in delight. The old boy took time to introduce his entire family, which included his wife, the chef, his waiter sons and his nephew who was rapidly preparing a gift-shop stall outside as we spoke. Then the man with the name of Delhi belly produced a postcard depicting the last living king of the Hittites, adorned in traditional costume, proudly standing in front of the grand Lions' Gate.

'You are British yes, the BBC make film documentary here with my son the last king of the Hittites. It was called The Lost Civilization of the Hittites, you watch yes?' the old boy enquired enthusiastically. 'See picture, this is my son, he is king, BBC very very interested in him.' This was turning out to be quite a night. I politely enquired whether he was still alive? Was he conducting state affairs overseas? Did Turkey regard him as royalty? Where was the last king of the Hittites now? 'He is here my friend, he is your waiter.' I nearly choked; the Hittite sovereign was unfolding my napkin and passing out the baps. 'You want autograph on postcard?' 'Oh, yes, please,' I said. I was full of questions, the old boy's family obliged with answers and my soup went cold.

Carolyn and I had a made a pact of buying no souvenirs; we just didn't have the space and if we bought one then we would have to ditch something. The nephew introduced himself outside on our departure. 'See I make these carvings all myself,' he said, eager to seal a deal under the floodlit stall. His breath shimmered in the cold night air. A hastily arranged collection of ancient Hittite-style green stone carvings lay before us on a brightly coloured batik-type tablecloth. 'Watch me carve, see detail, see.' Every item was picked up and stuck under my nose. I couldn't leave this stall on a cold evening seeing the desperation in his eyes, so as usual I bought something I neither could afford nor wanted.

The long hilly road had a surface resembling the complexion of a spotty teenager. Chitty rumbled over it with ease, just raising the odd inner fear of whether my welding was up to it. Nothing had prepared us for the diverse and forever changing scenery central Turkey had to offer. The view was a constant surprise, one minute we were in the Rockies, the next in the Prairies. Down the hill and round the corner, it was the Tyrol or was that New Zealand; the world is so different and so much the same. Just in case we were a bit homesick we were now ogling the countryside of Surrey.

The eighteenth of October was always going to be a funny day. After settling on heading north to the Black Sea because of the impassable snowy mountains, we had now changed our minds. The road east came from another petrol pump encounter. Having feed Chitty's never ending petroleum habit, the proprietor took my hand and escorted me over to the forecourt shop for more sweet tea and a photo. I was now accustomed to holding hands but never really at ease. I was always flattered with the interest Chitty generated and I'm sure there was a misconception that we were rich, based on the constant question how much was the car worth? 'You have very good car, your Shi-tty Shi-tty Bam Bam 1 million euros I think,' he said, showing off his cars to me while completely ignoring Carolyn.. I could see this was starting to grate, but the male was top dog, so it was me who got entertained with a cuddle and a kiss thrown in. I gave the leather jacket-wearing middle-aged man the low down. His black balding hairline was greased back and he carried off a second-hand car salesman look with ease. 'You must not drive north, guns, bandits, mafia they will rob you,' he explained with a grin from ear to ear. 'You go home, not north.' I laughed inwardly and so we headed east.

We pulled into a petrol station in Yozgat, set back from a dusty half-made road. I jumped out of the car to fill the tank as a job lot of policemen arrived. Chitty had really come into her own; nobody has ever heard of Dick Van Dyke but as far as they were concerned the circus had just rolled into town. Getting the tank filled was almost impossible what with photos, tugging on shirtsleeves and a thousand questions all in Turkish. The police treated us like royalty, full of respectful body language as not a hint of English was spoken. Carolyn took the opportunity to ask about an ATM by showing her bank card, The the young uniformed and gun-wielding officer introduced himself by patting his hand on his chest, saying, Abraham A-bra-ham' and beaming a genuine smile. He beckoned us to follow, so now with a police escort front and rear we were funnelled through the suburbs to the town centre. Toytown had nothing on this place and I half expected Windy Miller to pop over for a chat; it was typically European dipped in Turkish delight. Bakeries, greengrocer and coffee shops surrounded the Central Square with a clock tower piercing the clear blue sky. We come to a rest, parked with police vehicles front and rear. The carnival atmosphere had followed us into town and a few interested bodies sparked a riot so to speak. I couldn't even get out of the car, there were literally hundreds of people round us with more scooting across the road in frenzied panic. The road was now completely blocked with the multitudes of people all looking at us. Actually they were all men, not a woman in sight. The overwhelming din of questions and chitchat was reaching fever pitch. There were smiles, handshaking and tutting (strange but true, a sign of approval is to flick the car body with a finger and tut at the same time).

Steve and Julia came to our assistance, standing by both doors as we alighted. Abraham took it upon himself to post policemen round the car and reluctantly I followed him to the ATM. I looked back and I was genuinely astonished at the sheer number of people standing around Chitty. Carolyn hitched a police escort by foot to the internet café and Abraham gave me a loaf of bread. He was insistent I accept his kind offer and wished to take me to the customary teahouse. This was a humbling moment. He was so genuinely full of Turkish hospitality. So far I had received a police escort, guarding duty, been shown the ATM, given a loaf of bread and been taken for high tea. I never get that kind of service from the police back home and I'm married to one! I returned to Chitty only to find a TV camera crew had been added to the huge crowd. Just as I attempted to kindly request a person to refit my brass fuel filler cap and somebody to stop going through the contents of Chitty's wooden fruit-carved glovebox, a tall, well-built, imposing man put his hand on my shoulder. The very smartly dressed TV presenter pushed a microphone under my nose, nodded to the cameraman and rolled his fingers over and over on his free hand to suggest that I talk. I figured nobody would be able to understand a word I was saying. However, I am not one to shy away from a camera so I began. I talked about the car and how I built Chitty Chitty Bang Bang. There were no questions because of the language barrier. I talked about the film and the idea to raise money for charity and then I stopped. With a wink of his eye he rolled his fingers and wanted more, so I talked about planning the trip and the adventure of driving to Australia. After twenty minutes or so I stopped to take a breath. I was running thin on ideas. The camera was still running and so I talked about the Queen and her corgis, the Beatles, you know the sort of thing.

Glovebox shut, fuel cap on and luggage secured, we departed to waves from the onlookers. Abraham and his flotilla of police cars saw us to the city limits. After a truly exhausting yet surreal and humbling morning we relaxed on the long and winding road to Erzurum. Rolling down one of the most beautiful roads carved out of the most spectacular rugged mountain, Chitty nearly took to the air. moving faster than ever before. Chitty hit a top speed of near on 80 mph, and boy did we know it; the front fenders vibrated, the leather bonnet strap end flapped wildly and the roof was lifting off.. The old Land Rover's running gear whined at the lack of power and as we succumbed to a more gentle speed I tried to engage fourth gear. It just wouldn't select, probably because of the limp and lifeless clutch pedal. 'Oh fiddlesticks, the bloody the clutch has gone? Not now, please not now.' 'Is that bad,' asked Carolyn. 'Don't know, but it's new so it's got to be fluid,' I said talking as if I knew what I was on about. It's at times like this the world starts caving in, but somebody was smiling on us.The road in the middle of nowhere without a town or settlement in sight levelled out and into view came a lonely ramshackle service station and we rolled in. In the engine bay, bonnet up, I investigated the problem. 'Yep, it's the bleeding clutch fluid.' I yelled out. 'What's the problem with the fluid?' was Carolyn's concerned reply. 'Well there isn't any, simple.' The master cylinder was leaking, the seals were well worn and the clutch fluid was completely squeezed out.

For a place devoid of civilisation there was a surprisingly high number of homo sapiens. People appeared from thin air and guess what everyone was a mechanic. Someone was tugging on my now oily shirtsleeve..I left the engine bay expecting the tugger to take a photo or something; but no, the kind, oily, unshaven, windswept man handed me a set of overalls. Carolyn was impressed. Half an hour later the clutch was functioning agreeably. Five Turkish men, Carolyn pumping the pedal and me around the steering box finely brought life back to Chitty's transmission.

Camping was now looking slim with the sun hiding below the horizon. Dusk changed our plans on the accommodation front. So we sought advice. The man who should know the answers, the service station owner, couldn't speak English. However, rescue came in the form of three black limos with a group of young Turks kitted out in dinner jackets, who understood the word 'hotel' and enthusiastically insisted we join the convoy. Nightfall fell. The military dominated the view; row after row of troop personnel carriers passed us heading towards the Iranian border. Military establishments were dotted along the roadside with endless acres given over to tanks and armoured vehicles. There was the roar of night manoeuvres and tanks in convoy heading east. For the first time nobody was waving as the military mood was sombre.

We came to a vibrant city where the nightlife was in full swing. The limos ground to a halt and a dapper young lad leapt out pointing to a narrow cobbled alley, 'Hotel, hotel' and then they were gone. Steve in his Discovery followed us into the hubbub of neon signs and markets alive with night trading. The hotel was confined to a seedy corner. I negotiated a cobbled parking space adjacent to the tatty doors guarded by a porter. Stopping here was a disaster, the world and his wife had descended on us and it was frantic. This was starting to grind us down a bit; the day had been long, fraught with mechanical problems, and now finding a place to stay with secure parking looked impossible. Most people were genuinely courteous and respectful, but tonight the late-night rabble of men crowding round Chitty looked as if they had turned up for a fight. The air was intimidating. One guy climbed on to the car's running board and shouted out at me. He slapped his hand down hard on the roof and unwittingly flicked his ash into the cab. Tyres were being kicked, the front wings had the full weight of downward pushing to establish the build quality and the bodywork was being flicked again. We had parked in a human bottleneck and the enthusiastic onslaught was emotionally draining. Fingers found their way into our luggage, bungee grips were unfastened and our personal belongings became fair game. A couple of older guys debated Chitty's pedigree and rummaged around in the cab through our maps and guidebooks. The fact that I was sitting there was of no concern! Chitty wobbled slightly as some trapeze artist climbed on to the rear tow bar and hung on fast . It was becoming a bit much, the porter had not an ounce of a Western tongue and our Turkish lingo couldn't even muster a goodbye.

'Why are you here?' said a pretty young student who popped up from under somebody's arm. 'I studying English, can I try you?' 'Hi, yes, you speak English,' I said, stating the obvious. 'Um, yes, we are here looking for a hotel with parking, secure parking,' I continued. 'Please can you put that back on,,' I said, trying to make conversation with a shifty looking, bearded man as he unscrewed the brass Spitfire plane mascot on the grille. 'See this my name here and my e-mail, I ask for you,' said the pretty girl with a name I really couldn't read or say. It seemed to be Dilara. She batted her eyelashes, so impressed with the car and our trip, and instructed the porter to ride on board and guide us to the underground car park. 'I like your name too please and e-mail please,' she said. 'I bet you do,' Carolyn piped up in my left ear.

Checking in, the oppressiveness of the dark, damp-feeling building was increased by a feeling of insecurity., 'I am no warrior, but we are going to war, you know about war?' 'What war?' I said to the receptionist. 'We fight Kurds in Iraq, eighty kilometres to them, and we fight Iran.' 'Sorry, Turkey is at war with Iran?' I enquired with concern. 'Yes, my friend, you must go home, it is not safe.' We closed our bedroom on a day of uncertainty and Carolyn put her arms around me. 'The kids, what about the kids?' she asked anxiously. Alarm bells were ringing as this warning and the build-up of the military confirmed hostilities. We returned to reception to have a brief catch-up on the internet. Sibling worries were voiced in e-mail chat. Carolyn's brother, Adrian, was always on the pulse with current affairs and bluntly said, 'Turkey goes to war, you need to rethink your route, PS where are you?' Not surprisingly it was not the best night's sleep.

Our spirits were lifted over breakfast by a chance meeting. 'Please sir you English yes.' 'Oh yes, we are.' 'I am living in Southampton back then, my English was good, not now.' The very tall man in his late fifties complete with a Turkish comb-over spoke the best English we had heard since leaving home. 'In the seventies I play professional football for Southampton with Kevin Keegan curly man hair.' ' Wow we come from the Isle of Wight.' 'Isle Wight I have been there too.' We told our story over sweet black tea and as he spoke there was genuine passion and pride in his voice over his links with the UK. His eyes were full of affection as he clasped my hands in his to say farewell. 'It is true, you must go home, it is too dangerous, our Turkish army have just captured Iranian spies in our mountains, just here my friend, and now we go to war.' This was not news we wanted to hear as today we were heading for the border..

Clutching the steering wheel and focusing on the road ahead we followed an army personnel troop carrier, the soldiers looking unenthusiastic, heads wobbling from side to side, guns secured between their legs and fag butts hanging from bottom lips.

At 40 mph, we had managed to find ourselves wedged in the middle of a camouflaged convoy. The line of trucks, rocket launchers and fully laden tanks stretched out as far as the eye could see. In this sombre mood of political cat and mouse and serious warfare, whatever did they think of us trundling along for the ride? The fenceless tarmac rumbled to the sound of caterpillar tracks joined by several overshoots of unseen gunfire. Were we worried? You bet we were.

Army barracks and tank enclosures caged in barbed wire were spread out along the roadside among the burnt, yellow vegetation. Traffic slowed to a walking pace, giving us a clear view of the seventh alive goat to be slung up on to the roof of a battered transit van. There was no roof rack and the rope was pulled down tightly around its hooves and neck to wails of bleating screams. Unpleasant, but it was part of the daily life we viewed for five hours from our convoy spot.

Armoured battle emplacements littered the lonely countryside. Two dogs, with blood-curdling howls, were tearing another to pieces and feeding on it. We took to looking at soldiers with nodding heads again.

Chapter 30 **W**elcome to Iran

Dogubeyazit, the border town known by travellers as 'Doggy Biscuit', sits on a dusty patchwork of unmade roads and barren scrubland and has a backdrop of the Iranian mountains. It is just a stone's throw from the Iranian gateway. Tonight we had time to emotionally prepare ourselves for whatever lay ahead. The bloody clutch was still not right, so first thing tomorrow I'd bleed the system.

Doggy Biscuit really wasn't anything to write home about, but it had an overnight camping spot.. We both woke with a sense of doom. The recent media coverage of Iran's capture of English subjects didn't help, nor did the news of war. It was at times like this that driving across the world in a replica Chitty Chitty Bang Bang seemed a pretty silly idea.

Carolyn handed me a mug of tea and I searched for the clutch kit. 'In, out, in, hold it, and release,' I shouted from within Chitty's ribcage. Carolyn didn't look too interested as she sat behind the wheel pressing in and out to instructions. After lots of pumping on the pedals a lively back pressure returned.

'You know what, sweetheart, I really can't complain. So what if we are leaking oil from the clutch, I've just got to keep an eye on it and top it up daily.' 'Yes, along with all those other engine things,' Carolyn replied. 'Okay, so what if we are leaking oil from the clutch, engine, gearbox, transfer box, front axle and rear axle, I've got plenty of oil, just gotta keep topping up, but lets face it, it's a hundred quid Land Rover and we haven't actually broken down.'

'Yet!' Carolyn added.

Two bottles of alcohol and a black scarf found their way to the front seat of Chitty as we departed for the border. As we turned off our camping spot on to a poorly maintained road an old man waved us over. I pulled up alongside and offered the gift of gin and ouzo, which we had received from an impressed group of friendly Greeks. Iran is an Islamic dry country and having alcohol on board was a no-no. They really would lock us up if customs found this lot. For the next few week we would be on the wagon. It didn't really bother me but Carolyn retained a cork to suck on and as for Steve, I didn't how he would manage. The old man's day was made and he rushed over to pick a bunch of flowers from his garden in return and then put in to practice his only known words of English, 'Sees yaz latas ally-gai-tas.'

Completing the border paperwork on the Turkish side wasn't a pleasant affair. An irritating man took control of our departure, which was pretty straightforward, then demanded 10 dollars for the official help he had just given. In no-man's-land another irritating man hounded us to part with our euros. I drove slowly towards huge, grey, iron gates and this unshaven, scruffy and smelly little man ran alongside stuffing Iranian rials in my face. ' Good rate, best rate ever, I buy euros, lira and English pounds, very good rate,' he parroted. I couldn't have given a toss about currency; I knew US dollars were acceptable within Iran and we had plenty. Frantic was not the word, the man was about to lie down in front of the car and wouldn't shut up. I really had too much on my mind so I relented and passed on my Turkish lira for Iranian cash hoping he'd leave. 'What about euros I buy euros.' ' No.' 'What about English pounds I buy English pounds.' 'No.' 'I buy dollars good rate for dollars.' 'No. No euros, no pounds, no dollars, now go.' 'Cigarettes have you got cigarettes.' 'Nooooo.'

Carolyn wrapped her black scarf around her head and pulled down her sleeves, sitting upright as we approached Iran. The imposing iron gates were set beneath a concrete gantry linking two formidable-looking buildings. Iranian gold-lettered text shimmered alongside two huge images of the current ayatollahs, below which was the sign, 'Welcome to I.R. Iran'. We were both quite nervous and were on our best behaviour. Flashes filled my mind of the downloaded foreign office paperwork that I had read last night.

If you are planning to travel to Iran you should monitor political developments closely. We strongly advise against all travel to within 100km of the entire Iran/Afghanistan border or to within 10km of the entire Iran/Iraq border.

Bomb blast in Zahedan, Eastern Iran.

British couple and an Australian man were detained after sailing in Iranian waters.

2006, two Swedish men were imprisoned for over a year on an espionage charge as a result of photographing a site the Iranians considered sensitive.

2007, the Iranian authorities detained 15 Royal Navy personnel and their boats.

There have been incidents of kidnapping of foreigners by armed gangs in South Eastern Iran

It hadn't made for good bedtime reading, However, when put into perspective, millions of tourists go on holiday to Madrid and if you read the Foreign Office travel advice for Spain you wouldn't set foot outside your front door.

After my frosty encounter with Turkey I was cautious to say the least. With both sweaty hands tightly gripping the steering wheel, the iron gates before us rolled back slowly and to a low rumble. A uniformed and well-armed Iranian policeman signalled us forward. Chitty cleared the border line and the instantly closed gates shut off the outside world. I was signalled to stop the engine. A very smartly dressed man appeared, a border official of some nature or another. He wore a uniform of dark green trousers with a pale yellow shirt topped with important-looking Iranian epaulettes and official badges. Clean shaven and with neatly combed back, thick black hair he looked me straight in the eye, smiled and in a polite, soft voice said, 'Welcome to Iran.'

What a relief, how reassuring that was. This was a good start. The man asked us to leave Chitty and to accompany him into the main building. 'I will handle all your affairs. I will deal with your visas and passports and the vehicle documents. Do you have a carnet de passages?' We were told to sit in a basic room which reminded me of a fifties headmaster's office. 'Please don't look so worried my friend,' he went on, God, do I look worried? 'I will also exchange your currency. Do you have US dollars?' We had 1,000 dollars in cash as we had figured crossing Iran would take some time. It was impossible to buy Iranian rials outside of Iran and the only acceptable currency was from their not-so-favourite Uncle Sam. Credit cards were not welcomed and despite having ATMs they were not linked into the rest of the globe. So it was hard cash only. Just as proceedings were about to start the Islamic call to prayer echoed throughout out the land. I started to panic 'Carolyn, what do we do?' Work had stopped and many disappeared to prayer. We were so worried about getting things wrong or offending somebody.

'So here are your documents.. We need to look into your car and luggage and check the chassis and engine numbers. Don't worry it will be okay,' the attentive man said patting me on the back. 'How much money would you like changing?' 'Oh money, um, oh, what do you think Carolyn, oh we'll change 250 US dollars please,' I said not having a clue and ignoring Carolyn's answer in my haste. 'Oh no my friend this is far too much, Iran is a very cheap country.' 'Oh dear, but we are driving across to Pakistan, can I have 150 then?'

Chitty was scrutinised for matching numbers and luggage probed for contraband while we sat waiting for our vehicle carnet and to change our money. The gates opened behind Chitty and a black, top spec Range Rover complete with blacked-out windows drew up and five big, intimidating, bearded men dressed in traditional clothing decamped from the vehicle. The car had Russian number plates. We had been processed with courteous attention for a good couple of hours. These guys were in and out like a shot; pausing only to take a photo of Chitty, with no dialogue they were gone. It really was quite a sight. I was flattered that even the Russian mafia wanted a photo!

'Mr Nicholas, I have your money,' said the attentive man. I followed him into a room entitled tourist office where he asked for my dollars and started counting out the local currency. Bloody hell, I thought to myself, I can see the problem. One hundred and fifty dollars was worth one and half million rials and they didn't make big notes. I had never seen so much money; it was unbelievable, there were literally wads of the stuff, bundles and bundles of notes. It just wouldn't all fit in my pockets. I was wearing travel pants with map pouches and they were stuffed full. I needed a bank robber's holdall and a Ford Transit to carry this lot. Carolyn found home for the remainder, including her cleavage which was well and truly hidden. Sitting in the customs office full of officials toing and froing, finally our man turned up with the completed vehicle carnet. I abruptly stood to attention awaiting the outcome. With a pleasing smile he said, 'It is all fine you may go and enjoy our country' and just to confirm any insecurities I might have, he patted me on the back again and said, 'My friend, please don't worry, it will be okay.' Clearly I had the persona of a condemned man about to be hanged.

Chapter 31 **R**ubbernecking Iranians

In blazing sunshine and with a shimmering heat haze distorting the road ahead, we progressed forward, leaving the well-ordered compound.

'Welcome to Iran, you need map 500 rials,' came a voice from an ever-growing bombardment of touts, taxi drivers and general onlookers. Leaving the uniformed world of the border, Chitty was now surrounded by at least fifty people. An outdated city map of Tehran was stuck under my nose and fifty pairs of hands were touching and flicking and photos were being taken. Women were conspicuous by their absence. 'No thank you, we have maps thank you,' I said. Chitty edged through the crowd only to come to a complete standstill because a white Hillman Hunter taxi was blocking the road by deliberately driving sideways across our path. Tabriz was today's destination but with an ever-growing mob of handshaking, photographing well-wishers this was looking unlikely. Apart from a couple of street wise touts working the border gates nobody spoke a word of English and communication was back to smiles, nods and a handshake which finished with the hand moving to the heart and patting the chest as a sign of endearment, accompanied with the word 'shalom'. We were soon joined by a few men on scooters with toddlers sitting on their laps and, of course, no helmets.

A contingent of old boys left their tea drinking establishment and insisted on a group photo. I stood proudly in front of Chitty surrounded by approving old gents. It really was time we made tracks so I bought a bloody map and drove off to the sound of horns honking loudly and the slightly distorted tones of the Chitty Chitty Bang Bang theme tune.

The road was good, very good, not what we had expected, but the buildings seemed to fit the bill. A ramshackle of yellow clay brick, single storey dwellings crammed together lining the roadside. Mopeds and scooters leant against rough, sun-baked walls. Litter, car parts and old oil drums filled dusty barren gardens. The small town was set in a rugged valley among raw, unforgiving jagged peaks. The mountainsides bore no vegetation. At the first sign of a petrol station I pulled in to claim my ration card.

Iran has about a hundred years of oil so I'm told, so there should have been plenty to go round you would have thought, despite the fact that refining isn't their strong point so everything they have is exported and bought back as petrol. However, petrol is rationed. Most locals are issued a free monthly fuel ration card whereas we as foreigners needed to buy one. The small office to the side of this border town petrol station was the only place I could negotiate my card. Now this was a bit tricky. I could only buy my card once I was told and I needed enough litres on it to get us across Iran, no card no fuel. How on earth did I know how much I would need? Petrol was amazingly only 5p a litre, but the appointed Iranian card supplier explained the cost. 'Four hundred litres will be one and a half million rials please.' Great, there goes my entire currency stash. It seemed so unfair. We were on a tight budget, with a fuel consumption of sixteen miles to the gallon, and the petrol cost us a small fortune, but Steve with his diesel Discovery capable of at least 2 million miles to the spoonful, had to pay only 1p per litre and needed no ration card.

As soon as a good stretch of tarmac gave us an opportunity to make a decent headway a police roadblock brought us to a grinding halt. The police officers ordered us over on to the hard shoulder. Their expressions were hard. One policeman signalled me out of the car and I leapt out sharply. There was no verbal communication, he simply flicked his fingers. In haste, Carolyn and I forced the leather, buttoned-backed seat up in search of our passports and the vehicle papers. The two policemen, uneasy about our intentions, stepped back, placing their hands on their gun holsters. Aware of the atmosphere I slowly turned round with two passports in my hand and offered them to the officers. The Iranian visas were scrutinised in detail. I then handed over the car documents and soon, without a word, a single nod signalled that we could go.

The first Iranian day was coming to an exhausting end. As usual we had no idea where to camp and twilight brought a decision to pitch our tents at the rear of a truckers' filling station forecourt. The pump attendants were more than grateful for us to sleep for free in return for the odd photo and a Chitty photo card. 'Flippin'hell, what is that!' Carolyn yelped. An Olympic-sized, grey, hairy spider was working his way between the tent and a stone wall. Carolyn doesn't do spiders. 'Kill it, you have got to kill it, I'm not sleeping here with that bloody thing roaming wild.' So I took a photo and nudged him along with a pencil until he disappeared over the wall. 'That's it, I'm filing for divorce. That was a bloody man eater and you've left it living. It will come back, I know it.' Carolyn went on and on and on, so I took up the kind offer of tea with an Iranian truck driver.

Harmin, as his name sounded phonetically, crouched down close to a side compartment fixed under the truck between the wheels. The tatty aluminium door fell open revealing an old teapot and a collection of chipped and tea-stained mugs. It was now dark and his wiry hair and bearded face were illuminated by the glow of a flickering candle. Communication was down to smiles, raised eyebrows and the odd pat on the back. I reeled off in English all the countries we were passing through and on saying Pakistan, Harmin said 'Waaa, no no no.' His face full of concern and nodding left to right, he reached over and put his hand on my forearm and pointed with his finger and said, 'No Pakistan', then smiled and took a sip of sugar with a spitful of tea in it.

Zanjan looked like the next major town which could offer a diesel fuel stop for Steve, as Tabriz had run dry. Every fuel station had a queue of cars stretching into the distance and lots of trucks were parked up as if they were abandoned. I had filled Chitty to the brim at the border, topping up the two red jerrycans, the fifty-litre brass tank on the rear and the standard Land Rover fuel tank tucked underneath, making good for a thousand kilometres. The overwhelming circus of events we received every time we stopped was becoming manageable. We were prepared now and we could assert a degree of control. However, I never expected it on the road. The Iranian roads stretched as far as the eye could see, cutting through rough mountain gorges and dissecting the desert terrain. Traffic was sparse between towns and the perfect road surface made for easy driving. Colourful lonely trucks rumbled past with their drivers waving frantically and sounding hooters fit for the Queen Mary. Only as we neared the outskirts of Zanjan did the Chitty carnival feeding frenzy commence. The weight of traffic grew along with the attention to Chitty. The duel carriageway allowed cars to slow up alongside, wave, beeb the horn and move on, allowing the next in turn. 'Where from, where from,' shouted a young driver in his fully loaded white Hillman Hunter. 'Great Britain,

UK, England,' replied Carolyn. The back seat was home to four squashed Iranian women, covered in black from head to foot, with only pretty dark eyes on view alight with smiles hidden beneath the veils. The two bright young men in front looked liberated and were adorned in Western culture with dark sunglasses and crisp white shirts. They held mobile phones at the ready to snap away at Chitty. 'Where you go? Where you stay?' they shouted. The rear window opened and an offer of food and fruit was given. The car drew in close and four apples in succession were thrown in to Chitty's cab. An arm was extended from the driver's window and Carolyn reached down to make contact. We all waved and smiled frantically. We were left a real sense of Iranian hospitality. Beeeeeeb. My heart leapt into my mouth. The queue of cars behind was getting impatient, as clearly it was their turn. One after another the constant stream of vehicles filtered past, waving, taking photos and generally looking amazed at what was trundling down their roads. Every car was laden with incredibly friendly people, women always in the back. By now we were getting used to the fact that we had a car in front with the passengers looking back taking photos and a car on our left with one on its left. doing the same A car would drive on the hard shoulder on my right, eager to get a good view. Behind would be another car and a never ending supply of rubbernecking Iranians stacking up for their photo opportunity. It was just unbelievable to see, and if that wasn't enough as we became within spitting distance of any town or city, fifteen to twenty mopeds and motorbikes would circle us like a pack of friendly wild dogs. My concentration really was stretched to the limit.

Concentrating so hard on not crashing into somebody or knocking off one of the kamikaze moped riders, I nearly missed the army checkpoint. As we became level with the nose-to-a-clipboard military officer, he raised his head and caught sight of us. 'Ahh-ay, 'he shouted and in my rear-view mirror I could see him jumping up and down, waving his arms. I pulled in sharply, locking four wheels and skidding in the hard shoulder gravel, creating a temporary dust storm. The officer was not happy. 'Stop stop stop stop,' he said, running along side. The man had a thick black moustache, greased-back hair and was slightly unshaven. Looking very intimidating and a bit out of breath, he pointed to me and said angrily, 'Passports.' I searched around and pulled out our documents. Still unhappy with us, he pointed to the spot where he had been originally standing and said 'Stop stop.' I nodded and looked very concerned to express that I was sorry. He spent ages looking at the wrong visa for India then handed them back satisfied. As an offer of goodwill I passed him a Chitty photo card and a picture of the old Land Rover as it once was, visually explaining our route and the charities were supporting. He smiled, beckoned over his colleagues and they all posed for photos. It is surprisingly easy to put pay to any suspicions with a kid's movie car, especially when Carolyn is driving.

Chapter 32 **D**on't go east, take a train

On the brow of a desert hill a filling station came in to view. 'Pulling over for fuel,' said Steve on the radio. The station was full of waiting cars and again dry to the bone of benzene as petrol was called and not a sign of diesel. The situation was now becoming dire for the Discovery Land Rover, the reserve jerrycan was empty and Steve had been covering miles on the sniff of an oily rag. 'We are going to have to wait,' Steve announced. Nobody could speak a word of English and the attendants were very dismissive at our gestures for fuel, so we both parked up and deliberated the next move. It was not long before the world and his wife and his kids were congregating round Chitty, flicking, tutting and asking the same old questions. 'Benzene? Diesel? Cylinders?' showing four fingers then six. And the one that always flattered me: 'Rolls Royce? Mercedes? Bentley?', after which I sadly shattered their illusions: 'Land Rover me old mate.'

Among the hysteria a small white unbadged car pulled into a parking space. The driver, a middle-class guy in black formal trousers and the obligatory white shirt and with a thick moustache, offered his hand to shake, smiled, then returned to his car bringing back a pitta bread sandwich. Insistent that we eat and share his kind offer of food he divided his tea into four. Extremely grateful and hungry we scoffed the lot and then tried to explain our predicament. Really trying to help he gestured to a petrol station further down the road. 'That's it, I'm not waiting around this bloody place any longer.' Steve piped up. 'Bloody Iran, one of the richest oil-producing countries in the world I don't think. They couldn't start a bleeding war; I don't know why the world's so worried, they can't even fill your tank let alone fuel a war.'

The light faded and fifty kilometres down the road Steve's diesel finally ran out. We were stuck with no idea what to do. It was now dark and the gravel verge was home. Just as the pitta bread's spicy aftertaste repeated on me the guy in the little white car pulled up. This really was a stroke of luck. He leapt out into the middle of the road and waved down the oncoming truck. Amazingly the driver reversed his huge yellow lorry on to the verge and after a quick Iranian chit-chat drained off forty litres of fuel. Before our tanks were refuelled a passing petrol tanker stopped opposite; the driver engaged in conversation with our new-found friend, climbed from the cab, untied a filler hose and offered it over. This was unreal; one minute you couldn't buy a drop the next we were being given as much as we wanted for nothing. I was so impressed with their genuine kind gestures and offers of help, just because we were foreign, oh and driving a flying car. Nobody would accept any payment, nobody wanted the cigarettes we bought in Turkey for potential bribes, and so a gift of a Chitty photo card did the trick, again. I was bloody glad I had brought them along. The city lights of Zanjan were a pleasing sight even if it meant we had to endure a flotilla of motor vehicles and mopeds. Too late to find a suitable camping spot, we opted for a hotel we couldn't find.

Tehran held the greatest fears of insecurities and it wasn't helped by a discussion in the hotel reception with a well-to-do, English-speaking German lady who had married an Iranian. 'Believe me, play by the rules; don't camp it's illegal, be careful what you photo and don't travel east,' she said with authority. 'Oh and if I were you I would inform the British embassy that you are here.' Before we checked out of our extortionately priced room, 250 US dollars I will have you know, I just had to see if like many hotels around the world would there be a Gideon's bible in the top drawer, and blow me there was! Well, not the Gideon's book but the Holy Quran, of course, in the Islamic Republic of Iran.

Tackling the capital was not going to be easy if what we had experienced so far was anything to go by. Leaving just after nine and a bombardment of photo taking from the hotel manager and his staff, we joined the flow of traffic eastwards. I thought we had experienced the worst of mobile paparazzi but the motorway to Tehran was a complete nightmare. Camping around the capital was out of the question so on recommendation we aimed for the Homa hotel. It was my turn for fuel and with a queue looking longer than the old 'Labour isn't working poster'. The time edging to the pumps I could handle, but the swelling crowd of interested fingers and twenty questions was hard. By the time I filled the brass fuel tank, it seemed as if extinction of the human race would have taken place

My cocky claims to carrying 600 miles of fuel had bitten me on bum. First, it worked out more like 500 miles and, second, the main tank was messing about, every time we stopped to fill, it would only accept about sixteen litres then spit it back and as we drove off litres would flood out from the overflow pipe. Just when we needed it most crossing the Iranian desert we were down to the brass tank and a couple of jerrycans.

The onlookers made filling up a complete disaster, engaged in conversation over how many cylinders and was it benzene or diesel I just kept pumping in the gas until it overflowed. The back pressure shot a spout of fuel into the air, drenching my hair, eyes, and the enthusiastic group nearby. My eyes closed tight, I nearly dropped the nozzle still pouring petrol over the back of Chitty and swamped the forecourt. With eyes shut the nozzle was relieved from my hand by who knows? Carolyn took to the wheel but the attendant dragged us back to pay, which was just as well as with so many cars packed in around us all taking photos we weren't going anywhere.

Back on the road I was starting to wish Chitty would just go that little bit faster. I looked at Steve's new Land Rover Discovery with envy, no oil leaks, no dodgy clutch, comfy seats, air conditioning and no mechanical worries nibbling away at your insides. I then looked with envy at the desperate excuses for light haulage trucks working the Iranian highways; they weren't leaking oil, and they were going a lot bloody faster than us, I griped to myself.

Moaning was a new side of me I hadn't seen before and now it was about to get worse. Thick black smoke was filling the air from behind, compliments of Chitty. The choke was playing up and the engine was more inclined to cough and splutter. An offbeat samba band had replaced the purring pussy and our carbon footprint was now being stamped out by the jolly green giant.

Driving was becoming impossible, all roads led to the capital and everybody was on them. Who were we? I thought, it's only an old car, nobody knows who Truly Scrumptious is, so what's all the fuss. We were enjoying the attention but this was ridiculous. If I had an Iranian apple thrown in the car for every photo taken I'd be the proud owner of the 'Wight Cider Barns Trading Co.' by now. I could see a clear bit of road ahead but it wasn't round us. Apart from the two cars in front packed to gunnels, there was a stream of vehicles on my left and three cars driving up close on the gravelled hard shoulder, all taking photos. There were cars pulling up and parking on the carriageway waiting for us to pass by.

Nerves of steel were needed just to keep focused manoeuvring around abandoned saloons supporting their drivers on the roofs and with doors left open and a multitude of motorbikes weaving in and out, all in aid of the perfect shot. Flattered, humbled, overwhelmed and knackered were just a few words stumbling off the tongue at that moment, and the city lights signalled the next challenge. Gridlocked in a maze of traffic a man on a scooter stopped, leaned on the boat tail and smiled. 'Homa hotel,' I shouted over. With that he nodded and waved us to follow; we did so and an hour later through urban mayhem, life-threatening short-cuts and gaps in traffic which you couldn't fit a fasting limbo dancer through, we made it to the grand entrance of a very posh hotel which I know we couldn't afford. On our arrival the world jumped to their feet followed by a military salute from the head porter. 'How grand,' said Carolyn then laughed. 'It's all show, mate, where're on a budget don't you know,' I replied.. The well-to-do in Iranian society filtered out from the hotel and were all over us like a rash, business cards, offers of accommodation and meals out came flooding our way. Its great but we just don't know where to start. Steve and Julia are sat in the shadows and an unspoken resentment is setting in, the attention, media coverage and constant focus appear to be taking their tolls on our support crew's enthusiasm.

Staying in hotels just wasn't in the plan but with sheer under-the-spotlight treatment there wasn't any other option. Three hundred US dollars a night was very hard to swallow and we were only here because it came with secure parking, leaving Chitty was just impossible. We soon realised the 1,000 dollars to cover three weeks wasn't going to get us very far at this rate. In fact, our £15,000 budget was dropping like a stone.

Departing came with a barrage of confusing warnings. The hotel gift shop guy warned us about heading south-east in to bandit country and going anywhere near Pakistan. 'Come in, shut the door, you haven't heard this from me,' said the well-educated Iranian man in broken English who had lived in Britain before the revolution. The bazaar was teaming with local knick-knacks, gold, gem stones and seriously over priced sculptures that only a wealthy businessman would buy when he had forgotten his wife's birthday. Door secured shut, he said in a very serious manner, 'They won't tell you, it's just not safe, Zahedan in the south-east is very dangerous, drug smugglers, gun runners, they will kill you, but I haven't told you this.' Steve looked unfazed and determined to make for Pakistan. 'That's it, I'm not going there, I'm not on a suicide mission,' said Carolyn. 'I suggest we do as the German lady recommended and ring the British embassy in Tehran,' I said sticking my oar in.

Steve, insistent Pakistan wasn't a problem, made the call; the tone of his voice said it all. The very helpful and kind lady was amazed we were driving through Iran then when we told her we were ambling across in Chitty Chitty Bang Bang she thought we were having a laugh. I think she came to the conclusion we were barking mad but nevertheless she wanted details of where we were staying and our intended route, all our full names, addresses and dates of birth and gave strict instructions to inform the embassy when we had departed Iran. As for Pakistan it was a complete no go. 'I can tell you this, currently negotiations are taking place for the release of two European travellers held hostage just over the border in the Baluchistan desert area of Pakistan and a couple of Japanese motorcyclists are also missing. Frankly unless you are travelling in a convoy, discrete and with speed on your side I suggest you find an alternative route,' she said in a polite but stern way.

'I still think we should go for it,' Steve said. This was a real blow, not only was hostage taking a real threat but Pakistan was at war with itself; the new president Benazir Bhutto had been assassinated and a state of emergency had been declared. Forgive me for scaremongering but Pakistan didn't sound a great holiday destination. Studying the map didn't leave many options; going north meant either Afghanistan or Russia. Afghanistan was just silly and Russia was back-tracking and we would completely miss India; besides if we couldn't get into China, we would be stuck for ever in the former Soviet Union. 'My friends, take the train to Bandar Abbas on the Persian gulf, very big port, ships to all the world,' the guy in the gift shop had pointed out.

Chitty was revealed from under her canvas car cover and within minutes the hotel car park was full with attendants, porters, the receptionist and suited business folk. Carolyn was trying to pack down the luggage and I was topping up the gearbox oil along with the daily routine of ensuring the engine got a tipple and the differentials, clutch and brakes get their daily recommended allowance too. We had mastered the art of entertaining well-wishers and interested parties but today we hoped to check out the train station and if no good make tracks. However, a coachload of Japanese, government-approved company officials was treating us like a fairground ride. I fired Chitty into life, hoping they would get the message, and covered the entourage with thick black smoke. Before I could select reverse a hand was placed on the bonnet. A tall scruffy man in overalls stood in silhouette backed by the glaring sun. He made a gesture to open the bonnet, so I did. 'Land Rover,' I said, assuming he was some kind of hotel mechanic. He just nodded and started to adjust the choke and carburettor mixture screws. Within half an hour he had compensated for running on choke so the exhaust was clear, but really couldn't fix it permanently. I was very grateful for his out of the blue help and like so many times in Iran, he smiled, wanted nothing in return and was gone.

The heat was stifling and the brightness of the day made for a heady atmosphere. Tehran's main train station was like a beehive buzzing with traffic, army, police and thousands all coming and going. On approach all vehicles were being directed away from the building round a roundabout and back into the city; not good if you needed a train.

We hit the roundabout and were instantly signalled to park right in front of the station; how strange and how convenient. The police took it upon themselves to stand over and guard Chitty, fending off the masses while Carolyn and Julia went to enquire about putting the cars on the car train to Bandar Abbas. The queue for the ticket office was strictly a women thing, for the first time not a bloke in sight. The long tailback of black burkas snaked towards the exit; Carolyn joined the queue and waited for forty-five minutes. Still not even halfway, an old lady came up to Carolyn and sounded off a load of Iranian abuse. My wife stood there covered from head to foot in black wearing the traditional hijab headscarf and somewhat surprised at the onslaught. With more Farsi and gestures of clear off, the old woman started to push Carolyn out of the queue.. Carolyn stood her ground, insistent she was queuing in an orderly fashion; with that the old lady pushed Carolyn in the chest and grabbed two Iranian ladies waiting behind her and forced them in front of Carolyn. It was a sad incident as so many were so kind but a little bit of jealousy or animosity towards Westerners had a lasting impact.

Chapter 33 **H**onest men and frightened foxes

The train idea was a stupid one, so driving south would now take us through Esfahan, and Shiraz, which I thought was a bottle of wine, passing by ancient Persian sites. Back at the car we were summons by the police to see the head of tourism affairs at his office on the other side of Tehran. This was a little bit exciting and a little bit inconvenient; so much for moving on.

Carolyn had to stay with the car as this was a man thing, like just about most things in Iran. Taken upstairs Steve and I sat in a formal air-conditioned office drinking chilled water wondering what it was all about. The boardroom doors opened and several obviously important people ushered us in and we sat around a huge table which could seat the entire Conservative Party after a cabinet reshuffle. The walls were sparsely decorated with the odd tourist poster and a geographical map of Iran. What the hell does the head of tourist affairs do in a country with no tourists I thought and then it became clear, nothing! We had been spotted and this was an excuse for a polite con-flab over tea. The head man himself was well suited and booted and greeted us with open arms. 'So what can I help you with,' he said after a quick introduction. 'Um, oh, well we are driving to Australia and do you know if it's possible to ship a car to India from Bandar Abbas,' I said thinking on my feet and making out this was why we had come. 'Very big port is Bandar Abbas, you can go all over the world,' he went on to tell me something we had already been told. 'See this photo, this is my French friend, he is walking around the world, he gave me this signed card for helping him, I like this card very much.' Oh, I saw he wanted a card from us, a bit of street cred I would say. I pulled out a Chitty photo card and handed it over. 'Please can you sign it, please'; so I did exactly with the same wording as the French guy. 'To my dearest friend, thank you sincerely for all your help, Nick & Carolyn.'

'Goodbye my friends I am so glad we could help, enjoy our beautiful country', and with that he was gone! A rather mad experience but now it was too late to hit the road so it was back to the hotel, which was fully booked and could now only offer top-notch rooms for an extra fifty US dollars; bloody typical, we were now spending money like a teenage daughter with her first credit card.

A walk into Tehran was not a pleasant one, a crowded square brought home the reality of a strict political regime: a man was being held face down on a public seating area by two policemen. His shirt was pulled down over his beige formal fitting trousers and there anguish upon his unshaven face. After a slight struggle the two officers held him secure while another administered the public flogging. Adultery was his crime, but more importantly the whipping was a demonstration of control. A bit scary if you ask me. Carolyn found a traditional dress shop and purchased a very modern long-sleeved outfit in this season's latest colour; yep, you guessed, it black. The hijab headscarf and body-covering full-length tent which is forbidden to show any female figure was a cultural challenge for Carolyn to wear and without realising it she had pulled her sleeves up. A highly embarrassed lady in her mid-thirties approached saying, 'I'm sorry your arms, you cannot show your arms.' Arms what arms? It was six inches of feminine forearm, but enough for the concerned passer-by to tackle us. The lady felt awful for telling us and after pausing, said, 'I am very sorry it is the law, they will punish you, it's a stupid regime' and before we could move on the hijab police were on to us. Their manner in dealing with us was considerate and respectful to our nationality, only demanding we return to the hotel and dress correctly. A stark reminder to play by the rules.

Esfahan was a bit of a shock. The 400-kilometre drive had wiped us out and the uncertainties of avoiding Pakistan and rerouting for an unknown boat was taking their toll. A low point for all and not a night to be without a secure resting place. My fuel consumption had gone from bloody awful to the downright ridiculous. Coughing and spluttering a dark cloud of Victorian London smog our thick Red Arrows' vapour trail filled the bustling city outskirts. I had taken the carburettor to bits to release the choke and even the 'off the cuff' mechanic in Tehran had managed to leave the incredibly important plastic vacuum pipe lying on the engine so that it had now melted. Having your tyre kicked while driving into town wasn't good for East–West relations. A swarm of irritating wasp-sounding motorbikes funnelled us through the suburbs; our concerns at their dare devil antics turned their enthusiasm into aggression and suspicion. Holding on tightly to a submissive smile and filled with caution we stopped to ask for directions and again so did the world. Accommodating and obliging I patiently entertained the growing crowd. The 125cc unbranded motorbike in red and chrome shuffled forwards, The rider, still with a bit of dried lunch stuck to his facial hair, leant over to shake my hand. He was in his forties with crow's feet wrinkles gathering around his tanned eyes. Genuine warmth and friendship uplifted my spirits until some berk ran him over. With a mood change quicker than a menopausal redhead, Iranian men were showing an as yet unseen side. Wrestling bodies absorbed punches on the ground below me; ripped and petrol-soaked chequered shirts squelched in the pool of fuel that continued to ebb from the rider's tank. Emotions were running high and blame was pitched at my door in the heat of the moment. I asked the question to myself, how on earth did we find ourselves here? The commotion which had swept us off our feet was nerve racking and up to a point life threatening. The sortie of motorbikes, overwhelming crowds of onlookers and the resulting fight between the taxi driver and man knocked to the floor had caused a riot.

I was extremely concerned to say the least. Carolyn was in the local shops probing a bed for the night unaware of our predicament. Farsi was the only spoken words, full of vigour and with a clear message of 'you ain't wanted'. Chitty was being pushed left and right. The teenage boys sat abreast their mopeds leaning against the cab and revelled in the heated atmosphere; aiding and abetting they rocked the car in riotous fun. It was a situation that was really getting out of hand. In the chaos of hand waving and vocal misunderstandings I started Chitty's engine. I kept my head down and looked nobody in the eye. A clenched fist pushed into my right shoulder supported with verbal communication of an unpleasant nature, heightened my attempts to move on. The now 'on a bandwagon' old man finished bodily contact by removing his offending arm from the cab to drag on his weathered fag hanging from his mouth. He ducked his head down between Chitty and the kerb and hawked up a gutful of tar-filled phlegm and spat it into the gutter, discarding his lit fag butt on to the pavement just missing the road full of motorcycle petrol. The gridlocked traffic that had been intent on eyeballing Chitty was undergoing a forceful dispersion exercise by the police. I revved the engine and sounded the horn with purpose; the police, although not impressed with the situation we had caused, made an asserted effort to clear a path through the jumble of cars, bikes and bystanders.

The jeering mob adhered to police demands and the crowd parted, cars moved out of the way and two teenage boys on their bike tried to hitch a ride. As we rolled forwards a policeman removed Chitty from the grip of one of the boys and we accelerated now into a clear road. A few yards along another cop directed us across the main drag and up a small side street, where, hidden from view, I parked and took a deep breath. Carolyn joined me escorted by the long arm of the now very helpful and friendly law. Two minutes, I'm not kidding, just two bloody minutes and a fresh batch of finger-flicking general public all tutting in approval descended upon us. You want fame? This was wearing thin. Heads leant over, looking at Chitty's collection of brass dials, and a there was a wall of faces full of curiosity. And something stood out, yep a woman, with two small identical twin boys who for a photo opportunity had been lifted up and sat on the car's front wings, 'Nice to be asked,' Carolyn said. 'What the hell do we do now.!' A small, weathered, unpainted door opened on to the pavement just to my right and out stepped a little old lady clad in black, with a warm friendly smile and two glasses of hot tea. Just when losing faith in human nature, a lovely old dear puts things right.

Trying to establish a place to camp or a hotel we couldn't afford was proving difficult. In the confusion a middle-class man, whom I based on the fact he had a decent car, kept hinting to us to follow. Kindly, he was offering for us to stay with him for the night. 'What do we do?' I said to Carolyn. 'He might be okay, who knows.' Carolyn didn't look too impressed with the idea. 'What if he's not, he could be taking us anywhere.' The man had the thickest black moustache I had seen in Iran so far and was very smartly dressed. He was losing patience with our indecisiveness and his body language was saying 'Look, I am offering my home and if you don't want it, then to hell with it.'

'This man is an honest man,' said some busybody who had some

English and the need to butt in ' Very very honest, trust this man, good man,' he pushed. 'Ahh sod it, what have we got to lose,' I said sparking Chitty into life and taking any excuse to avoid the current mayhem. Nightlife was in full swing and the illuminated following of cars, motorbikes and folk intent on running alongside took to the road behind us.

The twenty-minute drive took us through a ramshackle of clay-brick suburban buildings, through a more traditional-looking Iran. Like a frightened fox hounded to exhaustion our flotilla of fired-up young moped riders continued to taunt and tease us by overtaking and cutting us up, missing the cars by inches. Slamming on the brakes only brought Chitty to a gradually slower speed but ensured the cocky little git riding four up and kicking the front tyres as he passed lived for another day. One drove, the other three made gestures and verbal assaults on each raid.

Further from the city, numbers dwindled only to be replaced with a fresh batch of eye-opening locals. Right, hard left, right again, 200 yards down a tight alley where the roar of twenty mopeds and fast-footed children echoed between the narrow walls, then stop. The man leapt out of his car and opened eight-foot high, pale blue, solid steel gates and beckoned us in. They then slammed shut to a resounding clang of steel and concrete and words of stern authority to the mob of thirty to forty people outside, which I assumed were Iranian for 'Now all bog off.' How grateful we were, an oasis, finally a bit of calm. Before anything was said or done, I shook his hand, smiled and thanked him. He hadn't got a clue what was said but clearly he read my humbled and grateful body language.

The small courtyard was just big enough to fit Chitty and Steve's Discovery. The high whitewashed and weathered walls were filled with hairline cracks and sprouting vegetation. The tiled floor ran up to a single-storey building with an outside toilet. A lady covered in layers stood by the glazed front door with two young boys. How many times had I read about the experience of staying with locals in far-flung places and now it was happening to us. 'Carolyn I think we need to take our shoes off,' I said, pointing to the collection of footwear by the door. I had read the Lonely Planet guide on dos and don'ts in Iran, and typical, I couldn't remember a thing. The guy pointed to his wife and said her name, which could have been Klingon for all I knew. Both kids bowed slightly and shook our hands, I patted my chest and said in a very Me Tarzan, you Jane stupid foreigner way: 'Nick, Nick, Ca-ro-lyn' pointing to Carolyn. The two boys had names trickier than a tongue twister from a place in North Wales, and our caped crusader without the underpants or cape for that matter was called FarzAn, which stood for being wise, and we had been pretty wise to follow.

Shoes removed we were welcomed in and invited to sit on the floor, mainly because there were no chairs; in fact, there was no furniture at all. The oblong room was carpeted from wall to wall in fine Persian rugs and cushions gave support to our cross-legged pose. The last time I sat on the floor was at primary school and then I had to cross my arms too. I had forgotten how bloody hard it was to sit like that.

We had no idea what was in store for tonight but the silence was broken by the youngest son who had an English phrase book from school. The odd familiar word echoed the white plastered walls decorated with family photos. Fortunately the hard-backed book listed short sentences and phrases in Farsi and English. The little ten-year-old ran his finger down to a line and spoke really fast in Iranian, eyes full of expression. I am not sure if he meant to pick for his opening statement 'you were born on the wrong side of the blanket' but it broke the ice. Soon conversations around the book exchanged gratitude and appreciation. FarzAn's wife, who remained strictly covered, pointed out a phrase in the book to Carolyn. It said 'you need a shave'. I laughed and then realised that twisting cotton thread over her eyebrows and arms would remove the hair with a quick yank. Carolyn was summoned to the washroom and invited to shower. Well, when in Rome. Carolyn stripped naked in full view of her female host, who turned on the water supply and set the temperature; she pointed out the shampoo sitting on a small broken ceramic shelf and ordered to her to wear the dirty old pair of flip-flops in the corner – another Iranian custom. The washroom was cold, stark and basic, lifted with green and off-yellow gloss paint on the plastered walls. Carolyn appeared to have nothing to wear as her only black clothing and hijab headscarf were was now going round in a twin tub at 80 degrees. 'Pssst, Pssst, Nick, my clothes are gone, I need my pink joggers, hoodie and a towel,' Carolyn said. I was given a white pair of jogging bottom to relax in, 'Chav' sprung to mind. Steve and Julia seemed somewhat uncomfortable especially as Julia was marched back into the shower naked to make sure she had washed her hair. Clothes returned shrunk to a size fit for a hobbit and we sat down to dinner. A white tablecloth was laid out across the floor and a selection of rice and kebabs filled our eating space. All sat cross-legged; it was a nightmare, bad back, twinges of sciatica and generally being uncomfortable. It's normally a challenge of dining etiquette to keep elbows off the table, now we were struggling with our feet.

Watching with caution, and being ever so careful not inflict an insult' we took our eating cues from the family. Now with a bit more confidence we dived in and poured the small individual bowls of creamy yoghurt stuff on to our rice and mixed it in. The family chatter came to an abrupt halt, they all looked at us, then they all looked at each other, a slight pause then the male head of the household picked up his bowl of creamy yoghurt stuff, acknowledged his guests in a bottoms-up fashion and drank it. Oh dear, thinking quickly we all grabbed the small glasses of tea, and made a similar gesture, politely giggled and then stopped giggling at the lack of response. A knock at the door turned a formal event into a great evening, The brother, wife and two identical twin toddlers turned up to meet the strange foreign visitors; traditional music was played and the two sons of ten and fourteen years took to the Persian rugs and danced the night away. They were fantastic and hilarious, full of male confidence and bravado; showing the mobile phone photos of the twins to themselves encouraged a bout of laughter that lasted all evening and made a truly memorable night. Periodically the men would retreat to a private room to fulfil one of the five daily prayers. The night's sleep was a good one as we were given the family room. No beds in the house at all just Iranian rugs to sleep on and patchwork quilts to keep out the cold desert night air.

Morning was equally as rewarding and a good friendship had been forged with an experience we would all never forget. We parted company after being escorted to the main highway and as a gift for their hospitality I handed over a Chitty photo card and a spare watch I had brought along just in case mine had broken or I had to offer it up as a bribe on a dodgy border.

Chapter 34 **E**lvis had not left the building

Burning fuel had left its mark; the 400-litre ration card I had been using was now redundant, our last fuel stop having used the remainder of the allowance.. We had about 800 kilometres to cover crossing Iran to Bandar Abbas and so it was going to be tight. I made rough calculations in my head and figured the 500 miles to a full complement of tanks and jerrycans was equal to 800 kilometres ish with an emphasis on ish! From now on rolling down hills was a serious consideration. No card, no fuel I'd been told. I was sure there was a black market somewhere but how did I find it?

The six or seven times daily army and police road blocks if not just a bit frustrating were increasing my likelihood of wasting petrol with every stop. At one encounter close to a military base a platoon of soldiers gathered round the car full of interest. 'Motor, what motor' came the constant question. I said 'Land Rover' they looked bemused but all understood. The group photo was broken up by a man of 'standing', full of authority and carrying an air of wealth. Butting in and waving arms in the air with approval he said to the men, 'Rolls Royce Rolls Royce' and jabbered on in Iranian. The confused squaddies all shook their heads, talking in a mixture English and Farsi, 'blah, blah, Land Rover, blah'. Defiantly 'Rolls Royce' was echoed, making out the soldiers were stupid fools who knew nothing about cars in his opinion. Maybe they didn't but I had just told them what the car was. It was entertaining to say the least and this small battle of words raged on for ten minutes or so including an inspection from under the car. Finally, after viewing from afar I returned; leaning into the cab the gentleman said in a positive and knowing way, 'Rolls Royce?' I started Chitty, engaged first gear, the group of soldiers gathered close, I looked him in eye and said, 'Sorry it's a Land Rover, bye bye.' The foreign version of 'I told you so' was sweetly impressed on Mr Know-all; it was priceless.

I could tell you about the long dusty road chasing the sun south, but it's pretty boring, not because the scenery wasn't forever changing and starkly stunning, just that after eight hours on the same strip of tarmac everyday for a week or so, talking about it becomes boring. The rock faces were unlike any others I had ever seen, ripples of coloured veins ran vertically, defiantly raspberry ripple. The road cut through a rugged ash-grey valley bed, pitted with huge moonscape potholes, where pebbled streams meandered and a darkened sky only enforced the mood of a granite quarry from Middle Earth. And just in case it may sound boring, I won't focus on the lonely clean straight road disappearing into a pinpoint on the horizon among a vast landscape, windswept by hot thermals carrying a mix of airborne vegetation and red ochre dust, which was eternally sucked up through our nostrils and filled our yawning mouths settling on gritty taste buds.

Our last tea stop halfway between Esfahan and Shiraz was quite enlightening, flashbacks of car boot sales rumbled through my thoughts. Among a rabid frenzy of normal upstanding citizens who turned in to a babbling team of rampaging Vikings in search of a bargain our pathetic attempt at selling all our junk before we departed raised less than the fee to take part. Books were what we had, books which nobody wanted. To my surprise the only one of interest was The Idiot's Guide to Elvis; just about anybody and everybody passing our feeble pasting table picked up the book, flicked through the pages and then put it down again. 'It's only 50p, I'll take 25p, go on make an offer,' I said repeatedly over and over again. Despite the interest Elvis had not left the building. Then Carolyn nudged me in the ribs, 'Look, have a look at him, there's your chance'. Coming towards us was a Teddy Boy rockabilly kind of guy complete with DA haircut, black leather jacket and a huge belt buckle the size of Memphis inscribed 'Elvis'. Not one to miss an opportunity, I darted out front thinking if I can't sell the Idiots Guide to Elvis to him I haven't got a hope. I looked down among the books and knock me down with a Vegas show girl's feather, some git had stolen it! Brewing up on the tow bar, our PG teabags squeezed out, we were joined by the usual passers-by but today an added extra, Elvis, yes you guess it Elvis Presley in the flesh, and where was my book titled The Idiot's Guide to Elvis when I needed it. No he was not filling shelves in Sainsbury's at Sutton Coldfield. He was here, hiding in Iran. Let's face it, there couldn't be a better place, no contact with outside world, no Western media to track him down; how could there possibly be a better conclusion, oh apart from him being American. Dark seventies-style sunglasses complete with the gold side bits, swept back jet-black hair and matching starched white shirt and trousers. In fact, there were three, and we figured the other two were just decoys. Very friendly young guys, they offered us an evening at their restaurant and somewhere to stay. Every question and offer of information I found myself replying to with, 'U-ha, U-ha'; how juvenile. I still can't get over the book though.

Declining the kind offer of accommodation because the place was sixty kilometres back the way we had just come from, we opted to carry on.

Camping was always tricky in Iran and avoiding military land was almost impossible, it seemed to be everywhere. I turned off the road and drove a few kilometres over rough desert in search of a hidden place to stay. Dust clouds marked our route and made seeing, driving and breathing extremely hard work and left a mouthful of dirt and grit to crunch on during teatime. Just as I was about to pull over I came level with three soldiers in a bunker with a rocket launcher. 'Bloody hell Wigs, we're on army land,' I said. I stopped, they looked at us and we looked at them. I wasn't really sure how this was going to go. They could be hostile and angry that we were here, they could lock us up and throw away the key. They could shoot us. Oh let's not get carried away, I thought. Standing still and showing no emotion, they just looked and looked. I smiled, waved and offered forward a Chitty photo card. One guy climbed up took the card, had a look, smiled and offered to shake my hand. Boy that was close.

A few hours down the desert road we pulled off again and this time we managed to find a small hidden valley in the barren land. The experience of setting up camp in a place you probably shouldn't be in, with only vast miles of sun-bleached desert all around you, is unforgettable. Plenty of fuel and water gave a limited sense of security but not knowing really where you were and what was involved made it scarily exciting.

The sun dipped beyond the valley ridge and we settled down to stargazing with a cup of tea. We contemplated digging a bush toilet, and believe me it was the cleanest toilet we had seen for months. The night was full of shadows and noisy unseen wildlife, which made our imaginations run wild. The wind laden with sand whispered through the valley. Those nights as a child when you couldn't sleep and wished for the morning to come were ever present. Dawn broke and it was bitterly cold, and neither of us wanted to get out of the sleeping bag to make the first brew. A strong smell of manure gave Carolyn a reason to sling my shoes outside the tent, only to find a flock of camels grazing around us.

Heat wobbled the road ahead. The cab temperature soared to a sweltering 50 degrees. We sweated, full headgear whistled in the wind and the only water, which was strapped to the rack, was warming in the sun. 'Unbelievable,' Carolyn giggled at 'Fasten your SAET Belts', one of the only English signs we had seen. Sadly, with my abysmal spelling I didn't get the joke!

Most of the women of Bandar Abbas in southern Iran dressed in a much stricter Muslim code. They were covered from head to foot in black and this time their faces were concealed behind a dark veil or brightly coloured mask. Carolyn after her telling off in Tehran bought a small red textile mask and followed suit. Bandar Abbas was a busy port city on the shores of the Straits of Hormuz, a natural bottleneck to the Persian Gulf. It was baking hot and the air was stale and dry. Life here was so far removed from any experiences we had encountered before; the narrow streets gave way to a broad esplanade lined with commercial boats and traditional trading dhows and had a gut-wrenching odour of death. Bandar Abbas was a hive of activity packed with more women than we had become accustomed to. The tightly packed markets were filled with unrecognisable fresh produce.. Tobacco and gold souks dominated; every pitch and trading space was filled with hundreds of black bobbing heads, weighing gold and flashing rolls of Iranian rials to a chorus of female chatter. Camping here was a joke so before we could track down a shipping agent for India we needed a hotel. 'Here we go again,' I said, bracing for the whirlwind of attention as we approached a secure parking space with a hotel room thrown in. Armed with a hand drawing of a car sitting on a boat with a rough map of India, the receptionist nodded and passed me a business card for a Mr Haddad Poor of Valfajre 8 shipping with a reassuring slogan written in gold italic type 'Transportation of cargo and passenger in Persian Gulf and Oman sea'.

Life really came alive as the sun dipped away so with no time like the present we tackled the general public paparazzi and embarked on a bold quest for the port of Shahid Rajaee. Waiting for hours and having to suffer port workers in their droves kicking the tyres, flicking the bonnet and tutting like an ensemble of unhappy crickets only made it worse to be told to come back tomorrow. But before we could come back tomorrow nobody would let us out of the port gate. This really was bizarre; an hour ago nobody would let us in. As we sat awaiting approval, more dock staff appeared and were interested in our nationality. 'American?' 'See they always think we are rich Yanks,' I said to Carolyn. 'English,' I shouted.' 'In-glis.' 'No, English,' I corrected. 'You not In-glis?' 'Yes In-glis,' I said, losing the will to live. I sparked up a conversation with the port guard and for the second time on this trip a machine-gun barrel was lunged into my ribs as he climbed into Chitty for a photo. Somebody was undoing the fuel cap; the bonnet straps were untied and four or five men peered at the engine. 'You like Iran, yes? We are nice people, yes you think?' Those were really interesting questions which I had been asked so many times, almost as if they understood how the country was portrayed politically abroad but knew confidently at grass roots level they were genuinely nice people. 'Where go now?' the guard enquired. 'India, we take boat to India,' I replied. 'No boats to India, ships go all over world, but no India.' This was a verbal bombshell; he couldn't possibly be right, he was only a guard. A whirlpool of emotions flooded our thoughts. The reality of dealing with constant attention was draining, the physical contact with onlookers was frustrating as they took it as their right to handle Chitty and now with no real plan of getting overland to Oz , we had to consider if we had bitten off more than we could chew.

Options were running thin. We were truly stuck between a rock and a lot more rocks. War in Turkey and a 2,000-kilometre drive were out, Pakistan was in a state of emergency and across the sea to the south was Africa, slightly off track a bit. If we could find a cargo agent maybe we should think about shipping straight to Australia as this was just becoming too much.

Mr Haddad Poor brought us plastic cups of cool water and explained, 'Ships go all over the world from Bandar Abbas, very big port, not India.' Well, we knew that now.

Our only option was to ship over to Dubai in the United Arab Emirates and then on to India, but we would have to come back tomorrow.

A salute from the guard, the secured parking made for an easy night's sleep but the only posh hotel was asking a king's ransom. Our budget hadn't allowed for shipping costs, apart from Singapore to Darwin, and you really can't enjoy the refinements of a plush hotel you can't afford.

We came back tomorrow, which was now today, after the hotel's laundryman posed a proposition. With Carolyn waiting out front, the middle-aged guy wearing a grubby white T-shirt wheeled out his pretty young daughter. 'This is Shadee, it means happiness, take her to England my friend, marry my daughter she is seventeen.' Well that's not an offer to be sniffed at, I thought, but I don't suppose Carolyn would be too pleased.

With second plastic cups of cool water, the shipping agent reminisced over serving with the Iranian Navy and undergoing training in Britain at HMS Sultan about 5 million years ago. Then prodding him in the eye a few times he focused on the matter in hand, outlining their cargo ship wasn't actually a container ship but a roll on roll off ferry no bigger than the old one in Yarmouth on the Isle of Wight. The jetty had just been dismantled and the ship was now tide-dependent so he couldn't tell us whether it would sail this week or not. It was best if we came back tomorrow.

Don't ask me about the cost, paperwork and bureaucracy and about how many times we had to come back tomorrow but the hotel staff were now on first-name terms and would have topped our Christmas card list if it weren't for their religion.

Keys eventually handed over to the well-rounded ship's captain we embarked on our alternative mode of transport over the Persian Gulf. The romantic notion of travelling on a commercial dhow was illegal and only for the likes of Michael Palin and the BBC.

Iran had awakened many of our feelings: trepidation, fear and Cold War suspicion. It was controlled and uniformed but ordered and respectful. At times, it was claustrophobic and yet lonely on a vast canvas. The strict religious rules of conduct, the heat, dust and mayhem gave an experience we found to be truly foreign. The people although insecure had a warming presence and had received us with open arms, which will be treasured for all time to come.

Chapter 35 **W**ings clipped in Dubai

Almost abandoned in a warehouse full of grain, Chitty sat lonely waiting the endless streams of paperwork and rubber-stamping. A delightful reminder of our visit to Iran had been written on our rack full of stickers; just above the orangey red, white and green Iranian flag was a penned message compliments of the Valfajre 8 crew, 'To dear English people, we love you, love Iran.'

Dubai was a complete culture shock. After acclimatising from a Western way of life we had embraced the simpler things. Eastern Turkey and Iran were a far less materialistic experience and quite frankly we had got used to living out of one bag, eating simple but fresh food and witnessing an earthy and contented way of life. Dubai was like winning the jackpot in Las Vegas, full on, full of people and full of money. It almost felt obscene. Gold, beaches, seven star hotels and shopping malls packed with happy holidaymakers.

Driving through the heart of Dubai was amazing, packed solid with posh cars, people and a pace of life that never rests. Well ordered, beautifully clean and manicured it was a pleasure to take in the sun, sights and the odd East Ender on holiday shouting out, 'Wh-hay Chitty Chitty Bang Bang.' However, could we find a place to stay? No. I pulled over as one guy called out, 'I read about you in the paper, you're off to Oz.' 'Do you know the Ascot hotel?' Carolyn said. 'Yeh I'm staying there,' he replied. 'Hop in then and show us the way,' I said cheekily. 'Bloody hell mate, what really?'

Apart from taking a day out to go skiing in one of the world's biggest indoor snow domes, we were on a mission to clear Chitty through customs and send her packing to India. Patience was the word of the day and it had to be. Two days was set aside for bureaucratic paperwork and this was hampered by the fact that Chitty was sitting in the port at Sharjah. Customs officials, bills of lading, import taxes, vehicle carnets and passports, it just seemed an endless exercise of red tape. Pay for a photo to go on the port pass, pay for the port pass, pay for release documents from the shipping agent, pay for a stamp for customs, pay for … Well, by now I was completely disillusioned and it wasn't just because I had to part with US dollars or dirhams depending on the mood but we were back to the 'come back tomorrow' scenario.

On the outskirts of the arid city the third day was full of bright sunny optimism. The grand sand-coloured port building was illuminated by natural light so brightly the contrast with the deep blue sky looked too real, as if it just been altered in Photoshop. Dhows lined the jetty, eager to take on board cargo and set sail on the next Arabian adventure. Clutching a fistful of legal documents I queued in my turn waiting to be processed. A white marbled corridor lined with glass windows edged in gold was home to a collection of official tellers. Called to the first, a very efficient Arab worker wearing full white dress and traditional headwear stamped my documents then sent me to pay a fee at another window. There I was sent to a window next to the first one and I was given a pink piece of paper. The teller looked up, raised his eyebrows and nodded his head over to the opposite side, where I paid another fee and received another stamp. To be honest I couldn't tell how much I paid and what the hell it was for, but seventeen different windows later, mumbling between tellers and shuffling about like I was lost in a pin ball machine, I was ready to enrol in the Ministry of Silly Walks. Come to think of it, I think I paid for burping!

We were going to be here longer than we planned and as usual Carolyn and I were getting twitchy at spending money we hadn't got. As for Steve and Julia they loved it. Steve was like a pig in clover, decent hotel, fine food and Guinness on tap, especially after abstaining in Iran..

In Dubai, tracking down a ship bound for India proved simple enough; getting permission to leave was another story. Mr Biswas was an Indian guy living in Dubai and working for an Iranian shipping company. He had had a great sense of humour and had a good command of English, speaking faster than the commentator at Chepstow. Oasis freight dealt with the Islamic Republic of Iran shipping lines and Biswas as the shipping manager was happy to oblige. Sitting at one end of the office was a long established Indian colleague, who piped up and interrupted every question we asked. 'So how much will it cost and when will the ship sail?' I asked.

'It will sail soon and cost, it will be okay,' replied Mr Biswas. 'No, no, no, they need to know now you bloody fool,' piped up his colleague in a strong southern Indian accent wobbling his head side to side. 'I said soon, so that's soon and the price is the price, so don't tell me things I know.' Biswas said ready to take centre stage in an Indian sitcom. They both engaged in Hindi with the odd English sentence thrown in, banter bouncing between them like an old married couple. Whether we knew how and when was being overshadowed by an extremely entertaining double act. 'Two weeks and she sails to Mumbai, 1,500 US dollars for your container.' 'Tell them about the stuffing, you must tell them when to stuff the flying car,' his colleague interrupted again from the far end. Mr Biswas went on, 'Yes yes, I know about the stuffing, they know too.' 'No they don't, you said nothing, your ears and mouth don't do what your brain is telling you,' came another verbal attack in our favour from Biswas's sidekick.

Walking out grinning from ear to ear we concluded stuffing referred to the day the car was sealed into the container, we had two weeks to kill and had to find a cheaper hotel and obtain a 'no objections certificate'. Mr Biswas warned us customs would not allow Chitty to be exported without the approval paperwork from the chief of police. Now this seemed stark crazy, we had arrived in a place we didn't plan on coming to, we only ever wanted to leave the car in transit so it could be sent straight on to India but red tape said no, and it had to be imported and then exported. So far we had only driven from the port to a hotel and we couldn't leave until the Dubai police confirmed we don't owe them anything for any outstanding fines.

Time was ticking on and our container was ready, a date was planned for clearing customs and the shipping agent had appointed a guy to handle the paperwork. The police headquarters was tricky to find but armed with our car documents and a Chitty photo card we were soon queuing to see the main man. I don't know whether we stood out like lost foreigners or what but instantly we were ushered out of the queue and introduced to the chief of police. On explaining the certificate we needed, I presented a Chitty photo card as a gift and by way of visually showing what we hoped to export. The mood changed like I had just been caught in bed with his wife. 'You can't drive this on the road, this is illegal, these wings are too dangerous,' the police chief said looking completely hacked off.. 'No, they are not there, we don't have any wings, it's just the car,' I replied in a humble manner. 'Listen to me, this car is breaking the law with these stuck out like this, it could kill somebody,' he said in a slightly lower tone. 'No, look, sorry you don't understand we have no wings,' I said again. This was proving really difficult, he really wasn't getting it. I leant over, covered the wings with my hands and said 'This is the car now, no wings.' Without a pause for breath he said, 'this car is still illegal you cannot drive this on the roads of Dubai.' 'Why?' I asked. 'This car is right-hand drive.' I tried to explain we were tourists driving across the world for charity blah blah blah and he slammed his hand down on the table, leant forward, looked me in the eye while pointing his finger at me and in a deep assertive scary voice said, 'Listen here, I am telling you, you do not drive this car on our roads, are you clear. It is right-hand drive, it is illegal to drive right-hand drive vehicles in Dubai.' Hell, I thought, I better not tell him we have been cruising around for the last two weeks and it's currently sitting outside in his car park!

After thanking him for his time and still with no certificate, we realised moving on was going to be tough. He wouldn't or couldn't grant a certificate of no objections for a car that wasn't on the road or shouldn't be at least. We couldn't get it off the road, which officially it was not supposed to be on, and back in to customs because we hadn't a flipping piece of paper from the chief of police. We were stuck with a car we were not allowed to drive and couldn't export. Now that was tricky! Customs informed us it was strictly against their export laws to allow Chitty through without the certificate, pointing out as the car has been imported on to United Arab Emirates'. soil, it could have fines against it for speeding or parking unlawfully regardless of whether it was driven or not.

Day two, now back at the police headquarters by taxi this time and no Chitty photo card, we endeavoured to explain our predicament. No hope and total stalemate. He couldn't issue approval for a car that was not registered here or one not on the system and not on the roads. A pint of Guinness in the Ascot hotel's O'Connor bar brought a bit of thinking time and with only a couple of days left before loading, things were looking rough.. Mr Biswas wasn't too happy and the option of having to wait another three weeks was not possible; we had to ensure Chitty was ready for inspection on Monday,, 5th November, or there would be fireworks!

The morning arrived and the shipping agent's men started the proceedings and allocation of container space at the port entrance. There was a painfully slow photo shoot by the Indian guy pulling together the legal bits – as if we were interested when time was running out. We shot off for one last attempt with the chief of police. Waiting in the office we sparked up a conversation with an English chap on a government contract, liaising with the Dubai police. What a stroke of luck that was. 'Leave it to me, it's just another world out here, rules for the sake of rules,' he said smiling. Ten minutes later he returned with a letter on headed paper saying 'no objections certificate' not required, please allow export, and signed by the chief of police whom we never saw again. If I come across that chap again in England I owe him a pint.

Customs was happy apart from arguing between our agent and the inspector; I overheard something out personal effects, which weren't ours.

With Chitty tucked inside the container and lashed down with straps and wooden blocks we waited for the doors to close. 'You go now,' said the agent, hoping to hurry us along. I wasn't going anywhere until the seal was on and I had recorded the number. The Indian agent looked pretty angry to say the least. 'You can go, your car is safe, no seal until later,' he insisted, You didn't need a degree in psychology to work out he was up to something, so we stood our ground and waited two hours for the final seal to be locked on the grey container doors. Now most unhappy the agent stormed off, forgetting the return lift he had promised, leaving us to walk.

The clash of cultures made Dubai a melting pot of experiences. On one hand, the shopping malls were modern, spotless and oozing wealth with top-end fashion brands and car parks laden with mobile bling. Even the public toilets had an attendant standing behind you at the urinal, who handed out a perfectly formed quilted paper towel to dry your hands. On the other hand, the gold souks bustled with Middle Eastern and Indian traders who seemed to make gobbing and spitting a national pastime. Not forgetting the camels, whose constant sounds of revolting up-snorting, followed by a whistle of spit as a revolving dumbbell-shaped dollop of gob flew past your ear hole, made tiptoeing on the pavement a necessity. Dubai is one place in the Middle East, which maintains strong traditional values mixed up with the very best of Western aspirations.

Leaving Dubai had been bloody hard work with Chitty and now it was proving hard work for us too. They wouldn't allow us to travel with the car on the container ship; taking a traditional dhow was now illegal because of smuggling and pirates and planes were completely fully booked because of the Indian festival of Diwali. Checking back into our accommodation was impossible as the hotel was fully booked and so was the rest of Dubai. The evening drew to a close with another dilemma filling our thoughts. Driving across the globe was never going to be easy but the frustrations of not being able to leave were capped with those of not being able to stay.

Chapter 36 **T**outs, tourists and trains

It doesn't matter how many books you read or travel shows you watch they can never fully prepare you for the cultural shock and senses overload of India. Arriving in Mumbai at 3 a.m. was comical. Yes we were tired but so were the staff . Clutching visas we entered passport control. The official at first manned immigration point was asleep and so was the one at the second. I hesitated as to whether I should wake him up or not, then noticed an army guard standing behind. I looked at him and he nodded his head leftwards, signalling me to move on to the next booth and that official was asleep too. I looked again at the guard and he nodded left once more. At the fourth point, snoring similar to a mumbling warthog with a sleeping disorder resonated from a huge, fat, round immigration official, complete with wing commander's moustache and with his feet up on the desk. The guard signalled left again and the fifth post was also in the land of nod, the sixth also as was the seventh. Finally, at the eighth a yawning immigration guy stamped our passports with as much interest as a David Beckham interview then turned over and went back to slumberland. Now what am I going to do with sixteen machetes, hoards of diamonds and fifty kilos of cocaine!

Getting across the airport used to rely on local taxis. They grew tourist scams into such ridiculous proportions that the airport authorities banned them and introduced shuttle buses. Unfortunately, buses could only operate across the runway between flights and most of the time the drivers missed their slots because of sleep. Hence the three-hour wait.

The Air India flight we had just suffered lived up to my 'plane with the outside toilet' jokes. Nothing ever leaves on time here and ours was no exception. The captain had smuggled a pretty young girl into the cockpit and was arguing with a passenger who felt this was a security issue. I wasn't concerned over safety only whether she was familiar with his joystick.

Everybody standing up and a chorus of the Indian version of 'Here we go here we go' accompanied taking off. Landing in what was Bombay gave light relief after wrestling with my seat, which had come off its rails and flopped around like a stick in a bucket, and the meal tray, which kept falling down on my knees. My own self-preservation flying tactic was to always listen to any disturbing sounds and then ignore them. In this case clearly the undercarriage was containing a herd of Spanish bulls who had just come to a dead end in stilettos. It wasn't this bad flying over the Persian Gulf with Aseman Airways!

This was now going to be a waiting game, Chitty wasn't arriving for at least a week and we needed to spend that time organising an import agent and locating the container port. Mr Biswas had given us a few contacts and it wasn't long before we were sitting down in the back streets of Mumbai talking over the details with a man called Jay Pavel. Jabbering Jay talked for India; he was about fifty, bald-headed and wore a short sleeved shirt made from the finest Indian fabric he kept telling us. Always smiling and wobbling his head in agreement and smiling and wobbling his head in disapproval made it really difficult to pin down an answer. Jay would handle importing and all the relevant customs details for a fee, which alarmingly would remain flexible, and suggested we did a bit of sightseeing in the meantime. We took the opportunity to laze around on the sunny southern beaches of Goa. This broke us in gently to the Indian way of life. A beach hut on the sands of Palolem costs nothing in the big scheme of things and instantly put into perspective the standard of living here. Flocking tourists were something we hadn't seen for a while and now the wooden sun loungers, compliments of Café Del Mar, hosted a mixed bag. Witnessing the frenzied assault to claim one, left an interesting line-up. Two German backpackers were next to a large Indian family complete with grandfather, two babies and a dog with only one ear, who kept herself entertained by continually scratching, rolling over and chasing flies. Then there was me without socks and sandals as it really was too hot, then a cow, and a freshly made cowpat with an enthusiastic bunch of flies. Carolyn was next, perspiring in the midday sun, and the rest of the herd was on her right. A large black bull and a harem of cows all chewing the cud.

Beach vendors tiptoed around the hot golden sand full of rubbish and cowpats, stopping at every Westerner delivering a foolproof sales' pitch. On day one and within the first hour we were approached by a collection of sellers, beggars and entrepreneurs. The drum trader was the most annoying, slapping the skin and sliding his finger across to warp the sound. I could handle it once but every five minutes, I ask you. The little deaf boys presented a letter asking for 500 rupees and showed up daily, as did the bead seller, the henna tattoo artists and the sarong seller. Saying no over and over again left me feeling really guilty, especially to child workers who always claimed they were sixteen even if they only looked four. The coconut seller and the melon sellers came in handy but the newspaper guy really grated on me by sticking it under my nose and saying, 'you buy, you buy' every twenty minutes. When does no not mean no? The map seller of Goa and India was a very polite and friendly man but we had more maps than Google. If you shut your eyes for two minutes, somebody would come and sit on the end of the lounger and start displaying their wares. From hats and sunglasses to jewellery, postcards and seashells, there was everything. Want a relaxing beach holiday? Um. We both wrestled with our thoughts over seeing such poverty and succumbed to parting with rupees for things we didn't need. Sadly seeing a 11-year-old girl wearingl dirt-stained rags carry her younger baby brother of no more than aged two on her back is touching, then it's disturbing as she belts him as hard as she can, slapping him round the face, leaving a reddened hand print, only to make him scream and cry as she holds out her hand begging for money.

Goa took it's toll on our emotions and our stomachs. a simple golden rule: never eat in a place that is empty, never eat something which is not cooked or peeled, and never eat something which looks, tastes or smells bad, simple. So why we avoided the busy restaurants to find an empty one, ordering a salad of local prawns which weren't local and then didn't question the overcharging, I'll never know. Yes, I do. I could blame the sun, but really that's being politely British and a bit stupid. The rat scurried past me as I was on my knees at the toilet throwing up all that night, and I was wishing I wasn't here.

On the beach, the early morning air was filled with smoke as the funeral pyre burning the body of a local fisherman who had sadly lost his life the previous night took place. The beauty of the shore lapping the Indian Ocean and lightly windswept coconut trees contrasted starkly with the crackling of burning timber and the cries of hungry children.

Fuel prices had gone up compared with Iran but they were still half the price of the UK; even so I couldn't afford wasting money on a smoky engine. Time gave me the chance to ring home and order a new Land Rover carburettor to be sent to the shipping agent's address in Mumbai hoping it would arrive before Chitty did.

A week of well-spoken young girls sent to the southern beaches to ply the tourist trade became an endurance. They were genuinely hard working and sometimes desperate, shipped off by their parents from the northern states of Gujarat and Rajasthan. As much as it was a pain in the butt, these girls in their very early teens brought younger brothers and sisters to look after and carried a huge weight of responsibility. Sarah was Gita's adopted Western name to make it easy on the foreigners but at her acclaimed sixteen she was having a laugh. They either lacked imagination when it came to names or were having a joke on us because before we met Gita came Rita, along with Bigita and her sidekick Anita. After the normal chitchat Gita acknowledged she was a bit younger but genuinely didn't know when her birthday was and what year she was born, only that it was in the monsoon season. She stressed the money she made was sent home to look after her parents, only keeping a little for herself for food and rent, but a large chunk was physically removed from her each day by the local policeman otherwise he would ban her from the beach. Gita's eyes welled with tears as she tried to talk of the burden she carried. 'Girls don't go to school, only boys if they have rich parents,' she said. 'I learn English on the beach and now I have work.' Gita was so interested how life was for our 16-year-old daughter back in England, but with envy in her eyes we chose to play it down.

With these sobering thoughts in mind we caught the 4 a.m. very budget friendly and unbelievably slow train to Mumbai. I wasn't sure whether to blame the British for the introduction of the railways moving slower than continental drift or the Indians for their lack of maintenance and overloading. Steve and Julia after taking the air-conditioned option in the Palolem beach hut department opted to fly up instead. Booking a sleeper car for the twelve-hour journey we boarded only to find two fat and very smelly people asleep in our bunks.

The word sleeper is a bit misleading; basically it's a train travelling through the night full of people, asleep, which can be absolutely anywhere including the beds we booked. In our car there were fifty bunks and over sixty smelly, snoring locals and air conditioning we had paid for but that didn't work. The guard woke the now very grumpy bodies in our bunks and a wave of guilt ran over me, God knows why. Somehow getting in to warm and sweaty bunks didn't seem so appealing, so feeling tired we crashed on the top covers, and if it wasn't enough to sleep in my bed Goldie Locks was now sitting on the end of it sorting out her luggage and squashing my feet! I was too tired to care!   I hoped it wasn't porridge for breakfast. The next twelve hours saw a collection of tea boys, guards, newspaper sellers and food sellers all pass through our carriage and at every train stop, traders of every description boarded. Lunch was two curried vegetable balls in deep fried batter squashed into a bread roll. It looked crap but tasted lovely despite everything being passed around by grubby hands! I had given up worrying until I watched our rail trader stick his hands in his pants and rearrange his testicles, sniff his fingers and then blow his nose wiping it on his service tea towel.

India runs on deals, scams and bribes and arriving in Mumbai's Central Station was no exception.   The grand Victorian station is a building with presence, lovingly cared for. Its detailed beauty together with its with opulence and splendour shone out in a sea of 'live for the moment' hustle and bustle. The platforms were packed with commuters, traders, lost souls and touts setting up camp. Before we disembarked two young guys grabbed our bags, saying, 'Your taxi is waiting,,,sir.' 'No, your all right my friend, we are sorted,' I said, grabbing our bags back. 'Very cheap taxi any hotel you like, which hotel?' Now with five or six Indian touts fighting over our luggage we tried to ignore them all and opted for an auto rickshaw. The station was teeming with rickshaws parked as if abandoned, hassling for a fare. Trying to get in was unreal. I put the bags in and a tout took them out. 'This man is not honest he will cheat you,' he said. The poor fellow at the helm looked ready to commit murder. Walking towards a cab the tout was pushing away other drivers trying to manhandle our bags. I really wasn't having this, so I grabbed it again and politely told him to go away using just two words. Back at the auto rickshaw I said, 'How much to the Manama hotel.' 'One thousand rupees,' came the reply with a big cheesy grin. Turning to the ever growing group of taxi drivers I said, 'How much to the Manama hotel.' 'Five hundred and we take tour too.' 'I'll give you 300, now put your foot down,' I said feeling slightly bewildered and defiant.

Chapter 37 **M**umbai mayhem

The flamboyant colourful city of gut-wrenching smells wafted by. Grand colonial architecture dominated every corner but had succumbed to the progress of new India and was left sun bleached, moss covered and unloved. Beggars worked the junctions and traffic lights scratching a living in the shadows of far too busy people. Life was made up from contrasts of, affluence and well-heeled high rises against unbelievable filth, poverty and traffic-jamming cows. Twenty minutes in an auto rickshaw and we had witnessed the world on overdrive; we had touched it, smelt it and tasted it, apart from the two squatting down in the gutter taking a dump.

After we had clambered over a no-man's-land of broken pavements and moonscapes of rutted holes large enough to swallow a complete troll, green and leafy the hotel sang the song of the 1930s but now danced to the tune of a grand piano with a wonky leg and broken keys. Camping really was the better option but the tent was lashed to the back of Chitty so eating away at our rupees plagued our conscience. A loud up-snort of phlegm filled the mouth of the porter who was clutching my rucksack, the steel mesh lift took off and so did a gob of red stained beetle nut spit. The porter spat through the mesh on to the passing wall, the gob spattering and joining a concoction of coloured saliva. Unfazed he turned and smiled as if he had just sucked the blood from a thing invented by Bram Stoker.

Was I loving India for all the wrong reasons? It smelt, nobody left us alone for five nanoseconds and the world and his wife were trying to rip us off. But vibrant energy rubs off.

A night catching cockroaches crawling over our faces was slightly unsettling and the pillow with the odour of five wrestling lesbians kept the mind working on overtime. Thirsty because the tap only expelled air followed by thick black sewer-tainted water encouraged Carolyn to demand a new room in a new hotel. Jay delivered a message, which meant we would be getting to know Mumbai intimately. Customs, port officials and shipping agents were holding on to Chitty for another week and Jay reassured us he was on the case. 'See theses are all my friends, they still write, I help this man with his motorbike,' said Jay proudly, producing a photo from his top pocket. Slightly frustrated we headed into the heart of the city in search of food and some clean water. Checking the bottle seals had become a top priority after watching the 'Going Green' recycling efforts of one man and his rod.

The Gateway to India is a huge imposing archway built to commemorate the visit of King George V and Queen Mary to India in 1911 and significantly the place from which the last British troops departed in 1948 at the end of colonial rule. The location was full of pushy vendors, taking photos, flogging ice cream wrapped in newspaper stored in an old oil drum and enormous multicoloured balloons the size of a fridge freezer – as if we wanted or needed one of them! Fire ants on the attack look relatively lonely and docile compared with the activity going on here. Hassled is one thing; having a finger stuck in your ear is another. 'Something in you ear, sir, soap soap please.' 'What the hell?' I said as the fourth ear-cleaning, tourist-pouncing trader tapped my shoulder from behind and tried to stick a used cotton bud in my lughole. Just me, not Carolyn of course, had been bombarded by ear cleaners, shoe shiners and perfume sellers. I was starting to get a complex.

The steps to the waterfront were a rugby scrum of city siders commuting, tourists from the Punjab and day-trippers to Elephant Island. The quay left not a drop of ocean on view as wooden double-decker ferryboats filled every available sea space jostling for a fare. Dodging the tourist horse and carriage rides plying the short esplanade, a moped driven by dad supporting mum and two small Indian girls made for the sea wall. Black bin liners balanced on the handlebars and others wedged between the kids, the rider was unable to see the road ahead let alone the overworked skinny pony baring his ribs and filling his mouth with equestrian froth in response to the lashes from above. The thick sewage and rubbish that was hiding the sea beneath was added to as the bin bags were emptied over the side, retaining them for further use. I thought how environmentally friendly of them, especially as standing on a raft of waste and rubbish so packed solid with litter and crap it floated was a thin old man with white hair casting out a bucket collecting up the discarded water bottles. Saving the planet! No, I was saving my stomach Resealed sewage-laden plastic bottles filled with tap water, I was off for a Kingfisher beer a short walk from the Harbour View Hotel.

Now called home, the hotel was enlightening to say the least. As we looked out over the veranda, to the right was 'pee corner'. It stunk because of a constant supply of men parking up their taxis for the open-air urinal. In two minutes Carolyn angrily counted twenty-three unzipped wee wands. To the left was a family sleeping on the pavement, a mother of about of twenty-five with a toddler boy and a young baby. Her eyes caught ours each day as we passed, saying nothing and giving only a gentle smile and a helpless touch of envy. Her only belongings were left hanging in the tree for security and all she had was a sheet of cardboard to lie on. As night drew on, we would tiptoe over a never ending crèche of pavement beds, mostly tiny children with snot-dried noses lying cheek to dusty concrete, close to a desperate mother and usually a gatecrashing scabby dog full of fleas and sores, carrying the scars of cars and broken limbs, starving, scavenging and sadly left living. The wide awake children and babies followed us with begging hands and solemn faces, making guilt run high.

Making our way through overrun slums of tarpaulins and rusted corrugated iron roofs, life for the not so lucky eking out a living unfolded before us. Traffic diverted around a lifted manhole cover where a mother bathed her naked children in sewer water. 'In road' washing was just one small hazard for such young lives. Stumbling through the shanty land and controlling retching among the rotting smells of human waste, we were faced with a hopeless soul who had just given birth on the pavement, her eyes filled with despair as she clutched her newborn. Carolyn was unable to hold back her emotion and we offered water and parted with rupees, which we considered could make a difference. Her entire worldly possessions were for all to see: a small fabric patchwork bag, the clothes she wore and a sarong for her baby. Her caste status kept her looking down, struggling to smile with a sense of the unworthy.

'Excuse me where are you from,' came a direct question from a trendy young guy, sporting sunglasses clipped to V-neck T-shirt. 'I'm a scout for Bollywood films, would you like to work as an extra?' No sign of a toggle or short trousers confirmed he was a talent scout. I looked at Carolyn, smiling as if it was a joke. 'What for real?' I said. 'Yes. Here's my card, you get paid 500 rupees for the whole day at the studios, transport, lunch. I'll pick you up 8 a.m., okay,' he said as though he was on commission.

We couldn't find anything we considered safe to eat that we could afford so we didn't bother and returning past pee corner Carolyn heard the cries of a small kitten. The once grand harbourside house with broad walkways and leafy gardens was home to a little white moggy stumbling on its feet, with patchy fur and fleas leaping to and fro.

Carolyn knelt down to stroke him and offered some comfort; it wasn't a good life for cats in India among poverty and slums and this was the first we had seen. Carolyn picked him up and he cried out with hunger pains. The more she gave comfort, the more she needed to help. Sitting in the driveway entrance was a khaki-uniformed security guard looking unimpressed at our attentions. Carolyn asked the man if he had access to a little milk; talking in Klingon would have had more effect. Desperate to save his little life, we headed back to buy a carton of milk and purchased a pack of chewing gum so we could have the packet tray for a bowl. Turning the corner and calling for the kitten Carolyn's eyes filled with tears; there was no sign of the starving creature, only the guard who had taken the matter into his own hands returning from the sea wall. A not so polite term springs to mind.

Chapter 38 **B**ollywood dreams

We still loved India for its vividness of life, explosions of colour and cultural diversity but there was an element that was grinding us down because of our upbringing in comfort and Western values. India didn't have a problem, we did.

Bollywood beckoned, so after giving fresh bottled water and soap to the family on our doorstep we caught the 8 a.m. bus to the Mumbai studios. Lucky Charm was the film and a couple of backpackers in search of fame and a fistful of rupees joined us. Ushered off to the wardrobe department, which was the back of a truck, we were kitted out in musty seventies-style nylon outfits smelling of fish and stale sweat impregnated with curry. The studios were heaving with Bollywood dancers, technical teams, directors and egos. The two Australian backpackers, who were doubles for Leonardo DiCaprio and Ewan McGregor, saw the whole affair as one big party and took the piss all day. They were in for the cash but made our day a cracker. The young dashing stars of the film were only for show – two pretty boys with stage names of Michelle and Charlotte – yes we were confused too. As the countdown for cameras rolling was announced, one took to the floor pushing out ten press-ups, pumping up his biceps; a dab from the make-up harem and a comb of his locks and they were away. Dressed in a deep purple suit I looked like a pimp from New York. Instructed to carry furniture and timber in the background, left unattended we opted to act out a classic Laurel and Hardy sketch; turning left and right swinging planks around, ducking under them and banging heads made earning 500 rupees a pleasure. Carolyn griped over her static brown polka dot nylon cocktail dress, which I thought looked rather fetching. There is no such thing as a free lunch, apart from today when we had a free lunch, a mix of rice and rich Indian dishes. The day soon came to a close with an offer of a few weeks' work for us as a Western couple and a speaking part, but the limelight wasn't calling, Chitty was.

The mix of wealth and poverty that live alongside the film industry brought home the contrast of millionaires growing out of city slums. Ferried back, the drive in through illuminated vibrant city life was as exciting as it was dangerous. Hard on the brakes, swiftly to the left our driver made wing mirror clipping a national sport; not that there were many left to clip. A shantytown of market stalls dotted the churned-up wasteground, selling catfish the size of Wales. At a flick of the wrist the moving carpet of flies lifted into the air, avoiding the toothless old dear waving a short stick with string attached. The dark fogbank of bluebottles hovered in a swarm then settled again for the next feed. I was glad I'd had the curry.

The main artery was a dual carriageway separated by a small central barrier; this was no more than two feet high and three feet wide but astonishingly was home to many. The traffic flowing towards us out of town was fast moving and packed with lorries, private cars homeward bound and a million taxis fighting to gain ground. Our side was another story, a few concrete blocks from the central barrier had fallen into the road. No one had had the sense to stop and pick them up; therefore, we were bottlenecked at 5 mph all trying to get round it. However, what was so amazing was the fact weeds had taken root and this was obviously a long-term problem. Pausing to watch the world go by, a stark reality took hold. Many families living in this motor-mania they called home had kids. A few men lay fast asleep finding an open-air comfy spot following the contours of the rubble. A couple of older women sat in conversation over a boiling pot and a tiny girl barely walking stumbled her way over the minefield of broken concrete obstacles. I could hardly believe my eyes as she constantly fell forwards tripping over blocks. High-sided commercial vehicles raced so close the slipstream of wind lifted her hair and the vibrations of heavy haulage sent her flat on her face.

The traffic roared past on the opposite side knowing, as in so many cases, this dear little girl in a tattered and torn dress could so easy stumble the wrong way.

The free lunch was now asking for payback and I was spewing my guts up; both ends erupting violently made the ride unbearable. Once again I worshipped the porcelain all night, hot and sweaty, covered in goose bumps, and slept on the tiled floor in a sea of curry, carrots and dribble for the next three days.

Mumbai was nearly ready to release its grip on us with a meeting called by Jay Pavel. Like all these things it was going to take time and money but India had added a little extra ingredient of counterfeiting and bribery. Before Chitty could be released from customs into the country they had to confirm the vehicle's travel carnet was original. India deals with so many scams nobody knows what's what any more and the RAC carnet could be fake. Waiting was becoming an occupational hazard fuelled by false promises and scatty communication. 'Jay, a simple question: when will we get the car?' I said, trying to tie him down. 'Yes yes yes, you will have your car soon,' Jay wobbled on. 'When, what day, tell me a date. I can wait but I would like to narrow it down to this century,' I said with determination. Jay smiled and took hold of my hand as he walked me across the road bound for a taxi. There we go again, male bonding, at least I was prepared this time. In the taxi Jay explained we were heading to the WI. I was getting hacked off with Monday running into Friday and Jay was taking us on a day trip to the Women's Institute. An opulent art deco building came into view and ageing signage, weathered and chipped, revealed its true identity: WIAA (Western India Automobile Association). It turned out the WIAA had to fax a copy back to the UK so the RAC could confirm our carnet is legit. Then the very nice man would write a letter to customs, for a fee of course, to allow Chitty in to the subcontinent. Stepping back in time to the 1930s, we marched up a spiral staircase to a wood-panelled room full of framed road maps from a bygone age. Mr Dossa (or Dossa the Tosser as Steve called him) was the chairman and only he could sign the letter. However, this would take at least a week Jay pointed out. I suggested we left a Chitty photo card with the receptionist, who took it straight into the chairman's office. A week was the time it took, unless you just happened to have a Chitty photo card. Mr Dossa, a tall affluent-looking man in his late fifties and wearing a cravat, appeared pretty sharpish as though Shilpa Shetty was standing naked in his foyer. Inherited wealth and boasting a collection of fifty-four motorcars, he demanded to see the flying auto. 'No no, don't worry with faxing, get me a letter. You shall have your car,' he said, bossing around an army of staff.

Forget the low-cut dress, if you're after a favour start talking classic cars. Mr Dossa entertained us with tea, a guided tour of his boardroom and collection of die-cast model toy cars and a visit to the basement surrounded by WIAA men, mechanics and guards all standing round his drophead 1940s Bentley.

'Don't forget I want to see that car,' were his parting words. Not out of the woods just yet, Jay advised us motor insurance was very important considering the general state of the roads and the lack of driving skills. He just happened to know a rather glamorous-looking female, Varsha, who worked for the government-supported New India Assurance Company.

Juhu Beach was a Mecca for all and the sand was lit with fireworks and illuminated stalls. Jay insisted this company was the only option over the dinner we had paid for, which entertained him and Varsha. The rapport between them both was of a denied affair, with cheeky grins and shared food tasting not to mention the groping that went on under the table. Varsha explained that the engine and chassis numbers were needed and a pencil rubbing must be taken to prove we were insuring our vehicle, which we said we would do before the policy was issued. 'Far too many scams in India to take people's word,' she said.

...

Jay took us on a wild Raj goose chase, catching the harbour boat a few miles over to Nhava Sheva commercial port. I stood up photographing Mumbai from the sea, the Gateway to India and general life. I was aware of being watched with frowning eyes. I zoomed in across the boat to a group of deckhands leaning on the bulkhead and just above them was a huge sign displaying the message: 'Harbour Military Installations Strictly No Photography'. Oh!

With luggage in tow and a taxi ride later, fees to port officials, customs and a handout to the container rep, we were ready to break the seal. Over the last few days Jay would click his fingers to summons a financial contribution for one service or another and bribe our way through the system. 'What's that for Jay,' I enquired at another payment to some shifty guy not wanting to be seen loitering in the shadows of the container. 'Yes yes yes, oh just stuff, he sorts things,' Jay said smiling. 'It's the way to get things done,' he added, leaning into me and whispering. It was, as expected, very long-winded and there were one-off payments for everything! We paid the port, customs, the shipping company, the administrator, Jay! Including dinner in a restaurant he recommended and where he brought a friend. We paid the clearance charges, port entrance pass, the security guard, the man who opened the container, the man who took the packing out; we paid the taxi driver and the tea boy! There were a few other payments, which I never really understood exactly what they were for. At one point I'm sure I saw the same keen open hand and smiley face twice! The moths in my wallet went on hunger strike.

'Hang on a minute, that's the wrong seal number,' I said loud enough for customs to hear. 'Look this is a photo of my seal in Dubai; I'm not taking responsibility for anything illegal in there.' The customs man really couldn't give a hoot, so the doors opened to a well-missed car. The shipping agent in the United Arab Emirates had worked a scam to export his own goods into India under our name and for free. What a cheek! Just showed what a bloody waste of time a seal was. Nothing was stolen but curiosity had led to the bonnet being opened so many times one of the bonnet clips was broken, Bribing our way out, we finally took to the roads and made plans for travelling east again.

Chapter 39 **R**ules of the road

Out of hotels and back in Chitty made the news of China an easier pill to swallow. We were now heading north to the Himalayas and Nepal only to find out getting into China was impossible. I had spent weeks researching the internet and found mixed messages on whether we would be allowed to drive our own car through the country.

The Chinese embassy in London had given us no clues whatsoever and in a last attempt we contacted the British embassy in Beijing. They confirmed only vehicles with a special permit acquired in your country of origin three months prior to travelling would be considered. This we didn't have and even if we had it would cost 100 US dollars a day to pay for a government-approved Chinese guide to sit in our car. The guide would be paid for every day of the five weeks we had planned for and we were responsible for his accommodation and food. Having only two seats because of our luggage and tools we would have to also pay for a hire car for the guide to follow our daily routine. And to top it off, having organised this there was no guarantee we would be allowed in.

A bitter blow, we changed our forever changing plans and decided to take in Madras, heading for the eastern city of Chennai. Making decisions at a low ebb was not good at all. After nearly three weeks fighting bureaucracy, physically drained and a stone lighter in weight because of severe stomach upsets it really felt as though the world was against us. The topic of shipping directly to Australia seemed so appealing when insecure, homesick and financially backed into a corner. I was making excuses to myself on how Chitty would not fare well on India roads and how we couldn't afford the fuel. We found it hard to endure but Steve and Julia had it really bad as they had suffered with the trots – particularly Steve – from day one in India and it was taking its toll. There was a real discussion with them considering on calling it a day and heading home early. Then they made a phone call home which only made things worse, both of them now so depressed and in tears down the phone line. We suggested if it was that bad for them both they needed to go and we were happy to continue on our own. Negative and tired, this day needed to be forgotten and with good night's sleep welcome the next. Finding a place to stay left two options: a hotel or sleeping in the car. Hotels were never on the agenda, camping was, but finding a campsite here made cracking the Big Bang theory a tea break teaser.

Against all our convictions and with a tent strapped to the back of Chitty, we settled for the K-Star hotel five minutes down road from the container port. Jumping to his feet the doorman stood to attention and saluted me as I pulled up. I was getting used to this by now. Up at six, I removed the bonnet and stripped off the carburettor. Working for the next few hours and under the gaze of the porters, the cleaners, the doorman, a chef and the gardener I fixed on the new part and revved the old engine into life. She purred like one of Carolyn's much cuddled kittens and with no smoke.

Insistent on showing us to the main highway east the hotel manager instructed a tea boy to sit in the cab offering directions and this proved life threatening. 'Go straight' were the only words of communication. Every time I asked, 'Do I go right or left, which way?' he just said, 'Go straight', so I did. The road signs pointed out we were travelling down a one way street the wrong way but I stuck with it. 'Go straight' so I did over the roundabout, at which time he lunged his arm out pointing to the road we had just missed on my right and he said, 'Straight, straight, go straight.' 'Go straight to bloody jail,' I said under my breath.

One of the first road signs to spark a debate was 'Obey Road Rules'. The bloke who had gone to a great effort to fund, design and erect this sign was hopeful to say the least. His optimism was as misguided as the Titanic's captain ordering cornflakes for the following morning's breakfast. Road rules? Simple, there weren't any; driving was going as fast as what was in front of you at the time, which most of the time was a cow! Driving on the left or right was optional. The reality of a few thousand kilometres across a 'free for all' motoring wilderness in a car we really cared about was like being told you're pregnant at ninety-six. Concerning! The first day, no the first hour, driving in India was an experience! Where do I start? First, forget everything you have ever learnt about driving. Throw away your indicators, bin the backlights! Remove your wing mirrors and drive like a madman! Oh and any common sense you may have, leave that as well at home! The only modifications required are the horn. Fit the loudest, biggest monster horn you can find, which we did as Chitty's was just not loud enough. Nobody really cares what's going on behind or around him or her to be honest! The focus is clearly on gaining as much ground as possible and don't think about leaving more than an inch between you and the next car, as even an Indian on a bike will edge his two-inch wheel in to the gap! Sticking to a lane is for Westerners only and as for the road conditions, well imagine the M25 with three lanes running both ways then every five miles or so drop a bomb to create a minefield of potholes, ruts and dust. Here, in no-man's-land, it's a free for all, lorries, buses and cars jostling for the front like a scene from the Paris to Dakar Rally. The holes were so deep that Chitty, even though built on a Land Rover, bottomed out many times. The dust was so thick I couldn't see a thing and I even had to feel for Carolyn next to me to make sure she was still there!

The lorries looked very intimidating coming towards us. I looked up at the cabs as they passed by expecting to see a big burly skin-headed, bearded macho trucker. Instead as a lorry came close it disappeared into a huge pothole and the cab for a brief moment was at eye level and there staring back was a tiny thin Indian smiling. Finally, the gravel pit gave way to tarmac and a nice dual carriageway. I followed a bus and accelerated hard to overtake; just as I reached the maximum revs in third gear I changed up in to fourth and pull out in to the fast lane. Bang! I slammed the brakes on hard there a was a man cycling down the fast lane the wrong way with a bush on his head! I should have known to expect the unexpected as a few hours ago I had come face to face with a herd of cows and a huge ox and cart and just after leaving that morning the motorway or expressway as called in India was blocked completely with a combine harvester coming down the wrong way.

Soon driving the Indian way became a must, if only to actually get somewhere. We pulled up at a set of traffic lights, sitting among a swarm of motorised bees. All cars, lorries and motorbikes line up on the left side of the road, oh and the right side to! This is also happening on the other side of the junction and as the lights turn green it's like the start of a motor cross race, both sides scream at each other, fighting to gain ground and then spend the next twenty minutes trying to make it over to the correct side of the road – or not as the case may often be. Chitty was sucked along like a twig in a torrent of water. I didn't mind so much apart from I kept ending up in places I didn't want to be! Overtaking... don't! Leave that to the bus drivers as the general rule of thumb is to overtake where there is a suitable blind corner or a brow of a hill. Most of the time this coincides with a bus or lorry doing exactly the same thing coming towards you. Both charge together with a couple of motorbikes thrown in for good measure and the near misses are so unbelievable, they have to be seen to be appreciated. They get through the smallest gap where only a whisker on a diet separates them. Luck must be in their favour, probably because the only driving school I saw in India was called the 'Lucky Driving School'. Mind you there were plenty of stark reminders littering the roadsides when it wasn't so good. Burnt-out wrecks of head-on collisions lay rusting on the carriageway and overturned trucks would close a lane or two for what seemed like eternity. Witnessing an accident is horrific and shameful as away from the city ambulances are unheard of and medical care is sparse. Most casualties face the trauma themselves, expecting nothing and getting help from whoever stands by or sometimes they die.

Morning tea at eleven meant finding a quiet lane off the main road so we could enjoy a moment to ourselves. This was a bit of a joke in India, but we were going to try. Looking down I could see a track disappearing into some bush and this had potential so we turned up the narrow dusty entrance and hid behind a hedge. The kettle was not quite boiled when I saw a man on a scooter edging his way through the gap and then disappearing. Fifteen minutes later we were surrounded by a few hundred people, all looking but strangely not a word was spoken, it was complete silence. I should have welcomed this but no, I thought it polite to say hello, so I did. This act of introduction was the licence to open the floodgates. The Chitty circus and entertaining clowns had rolled into town and friendly handshakes, a thousand questions and every man and his very scabby dog was climbing on the car, scrabbling through the luggage and opening the fuel cap once again. Why did they always do that? Peering down the pipe what did they expect to see? Did the Indians keep small children down there working the pump? I'll never know. Just as Iran, the tactile flick of a finger to sample the brass, the polished bonnet or the varnished boat tail was a sign of approval but with several hundred finger flicks, the only thing I could think of was to flick off!

Chittoor was a place we just needed to visit and amazingly was home to a local tribe called the Chitty people. Camping just wasn't possible as on our first attempt pitching the tent hundreds people came to watch and were still watching at 3 a.m. Sleeping in the car became a necessity but two lying across the front seat was bloody uncomfortable and we couldn't sleep anyway with an audience who felt the need to touch everything and beep the horn in the early hours of the morning. The collection of hotels always made us very welcome and most had a locked car park and a guard that put pay to the need for my inhouse alarm system (the Indian handbell hung from the cab roof secured by taut bungee cords on each rolldown vinyl door), so if the door was opened the bell rang a little! I had no idea what they thought but the porters, guards and hotel management always stood to attention and saluted us on arrival. With so many backhanders the only way I could ensure Chitty remained safe was to tip the security guard with fifty rupees and tell him another fifty would follow in the morning. There were eighty to the pound so in the big scheme of things it was a price worth paying. Passing through the different Indian states was a frustrating nightmare in this bribery ridden country. Without fail a policeman would run into the road waving us down. I would stop and smile, saying, 'Hello, do you want to see our passports?' No words in return just a cheeky grin and a hand held out rubbing his fingers together. 'What for,' I would demand. 'Pollution tax, too much pollution,' he would reply. I would offer ten and finger rubbing would continue until I had given fifty. The thing is this happens every time you see one of the old bill. In the end, I didn't even question it and would just hand over fifty rupees whenever we were stopped.

Chapter 40 **T**ea stop talks

Bangalore is one of India's richest cities as we could tell by the sheer amount of traffic. However, along with the wealth came the poverty and every junction was no exception. Beggars stood waiting for the traffic to grind to a halt and open hands appeared from everywhere. Leprosy, I thought, was a thing of the past and I had no idea people were still inflicted and living with this awful disease. The lepers were horribly disfigured and tapped against the car windows looking desperate and down trodden. Drivers ahead of us quickly wound up their windows, choosing to ignore them. I felt so uneducated, I didn't know what to do. 'Carolyn is leprosy contagious,' I said, 'Probably, I don't really know,' she replied. I was torn between ignorance, fear and genuine concern. We had no doors, nor did we have any windows to wind up. I wrestled my wallet out of my pocket and shamefully I threw a collection of rupee notes and coins to the ground. The poor old lady had a face distorted and maimed and in her eyes was inexpressible suffering. The old dear was pushed aside by a kid of about ten who was carrying a younger sibling; she held our her hand to me which I ignored because of her treatment to the old lady. Again the girl thrust her hand out and into the cab while walking alongside as we edged forwards. She was vocal and demanding and slapped me on my thigh to gain my attention. I was pretty annoyed at this so continued to ignore her. She called out angrily and slapped me on the leg again. Yes, I know you're hungry but do that again and I'm going to poke you in the eye, I thought. There are some who melt you heart and you cannot but help give to them and then there are others …

Climbing out of the valley for the first time Chitty felt quite fast. It wasn't, but everything else was just so slow and we even overtook something once. The steep winding roads were the worst we had known so far and up front five or six overworked and overloaded lorries belched out thick black diesel fumes which mixed in with a blanket of red dust filled our lungs for the next three hours. Oh how we wished we had doors. Monkeys scurried across the cliffside roads and it was time to stop and wash down the dirt with a cup of tea. A quiet spot, don't you believe it. We were in the middle of nowhere so where did they all come from?

Gathered round, the rural community full of surprise and smiles asked many questions and then repeated my answers. It was so innocent and funny. 'What model?' they would ask. 'Chitty Chitty Bang Bang.' 'Oh yes yes yes shitty shitty ban ban.' 'Where are you from?' would come the next question. 'England.' 'Oh yes yes yes England.' 'Where are you going?' was another question. 'Chennia.' 'Oh Chennia, yes.' 'Yes we are going to Chennia,' I would say, replying contagiously. Banana half peeled and tea boiling we were now on view to at least a hundred people. Steve and Julia were most unhappy with the attention, opting to stay in the background fifty metres down the road. Julia was intent on finding a bit of peace and quiet and now grumbled at our travelling road show. Carolyn and I had always been comfortable with the interest. I mean, let's face it, getting constant praise for something you have built is extremely flattering. Understandably for Steve and Julia India had taken its toll on their emotions and the limelight we were receiving was getting on their nerves.

The dusty town of Tumkur with its unmade roads and jumble of dwellings had a sense of real India; rural and vibrant the place was alive with earthy living. Ever conscious of finances we parked Chitty under a hotel carport and made our beds on the front seat. Steve and Julia booked a room and took to the nearest eating-house for dinner. Chitty caused the usual stir, but before we could hide her under the car cover the hotel's owner, wife and two children turned up for a chat and a photo. We felt really guilty for not booking a room and parking in their spot, but as with so many people and experiences in this colourful country, they were so friendly and couldn't do enough to help. I gave both the kids Chitty photo cards and later they returned with a small wrapped gift they had made for us. Cooking our tea was a source of entertainment for the entire hotel staff and just about any passing local. The audience stood round while we sat down at our foldaway table and chairs in torchlight eating pasta and cheese. The night was unbelievably hot tucked in the cab under the car cover, which was lifted every five minutes. Counting sheep was rudely interrupted every time a passing shadow hawked up and spat out the usual recipe down by the front wheels. Grubby fingers at 3 a.m. pulled up the cover for a peek of the car now the word was out. Bleary eyed I looked back, waved and nodded back off to sleep. Did anybody sleep here? Apparently not. By 5 a.m. the attention was wearing thin, the idea of waking somebody up every twenty minutes with a honk of the horn was completely normal to these characters.

Back on the road and the day turned into another drama. After only travelling for a few kilometres, winding through a lowland forest, Carolyn shot up out of her seat, screaming her head off. 'Arhhhh get it out, get it out. Arhhhhh,' she panicked. So I panicked too. I slammed on the brakes and shot over on to the grassy bank. Before I could fully stop, Carolyn had leapt out of the cab. We were still moving at a fair pace but Carolyn was gone. 'Bloody hell, Wigs, what the –' I said, my heart beating crazily. I thought she had been bitten or that a snake had dropped into the car, but sitting on the floor was a bird, a pretty big bird I grant you. Somewhat shaken and minus a few feathers, the brown speckled bird took to the air again after his bull's eye. Nerves settled we pulled away and Carolyn screamed, 'It's still here, get it oooout, get it out', then realised the lost feathers were just that.

Eastern India and the port of Chennai was the hopping-off point to Malaysia. The sun-baked, diesel-filled dust roads had come to an end with a touch of sadness and the excitement of what was next. Staying at the Raintree hotel in the city's centre was something I really resented but a home for Chitty and a place to camp was just an illusion. Pulling into the forecourt of this fine hotel sent the concierge into hyperdrive. Cars dropping off were ordered to move on, taxis were temporarily banned and we were given pride of place under a grand canopy. The hotel manger turned up, bowing, handshaking and offering his personal attention. At this rate I half expected a handful of rose petals to lead the way and so I should've with the price of a room.

Vinita Venkatesh was the vice-president for Samsara Shipping. A very attractive lady, professional and full of confidence, she was well in control of our first meeting. Damu was assigned by her to handle exporting Chitty over to Port Kelang in Malaysia. He gave us confidence by promising that expenses would be minimal, explaining where they were needed, and told us that customs wouldn't go ahead until payments for this and that were sorted. This and the promise of a few days' waiting turned into ten days of watching our trip and carefully monitored budget disappear into the Raintree hotel accounts department. Steve was incredibly frustrated and referred to the agents and legal men as Damu who's done damn-all, the Indian Jibbering Jay and the Indian WIAA chairman as Dossa the Tosser. Clearly Western expectations were not being met, but why should they? This was all part of experiencing different cultures and the colourful mixed bag of travelling.

Chennai, rugged and worn around the edges, heaved with business and industry. Hot and humid the daily passage of life was ordered chaos and the suicidal road manners and incessant jam-packed traffic of the former Madras weren't helping Chitty's clutch problem. I had lost the complete reservoir of clutch fluid in just four days' driving so opting to leave Chitty in the care of the hotel car park seemed a good idea.

Carolyn fought off the beggars and touts while I politely told the rickshaw driver he was cheating me. 'No, we agreed 150 rupees to the beach, not 400,' I said as I was followed across the sand. I would have paid four hundred, it wasn't much, but he was pulling a fast one, knowing if I had insisted he used the meter it would have cost fifty.

There was not a tourist in sight on the city's main sandy beach. Strange, I thought. The entire beach fishing community descended on us with either a fish or shells for sale. Their local-style timber boats nestled on the wide expanse of beach front and as we walked a guy full of personality, who had given up trying to flog us something, launched into a story of how he survived the Boxing Day tsunami by hiding in his boat. One step forward, the very tall for an Indian storyteller, who looked more African, grabbed my arm, yanking me back to a chorus of yelling and dancing. On the one hand, I was thankful for being prevented from stepping on a now very angry sea snake; on the other hand, I was dismayed at treading in the human crap which littered the shore. Yes, I knew only half of India had got toilets and they all had to go somewhere, but watching a endless supply of bottoms crouch down and then carry the smell around on my shoe for the afternoon did dampen the romantic walk a bit. Dog crap I can deal with, but human faeces?

During the rickshaw ride back home the fare haggling began. A hundred and fifty rupees had now become 250, based on the fact our cheeky little driver was adding a tour guide fee for pointing out the obvious. 'See big hospital, very big in Chennai.' Yes, we could see the 'UDHYE' hospital 'Somewhere I'll be taking him if he adds another fifty rupees,' I said under my breath to Carolyn.

Apart from the unexpected delays due to a customs strike, Damu explained Chitty could not be stuffed into a container and loaded on board until we had booked our flights and could prove to customs we were leaving the country. However, we couldn't book a flight to leave India until we had a date to load the car. Mainly because we couldn't leave until we had driven Chitty to the port. The customs were adamant they wouldn't give us a date to accept Chitty until we showed the tickets. I felt we had been here before, and nobody was listening.

Vinita invited us to join her and her husband for dinner and took it upon herself to deal with customs and then kindly gave Carolyn and Julia each a fine Indian silk pashmina shawl. Topped off with more good news, as she was the vice-president of the shipping company and we were on a charity trip, she had worked it that the cost of shipping would only be fifty US dollars.

Chapter 41 **M**alaysian jungle cheers and festive tears

Malaysia was a breath of fresh air, literally! The roads were great, it was clean and most importantly, it didn't smell. Port Kelang was a working town and had no frills to speak about. Our container was somewhere between the Bay of Bengal and the Andaman Sea so making contact with Heung-A Shipping was top priority along with an encyclopaedia of red tape and paperwork. Nothing was straightforward, so we expected the odd surprise or two. This said, the message from our agent Damu back in India took the wind out of our sails. Not only did the Malaysian shipping importers know nothing of our container, mainly because it wasn't here yet, but more importantly it hadn't even left India. To leave the Indian subcontinent the agent wanted cash for the port workers, the crane driver and the group of guys who lashed Chitty down in the steel box. He then demanded a financial incentive to be paid to customs to ensure the container would leave as planned. The fistful of rupees along with a few packets of fags and a Chitty photo card which Damu had insisted we give as a gift via his top pocket was probably still there, or in his bank. Not that I'm cynical. Now another week's wait was on the cards. I knew the stress of enduring India had taken its toll on Steve and the frustrations topped with our latest news saw Steve's temper fly.

Kuala Lumpur, just like Dubai, threw us back into the twenty-first century. Retail therapy kept Carolyn on track. Even if it was only an M&S Christmas cake and clean water, it was so novel. Western culture and overseas investment lulled us into a secure sense of normality until I was reminded the Far East still had a few surprises. Rounding a corner, only one street back from the razzmatazz and bright lights of Kuala Lumpur's main drag, stood sixteen men in an urban front garden, bloodstained from head to foot, each wielding an axe and drinking Coca-Cola. One man was still on the case axing his way through a freshly slaughtered bullock. The garden was filled with eight or nine cows chopped into manageable pieces. Blood ran across the pavement and into the gutter, kids were playing nearby and interested local onlookers hung out of their windows for a better view. Clearly it was a sociable event. I've never seen so much meat and blood and if you think of the Texas chainsaw massacre, you ain't seen nothing.

It wasn't long before we downgraded from our hotel and embarked on a nitty gritty jungle adventure. The bright lights were akin to a hot shower after a week of pulling spuds, but a city's a city and it was time to get back to nature.

Taman Negara is a 130 million-year-old rain forest in the heart of the Malay Peninsula. We took a wooden long boat powered by a car engine balanced on a pivot with a very long propeller shaft, which was frequently waved around like a lethal weapon. From Tembeling jetty we navigated the river for half a day, working our way deep into the forest interior, and it was fantastic. I knew it rained a lot and the clue was in the title but it poured with rain all day and it just didn't matter. Anyway, if we didn't get wet through rain we got wet through sweat!

As the journey was so long we opted to stay in a floating cabin and explore the forest by night and by day. Evening brought teaming fish to the floodlit waters and it was from here we were escorted through the jungle with a local guide. In preparation Carolyn and I donned long sleeves and trousers tucked into our socks in a vain attempt to keep creepy crawlies out. Instead of looking like intrepid explorers we looked like a couple of anoraks missing a bicycle. The guide took one look at us and said, 'Oh dear, you need shorts.' 'Why?' I asked. He went on to explain that leeches will climb up your boots and as they are so fine will work their way through the gap between your sock and trouser and up your body to the chest, neck or somewhere suitable to feed! Now I was getting paranoid! I was already itching and twitchy! If there is one thing I hate it is leeches or slugs or snails or worms or even anything sluggy or wormlike. I could complete a bush tucker trial with ease, eat crickets and bathe in a pool of rats, but leeches? Oh no. Fortunately Carolyn has no fear of them so she could deal with my emotional breakdown if required. Her nemesis is spiders and that's what I'm there for!

The guide wearing shorts said if a leech gets on your legs then you will see it first or at least the blood and will be able to remove it before it does too much damage. Apparently tobacco, toothpaste, soap and mosquito repellent all work to deter them but we were already in the jungle on hearing this vital information. Plucking up courage we trekked deeper into the forest stopping every five paces to examine our boots. The guide stopped suddenly by a tall hollow tree and shone his torch on to a pair of eyes. 'That's a bird-eating spider,' he said. Carolyn gulped, swore a lot and went on to seek clarification of his last remarks concerning the huge hairy insect. This was fine by me; however, Carolyn had gone into twitchy mode zipping her raincoat to her neck and pulling tight on the hood strings. That night we saw sambar deer, metre-long monitor lizards, praying mantis and stick insects. Oh, and magic mushrooms. Initially concerned as trafficking drugs in Malaysia results in death, we then found out that they were magic because they glowed in the dark, which they did!

There are tigers, black panthers and Asian elephants in the national park but alas we didn't see them. The next morning after another breakfast of rice and chicken we explored the jungle by foot again. By now confidence was building and we were flicking off leeches left, right and centre. The guide had one sucking between his toes. And when he pulled it off, it latched on to his finger! In the afternoon we took a further boat ride up river to an Orang Asli village, meaning original people. I was expecting to see a well-established tourist village selling local souvenirs. To our surprise we scrambled up a muddy bank to a tribal makeshift village of five or six huts. I was really impressed to be here and incredibly embarrassed! We had just landed at a genuine tribal village and I had forgotten the word for hello! The Batek tribe look nothing like the Malay people and are quite unique. They still hunt and gather and move round the rain forest. Only in the last few years have they agreed to accept tourists and our guide explained they were honoured to share their blowpipe and fire-making skills with us. It was a great, unexpected experience, which we would have forgone if it had ensured their survival. The guide encouraged us to take photos, which felt inappropriate, and I asked him to thank the chief while I looked into his eyes. He had clearly seen too many tourists. The people seemed at ease and fun loving. The kids ran round naked, wielding machetes, and they all seemed to smoke tobacco from the age of nought!

The forest outskirts is home to an elephant sanctuary and when most people were rushing around trying to find brandy sauce and standing in a turkey queue we were headed into the Kuala Gandah elephant sanctuary, which is home to mainly baby orphan elephants. In addition, there is a mixed bag from the odd wild rogue awaiting a new home from the reserves, to ex-working elephants from Thailand and Burma to a collection of young elephants fallen foul of poachers' traps. In the sanctuary you can feed, wash and bath with the elephants, if you don't mind sharing a loofah. Feeding the elephants is like an extreme sport! Handing over a few bananas or pieces of watermelon was like falling into the mouth of a giant squid, all wet and slippery, but it certainly gave us an insight to their sheer strength. The trunk is a bit like a hand and, unexpectedly for me, can grip (boy can it grip!). The first attempt of a trunk coming my way was a bit like an introduction and I felt like I should shake it; the second time he took hold of three bananas and my whole hand and as I winged my way towards his mouth a rather assertive yank back brought my freedom. It was all very rewarding but saddening to see a 36-month-old orphan elephant who had lost a foot to a poacher's snare balancing on three legs and clearly distressed.

Unable to do anything except wait for the day when we could prepare Chitty for her onward trip overseas to Australia, and with Christmas Day looming, we decided to Part Company with Steve and Julia and spend Christmas on the beach. On Christmas Eve, we caught an overnight train to Butterworth and then hitched the only available taxi over the bridge and on to Penang. Secretly we had both bought a few small presents for each other and the Christmas cake we purchased in Marks & Spencer was our only reminder of home. The bright sunshine and sandy beaches of Penang wasn't like we ever imagined. The stories of turkey down under sounded idyllic but the reality for us was very different. We were homesick, unmotivated and sad. We both woke to the first Muslim call to prayer and passed around our little wrapped gifts that were mostly edible. We thought a lot about home and the kids, imagining what they were doing, and struggled to find the drive to head for the sea but made it a mission to tick the box for Christmas on the beach. I cut into our cake with a small penknife from Chitty's toolbox and Carolyn burst in to tears.

Chapter 42 **T**hai monkey

The Malay people had been extremely friendly, complete strangers acknowledging us as we walked by; they were full of beaming smiles and genuine warmth and now we were in Thailand it was just the same. It was a bit of a mission but a visit to the famous bridge over the River Kwai just had to be done. Ever since I had had the inclination I whistled the Great Escape theme. Unfortunately, music from the wrong film. Moving experience, yes. It's a tourist attraction on the back of a great film on that of a real heroic endurance. Slight flaw in the plan, though: the River Kwai didn't actually exist. Carolyn was taking time to digest the poignant war memorials and some geek is harping on about the facts. He had shorts just below the knee, a rucksack the size of the White House and thick bottle bottom glasses. The strong American accent blubbered out from a hairy face hidden under a baseball cap inscribed the 'U.S.S. Iowa'. 'Well actually Kwai is a water buffalo and the word in Thai also refers to male genitals, don't you know.' No I didn't and did I care? We were both humbled by the real historical events but for silver screen detail, come on it was a film. So the watery bit below was, according to Nobby Know-All, a tributary of the Mae Klong. The thing I liked was this: the clever chap who wrote the book, Pierre Boulle, never came here and he wrongly assumed the bridge was built over the Kwai. We, like thousands of others, flocked here to see a bridge over the wrong river. With a bit of quick thinking, the Thais just renamed it 'Kwae Yai' in the 1960s.

The locals always make my day with the unexpected and we were given the complete royal history about the Siamese King and I and various Thai kings and queens over a cup of coffee. One of the male waiters was called Vera and he answered to his boss Rosie Wong. Still separated from Steve and Julia, Thailand was quite simply a holiday and before going any further time on the beach came as a reward for long days driving and legal paper shuffling. Ko Phi Phi was our next stop and as idyllic as you could wish for although it is alas hounded by the marauding masses. Leonardo DiCaprio starred in the film The Beach which was shot just a stone's throw away and we could see why. A small limestone island with steep cliffs and virgin rain forest played second fiddle to a terrific beach and thousands of tourist-loving pubs and shops. It was all here, backpackers, sixties dope-smoking dropouts, adventurous adrenaline junkies and package holiday makers and, embarrassingly, many overweight Western sweaty businessmen on the lookout for free sex or a Thai bride. Getting there was no mean feat. The ferryboat leaves when it's full; however, the Thais have no concept of full or overloaded, as long as a few more backpackers were eager to embark the crew were happy have them. Full steam ahead was not fast, which was just as well with passengers packed solid to the gunnels. Sitting cheek to jowl, Carolyn and I sat on the top deck with our legs swinging in the wind over the side. The ferry listed heavily to port and with each wave the angle became more acute. Now with our feet about to get very wet the boat slowed to a near stop and the crew ushered us to our feet. All passengers including baggage had to move to the starboard side to balance the boat. Thankfully it worked.

Backing on to an intimidating cliff face of rugged limestone the far side of the bay was less lively. I thought this was just because it was too far to walk for the average hungover binge drinker. However, little did we know we were under attack. The dawn raid was in full swing as tourists lay unaware. The German family next to us were spread out on two large beach towels, asleep soaking up the morning sun while the kids played quietly on the sand. The Australian couple in front had just returned from a refreshing dip oblivious to the well-planned military operation going on around them. We, too, had no idea at the strategy the raiding party had put in to action. The first platoon arrived on the foreshore at 10.36 a.m.; two scouts circled the area and took up position at the rear. With that, a decoy was deployed into the field of view. Tourists looked up surprised and nudged each other. The troop has the upper hand. The tall German took to his feet and bang the secret runner was released. The brazen male ran at full pelt, made contact with a new unopened Pringles tube of crisps and was in and out like a rat up a drain pipe or a monkey on the beach if you like. 'Yeh wanna avoid Monkey Beach, it's a bloody nightmare,' I overheard a gap year student from Brighton say that evening.

Bangkok is a place that really never sleeps and for the time we were there it never stopped raining either. I'd moan again about having to stay in hotels but you have heard it all before, although this one came with entertainment. The loud music and smashing of furniture coming from above only served to balance out the noise of tuk-tuk speed trials at the Santa Pod raceway out front. I wanted to watch out of the window but I was in fear of my life in case a TV set came flying past. Go-go bars and cross-dressing filled our days with visual entertainment. 'Fifty gorgeous girls and a few ugly ones,' stated the teasing bar sign. The flavour of seedy dancing girls is now tempered with playing to the family tourists. We loved the city, it's hard not too, but a supply of single Western men plying drinks to giggling tiny Thais was slightly off-putting. Whether they landed a catch was one thing and whether it was male or female was anybody's guess. I spent 300 baht having a beautiful Thai girl leap all over me (for a back massage, of course), and just in case there were any misunderstandings on the service provided Carolyn had a foot massage sitting opposite. I really had a bad back, from too much time sitting down behind the wheel in Chitty, honest! The dimly lit room with shutters on the windows looked like a scene from the cult film Blade Runner. Neon lights flickered and collided with streams of bright car headlights that came and went. Five beds and groaning tourists filled the room. If it wasn't used for prostitution in a B rated movie it could have been. For one whole hour, 'Maily', who had started by pulling my pants halfway down, thumped, squashed and elbowed my body and it hurt like hell. Every time her forearm made contact with my vertebrae I gritted my teeth so hard that I ended up with toothache. I certainly didn't have time to worry about a bad back.

Carolyn on the other hand was wincing from the pain being given to her feet. Her idea of a foot massage was to have aromatherapy oil rubbed gently into her dry heels and to have her little toes tickled and gently pulled apart. What she actually got was sheer torture as her arches were pushed so hard and her insteps battered she could hardly walk afterwards. Not quite what we expected!

Time in the sun is reflective and thinking is what we both did. Sitting for eight hours watching life go by was great. Chitty was not fast but it meant we could see so much more. Our goal of reaching Perth seemed far more important than the trip itself. We were becoming too focused on Oz and in danger of missing the point. Touching down on Australian soil was what it was all about but we were missing out on the importance of other people and places. We had seen so much and it really had changed the way we felt. France, Belgium, Luxembourg and Germany had broken us in. Austria, Italy and Greece had given us the sense of adventure and bit of eye ache. Turkey had exposed us to a highly religious world fascinated by the car, with incredible kindness and a sense of worth. Iran was just another planet, an unforgettable experience and overwhelming, scary but so friendly. Dubai was like a wealthy tea break and as for India it was colourful, breathtaking, had heartrending poverty and was bloody smelly. Malaysia was far Eastern Heaven with its rain forest and jungle, and the people so warm and kind. Thailand was a party playground. We were both looking forward to Cambodia and then back down to Singapore, but it was Australia which held our imagination. Everything depended on Australia. Getting there was only half the battle, getting in was the other. Strict quarantine and immigration made this hurdle emotionally unbearable. Contacting the customs and immigration website I soon realised Chitty was going to be a problem. They don't mess about down under; the car had to be as clean as new, no soil, no bugs, no dirt and no oil leaks. Fumigation had to be completed in the container then had to be sealed and wood was a no no. Great! Half of Chitty is made of hardwood timber. Carolyn was reassuring but deep down being turned away was a realistic outcome and a heartbreaking worry.

Chapter 43 **W**hich road to Mandalay?

I knew we could never drive into Burma, or Myanmar as it's now called, because of the the military junta, but we were determined to make a visit. This could be hit and miss, depending on the day, the political climate, and which way the wind was blowing, and the key to success was money. The standard procedure was to part with ten US dollars to gain an entry visa from immigration. The snag was they would only accept a brand new, crisp, never been used ten dollar bill. Fine, I had a few. Not fine, you could only purchase a visa with one of their ten dollar notes, deemed suitable at the extortionate cost of twenty dollars. Setting foot in the country was only possible with a guide, who sorted passports and haggled with guards and fortunately had a boat to get us there. The border straddled the Kyan River at Kawthaung and the few miles of ferry ride was interrupted by offshore islands home to suspicious looking guards and platoons of soldiers. We left Thailand by long tail boat and passed through numerous customs and immigration officials. Eventually we managed to get in to Burma. On arrival a lad of about eighteen turned up and said, 'Hello, I am a tourist guide.' 'So am I,' said a smaller lad who had just popped up on the scene. 'So am I,' said a young girl of about eleven years of age. The town of Kawthaung only had a market, a Chinese temple and a jetty so the benefits of a guide were very slim and despite our request to visit Myanmar alone the three trundled on behind, occasionally pointing out the obvious.

Myanmar is a very poor country but the people were very friendly if not a bit cautious of us. I purchased a bunch of bananas from the market and they had pips! After eating two of the bunch and finding a suitable home for the pips and skins I offered the rest to the Myanmar three. They didn't want any so I had to spend the day holding them. The town was small with incredible poverty; people looked uneasy and afraid to smile. The market was raw as a real market should be; no cheap Chinese tat just wicker baskets, fresh produce and live chickens lashed up waiting for the pot. A dustbin full of severed goats' heads caught my eye, or had I caught theirs as they all gazed back with an expression of shock. Climbing a short hill we entered a Chinese temple, which the three young guides pointed out was a Chinese temple (they were trying hard!). As soon we had removed our shoes and entered I noticed a donation box and a Buddhist monk. I instantly realised I didn't have any Myanmar currency. We both felt a bit embarrassed searching our pockets for the odd lost euro. The monk smiled, walked towards us, and bowed his head. He turned to light an incense stick. The pungent smell of the burning embers filled the air as it was handed to us to offer up. I really felt bad now without a donation, then as luck would have it, I noticed a small table in front of the candles with offerings of bread, cans of food and, hallelujah, fruit. I didn't have to carry the bananas any more.

Standing on a roundabout on the outskirts of town was a clock tower giving importance to its location. Three roads joined the one we had come along, one to the town's main square and one with a signpost saying 'Mandalay'. I asked our three young guides the obvious, 'Does that road go to Mandalay?' They confirmed it did with enthusiasm, hoping this vital piece of information might secure a decent tip. 'Come on Carolyn,' I said, 'I want to go on the road to Mandalay.'

Chapter 44 **G**uilt and beauty

Border officials all look the same to me: stern faces, no sense of humour and body language which makes you feel as if you are up to something. Poipet is the border crossing from Thailand to Cambodia, and the contrast between the two countries was staggering. The man sitting behind the glass screen didn't even look up, just processed our passports and grunted. Caged in a building similar to a concrete bomb shelter, the queue edged forward past warning notices to report any suspicious characters engaged in paedophilia. Sadly, our first experience of this shattered and war-torn country was one of child abuse, landmines and casinos. Gambling is illegal in Thailand, and gamblers make for the border and poker free-for-all. The road east to Siem Reap and the temples of Angkor Wat was an unmade dust bowl; the surface was more enduring than in India, because there never was any tarmac. Lungs got a daily dosing of red dust and eyes were filled with grit. This I could handle; not seeing a thing was 'road doing Russian roulette'. Smog, fog and dust created a surreal atmosphere: the view was bright but obscured as if gazing through tracing paper. I have never willed so many dogs to get across the road, 'Move you mongrel, pleeease, quick quick quick.' Some just made it by an unconcerned hair and others dragged injured and wasted limbs along for the ride. Lorries and fast-paced independent taxis raced past to a plume of airborne soil particles, and as the dust settled six pigs appeared slung over the side of a moped. The little porkers weren't in a good way lashed down on the rear rack of a Honda 90. How they ever got them on there is a Krypton factor stuff.

In a country where old people are few and far between, and the echoes of the killing fields linger on, sticking to the road is a life-preserving necessity. Venturing off the beaten track risks losing a bodily part or your life to landmines. The countryside is literally littered with them, and stark reminders are everywhere in the shape of maimed human beings. Angkor Wat was what we had come to see, and apart from a truly amazing collection of fascinating temples, it was the people who brought this place to life. Elephants trumpeted their way up the hillside, laden with tourists, through thick monkey-climbing jungle. Fig tree roots worked their way through the crumbling buildings that captivated the imagination. The purples and yellows of brides and wedding parties clashed with the colour of orange monks, who pose against a backdrop of water-filled moats and architectural splendour. Beaming smiles radiated from landmine victim musicians – footless victims who earned a crust from the tourists with a bright jolly sound enlivened with the polite chatter of young schoolgirl guides. Humble, friendly and eager to please, one of them said to me 'Kim is my friend and where is he taking you, I go to the moon, sometimes by tuk-tuk and sometimes by butterfly.' How strange! Kim was a boy, a young lad ferrying tourists to the temples by rickshaw.

Everything was for sale, from T-shirts to coconuts and pan pipes to guidebooks. Pan pipes thousands of miles from the Andes? And kids: kids everywhere but none playing. Children as young as four and five worked the temple gates, selling whatever they could. Feeling guilty for passing by so many vendors I bought a book and five small brass elephants. Carolyn bought a pack of stickers, a woven bracelet, bottled water, and, strangely, we even bought two pan pipes. Now we were being hassled by two small girls wearing stripy shirts and with very pretty little faces full of smiles and only five or six years old. 'Hello sir you buy postcards just one dollar,' said the elder. 'Sorry sweetie, we have bought all our souvenirs,' Carolyn replied as she crouched down beside them. 'Just one dollar please, just one dollar.' We both kept walking through the temple gate of Ta Prohm as the two little girls ran alongside. With a face like a spaniel puppy and deep brown Malteser eyes, 'Please, sir, just one dollar,' said the five-year-old looking up and flicking through her collection of cards. 'See this is Ta Prohm, Angkor Wat, Angkor Thom, Bayon, Terrace of the Leper King,' she reeled off in a quiet voice. To be fair, she was doing very well for five, knowing the details and names. This was tough; we couldn't buy everything and round the corner would be more sellers. 'Please buy my postcards, sir, just one dollar.' 'Oh damn it, okay, I'll have one set.' I wrestled out my wallet and handed over one dollar, feeling I had done my bit. The next minute the other little girl was tugging on my shirtsleeve. 'What about me, what about me, you haven't bought anything from me.' Carolyn knelt down again to look at her cards. 'Please, what about me, just one dollar, you haven't bought from me,' she said over and over. Was that pulling at my heartstrings or what? 'Right that's it, there you go, one dollar and no more,' I said, like a dad handing out pocket money. There was so much more to this country than Angkor Wat but Australia was tugging us and we turned back towards Thailand.

'I bet that hurt,' said Carolyn as we passed the welcome sign of a small town called Bang Toey. Despite the long days, hair unwashed and feeling unloved, no pretty clothes to wear and lungs full of dust, she still had a sense of humour, and just like Cambodia, she was beautiful and touching.

Chapter 45 **P**andering to Perth

Singapore had left us with a bitter sweet, chalk and cheese, sweet and sour outlook and any other contradicting mismatch I can think of. Our immigration officer stamping the passports was called Ta-wit Choong, no prizes for guessing his nickname. Munching monkey-nuts in the long bar of Raffles and discarding the shells all over the floor was the done thing and sipping on a Singapore sling just because. A squeaky-clean shoppers' paradise where a slap round the face with a wet kipper was in order if you didn't flush the toilet. Being handcuffed by the Singaporean police was a more meaningful punishment for those who chewed gum but for all the rules and regulations it was friendly and safe. And here's the point: rules and regulations. I had spent the last six months moaning about bureaucracy but we hadn't seen anything compared to here. Permits and passes to drive and park, import madness and legal beagles demanding hoop jumping on an Olympic scale. Hell to that, great to visit but I think it's back to Port Kelang in Malaysia to set sail for Oz. Darwin was not going to happen from here with no ships on that route but Fremantle and Perth sounded just as exciting.

The quote by Maersk shipping was a few thousand pounds and as I choked on my bottled water, I was informed the bill did include cleaning of the cars and fumigation. Now back in Chitty mode and rejoined by Steve and Julia, at 8 a.m. we arrived armed with port passes and a cleaning bucket and were informed that two Indian guys had been assigned to us to clean the car and the fumigation process would take place once it was safe in the container. The two little Indian helpers had great intentions but wanting to scrub the brass and aluminium bonnet with wire wool and a scouring pad was not my idea of cleaning. After half an hour of 'No, don't touch that' and 'Yes, that is a nasty scratch, please put the chisel down', I sent them off with a flea in their ear and we cleaned it ourselves. Fourteen hours were spent on the car on New Year's Eve. We removed every bug from the radiator grille, every speck of soil, dirt, dust and suicidal insect from the exterior of the car. The tyres were scrubbed with a toothbrush so they looked as spotless as new and, I spent hours on the suspension cleaning between each leaf spring, flicking out stones and dirt. The engine was polished and oil free and the windscreen water drained as per the Australian quarantine regulations on potentially bringing in contaminated liquid. Carolyn tackled the tent, accessories, car interior and luggage; all our shoes were scrubbed, the tent cleaned inside and out and anything just beyond cleaning as new we ditched. The pressure and stress of getting it to the standards of Australian import rules sent my anxiety of failure skywards. Bret Rainer had agreed to act as import agent and was based in Perth. Via e-mail he outlined the importance of 'clean as new' and referred to the last 4x4 vehicle sent out from the UK he had dealt with. They had found traces of soil under the newly applied thick black underseal and as the process of cleaning appeared too costly they packed it back up again and sent it straight home. Bret also pointed out if we had any holes in the chassis, soil could be trapped within. His experience was to have the vehicle's chassis drilled every four or five inches to power wash out any contamination and cleaned at the customer's expense for a few thousand Australian dollars. I couldn't help myself, so I posed another question to Bret, who was proving very helpful indeed. 'What about oil leaks,' I said on my mobile wiping out all the credit, which had £50 saved for emergencies. 'Oh yeah buddy, for sure no oil leaks, if they let you through quarantine, it certainly won't pass the Rego.' Rego, what's a bloody Rego, I thought.

Emerging from under the car cover head to foot in oil and dirt and soaking wet with grimy water, Carolyn and I were both physically and mentally shattered. We had given it our best shot. Chitty had been kept tip top on the trip knowing how good things had to be to get into Australia and today we could do no better. Two Indian guys helped themselves to the various bits and bobs we had offloaded and I was glad they were going to good use but I did wish they would stop spinning the propeller round on the brass Spitfire plane mascot.

With Chitty sealed in the container, fumigated and bound for Australia, we booked two flights south.

Arriving down under was just overwhelming even if Chitty hadn't quite got there yet. We had both forgotten how good the Western world really was. Okay, so it wasn't as flamboyant and colourful as Asia and the

Middle East but it didn't smell and we could drink the water. Carolyn and I stood at a zebra crossing, instinctively we waited and waited and so did the queue of cars; engaged in conversation our sub-conscious minds knew for the last six months crossing the road on a pedestrian crossing had been a sure way of being killed as nobody ever stopped. Beeeeeeeeeeb. 'Quick, I forgot cars stop here,' I said, dragging Carolyn by the arm.

Hotel prices were exorbitant in Australia compared to when we were here four years ago and all of our camping equipment was still in Chitty, so we bussed it into town and bought a cheap two-man tent and took to the ground for a week and awaited the customs and quarantine inspection. With time to burn I scoured the internet for immigration and customs information. The more I read the more I wish I hadn't. It turned out Chitty had to go over the 'pits' to become road legal in Oz. This was basically a car inspection like our MOT; without it you couldn't drive on Australian roads. This was of great concern to us because if Chitty failed we weren't going anywhere. Apart from the normal lights and brake tests the car must have no oil leaks! There it was again, bloody oil leaks, I was getting paranoid. Oil leaks and Chitty were like bread and butter, Bonnie and Clyde, Fred and Ginger.

Liam Darlingston Jones sounded really posh and he was married to a doctor. I worked with his sister at Marks & Spencer and in an address book packed with 'oh you must look up etc,' was Liam's number. He had visited us at home a couple of years ago when Chitty was being built. He and his wife emigrated under the £10 Pom down under deal and asking his advice about going over the pits was a good excuse for an meeting. Freo, as the locals call Fremantle, has a trendy line of coffee bars along Cappuccino Street, where we joined Liam and he put the record straight. 'Ych your right on that one mate, it won't pass with oil pouring out of the sump,' Liam said alarmingly, looking over his square rimmed glasses. 'Fix it, it's no big deal.' It wasn't that simple, leaking oil from the engine and the gearbox was big money to solve, let alone the differentials and transfer box. Everything had to come out, new gaskets fitted and seals replaced and being an old Land Rover there was no guarantee it wouldn't continue to drip. But more to the point we couldn't afford it; we would soon wave goodbye to a few thousand dollars. Apart from having cash put by for two flights home and shipping Chitty back to the Isle of Wight, we had planned to enter Australia with about five grand. It was January, we still had six months to last, a complete continent to cross and we were now down to £2,000. Chris Balcombe from the Solent News Agency back in the UK was hot on our trail seeking out the latest developments. He wanted photos, highs and lows ready for a media push now that we had made it to Oz. This just didn't seem right; we hadn't achieved anything yet, Sydney was the iconic rainbow's end and that was 5,000 kilometres away and besides we might never make it with customs, quarantine and the pits looking as likely as my four times married sister parting with her drip dry wedding dress.

I felt very low at this point, we had come so far, seen so much and getting into Australia seemed to be slipping out of our control. Could we get the work done? How could we afford it? I had already fitted a new sump gasket in Greece and the day after, the bloody thing had leaked! Would quarantine officials be understanding? Would the inspector understand it's 35-year-old Land Rover? We walked back, hand in hand, along the coastal footpath to our campsite. Carolyn took it all in her stride, what would be would be, but I just couldn't let it lie. Questions, questions, questions. I was carrying a huge weight of expectation, I had built the car over four years against all odds. I had spent a further year planning the trip and fund-raising and lavishly making claims to drive across the world. Telling the world, enrolling the support of the Isle of Wight County Press and Isle of Wight Radio, I just needed to make good on my promises. Carolyn had great faith in me and for the first time the pressure I put upon myself was beginning to show. The more I rattled on, the more the emotion increased, and to save face I had to stop talking as tears welled up behind my sunglasses. I gulped a few times, took a deep breath, waited for the quivering to disappear from my voice and then said, 'What's for tea then, Wigs?'

Chapter 46 **O**ver the pits

Bret Rayner took the relevant paperwork and by lunchtime customs had broken the seal. Bret was the only one authorised to cross the yellow line so he took the keys and reversed Chitty out of her metal box. It really was like meeting an old friend, a bizarre bond with an inanimate object, yet full of heartfelt emotion – that was until we both instantly noticed the brass Spitfire plane was missing, stolen., Some bloody thief had removed the grille mascot. I was angry, Carolyn cried. Yes, it had only cost £5 in a jumble sale but it was part of the car and the small propeller had spun in the wind across the world. Along with a few videotapes, tools and some spares, Chitty had been ransacked. Our concerns over passing the inspection turned to those of a tapered seal. Carolyn addressed the customs official: 'If there is anything in there that shouldn't be it's not down to us.' This was the second time the seal had been broken and rightly or wrongly we were blaming the Indian cleaners who had shown so much interest in the mascot. In agitation we paced up and down and whinged to Bret until a guy in a fluorescent jacket holding a torch returned from under Chitty. 'She's a beauty mate, tip-top, the best I've seen.' The guy stood in his hobnailed boots and shorts completing his paperwork. 'It's blinding under there, buddy. I wish they all turned up like that. Now, got any foodstuff or plant material on board?' he asked. Was that it? but I thought. What a sense of relief, Chitty had been stamped, passed and approved into the land of the didgeridoo. Great. I just couldn't drive her on the roads until she had gone over and passed the pits test.

We had purchased a two-day import licence allowing us to drive legally to the pits. We found a 4x4 dealership where they laughed a lot when I asked about the cost of work to plug an old Land Rover. 'What do you expect, you Pommies and those bloody old Land Rovers. What you want, mate, is a Toyota Land Cruiser.' With my tail between my legs I cleared off, calling him names under my breath. I parked Chitty up around the corner from the testing station. I spent a good twenty minutes under Chitty mopping up any signs of oil and then joined the queue, praying the wait would be short and it was. Being signalled forward, an old guy took one look at the car and said, 'Interesting Land Rover.' He obviously knew his stuff, spotting Chitty's pedigree. Time stood still as lights flashed and horns honked. Politely I answered his questions like you do to a police officer with your driving licence and holding a radar gun. 'This steering relay arm needs replacing, there's wear on the spine,' he said. I was signalled to move forward and follow him into the office. I joined a line of disgruntled Aussies moaning about work which required doing, rebooking of tests and the cost. The old guy disappeared and finally returned one hour later. 'Excuse me, what do I do now. Has she passed or have I got to get some work done?' I said in a pathetic please-don't-beat-me way. 'Yeh, it's passed, fill out that, pay the lady over there and don't forget to get that steering arm sorted,' he said as if I should have known. She had passed, thank God. I was stunned and pleased and thankful. 'Carolyn she's passed, Chitty's passed. What a relief, whatever happens now I really don't care, we're in Australia and she's passed.'

Chapter 47 **A**nd they think the Yanks are mad

A week on a campsite without Chitty and we had been nobodies. I received the odd nod and 'how ya going', to which I replied with a rather formal, 'Oh, yes, I'm going very well thank you.' What ever happened to G'day? That seemed to be reserved for TV adverts back in England. The day we rolled up in Chitty at the 'Village' campsite we caused quite a stir. Our neighbours of seven days on both sides came over to introduce themselves. Our Coleman's petrol stove had been with Chitty so we had eaten Weetabix and sandwiches. Now that we had Chitty and our cooker, everybody was inviting us to a good old barbie. Patricia and her South African husband had been touring round Oz for the last five years and she wrote for Australia's Camping and Caravan Magazine, and tomorrow before we headed south she wanted the full story and some photos. It was very rewarding being flavour of the month, it was infectious. Clearly Chitty deserved the credit but yesterday the only hospitable human interaction was 'Yo, buddy, you got a light' from a bloodshot-eyed, red-nosed, pony-tailed guy staggering towards us.

Gordon and Michelle played host cooking a mountain of chops, steak and sausages and supplied freezer cold beer. Their caravan was the size of Wales, brand new, had rugged off-road tyres and was compliments of an engineering firm who had sent Gordon deep into the outback selling parts to mine companies. The truck pulling this thing made Chitty look like a Smart car. Gordon was a character to say the least, tall, grey haired and full of Aussie bravado. Like a stand-up comedian he was full of it, and so entertaining. His wife assuming the British liked Pimms offered me a glass. Carolyn thought that sounded great and jumped in with 'Oh yes please' and so I said I would have the same. 'Pimms, bloody Pimms, you gotta be a bloody homosexual to like Pimms, Here, Michelle, this bloke likes Pimms. You must be porking boys or something,' Gordon said full of mickey-taking wit. 'I'll tell you what, you bloody Poms do some bloody stupid things. You know what an Aussie poof is?' 'No,' I replied. 'Somebody who thinks more of his bleeding Sheila than his beer,' he said and before anybody could get a word in edgeways he had moved on to the Yanks, which was equally entertaining. Mind you, this hilarious, male chauvinistic bigot soon jumped to his feet when Michelle had a go. Gordon was full of useful dos and don'ts and he emphasised the importance of water. 'I'll tell you what, buddy, don't tackle the Nullarbor with a dodgy radiator, hot, you'll be sweating your knackers off. If your radiator goes on the Nullarbor you couldn't drink all the beer in the world and have enough to piss in the rad to get two miles let alone a thousand of the buggers.' I got the point, then laughed a lot.

Australia does camping big style and with a handful of people in a country the size of Europe free camping was everywhere – apart from the campsites, of course. The Camps 4 book was the definitive guide to sleeping for nothing so our route to Sydney was mapped with this in mind. We had all the time in the world although Steve and Julia now didn't as they had made plans to head home early. Steve felt he had stuck by his word to follow us here and the deed was done. Julia had said she was missing her kids back home and had no real desire to see too much of Australia. We agreed to part company and possibly meet up here and there before they shipped home three months early.

Easy driving, good road manners and back to the left-hand side of the road although the attention to Chitty was just as frantic but well ordered. Our speed was just too slow for the city train running alongside in Perth; plenty of waving from the commuters and a disappointed train driver who had just missed his opportunity for a mobile photo. Five minutes later a confused bunch of passengers peered back at us. The driver had stopped the train midway just so he could get the ideal snap as we trundled by on our epic transcontinental journey.

Open your mouth in Australia, give the game away you're a Pom and standby for a bit of flack, and you know what, we found it hilarious. The Aussies have a great sense of humour, were continually ripping the mickey out of us and offered great hospitality. Oh, and advice. 'See you Pommies come out here drinking warm beer and la-di-da,' said the Kenworth truck driver. It was our first fuel stop en route to Busselton and Margaret River and this fair dinkum Aussie walking information bureau explained, 'It's a big country you know, it ain't two minutes down the road like in Pommieland.' 'Yeh yeh yeh, I know,' I mumbled under my breath. 'Sees there's the heat too, you need plenty of water, where's you heading,' he added. 'Brisbane,' I said. 'What in that?' he asked, rolling his eyes. 'Yes, well via Adelaide, Melbourne and Sydney,' I added. 'Bloody crazy Poms and they think the Yanks are mad. Bit of advice, buddy,' he said, putting his arm on my shoulder, 'it's 3,000 miles west to east across the Nullarbor, pure outback, nothing for miles, don't break down and if you do don't leave your car.' I was listening and taking on board everything he said but it was patronising. 'You gonna need to carry loads of fuel, mate, and water. How much water you guys carrying?' I answered him but started to question myself. 'Take it from me, mate, most Aussies haven't driven the Nullarbor. Make sure you inform the police when you leave Norseman', and with his beer belly and shorts he climbed two miles up into his cab and leant out the window to say, 'By the way where have you guys just come from in that?' 'England, we have driven twelve thousand miles overland through Europe, the Middle East, Iran, India and Asia. Shipped her into Perth yesterday,' I said proudly. 'Strewth, no kidding. Hell you'll be all right along the Nullarbor' and with that, he left.

Chapter 48 **B**eauty and the outback beast

The south-west coast of Western Australia was just unbelievable, not a soul in sight, beautiful beaches and stunning tropical turquoise water. Driving with extreme caution because of no car insurance, we tackled a steep dusty track down to the beach. We were a hot potato when it came to insurance cover as nobody was prepared to take us on with an imported modified car, so the third party for personal injury only which came compliments of the Rego car tax thing was it. Mind you it was more than we had travelling across the globe., Meelup Beach and Eagle Bay were stunning but were only good for a lunch stop. Hugging the coast we camped for free in the bush that, conveniently, backed on to the beach. We washed in the sea, watched kangaroos, had words with the scorpion on our tent door and were slightly apprehensive at the brown snake asleep under our ground sheet. We were pretty blasé until a girl popped out from inside the pit toilet and said, 'God I hate those things.Mozzies, it's full of mozzies, be careful they carry the Ross River virus. Oh and ticks, they're everywhere.' 'Hi, thanks,' said Carolyn. 'Yeh and snakes; check your sleeping bags, apparently they love the warmth. And spiders, yeh don't touch the spiders,' she added just when we were getting comfortable with the place. However, we took heed as she was obviously a local girl and sounded pretty knowledgeable. 'Where are you guys pitched,' she said and then my illusions were shattered when she went on, 'Camping, God I hate it, this is my first time and never again.'

Carolyn was becoming a bit twitchy by now so when I brought a huge huntsman spider into the tent she was a little hysterical to say the least. Mind you, I didn't do it on purpose. We were both lying looking up through the mesh window at the clear night sky. The brilliant stars and Milky Way shone so brightly when suddenly 'There's spider on the window,' Carolyn said in panic. 'Oh go to sleep, it can't get in,' I said. 'I don't care kill it,' she squealed. 'Oh, for God's sake,' I muttered grumpily. I unzipped the canvas door, stood up in my boxers and couldn't see a thing. 'There's nothing here, he's gone,' I reassured her. 'You're lying, I saw it,' Carolyn jabbered on. I didn't know it was crawling over my head while I sorted a guy rope. I entered the tent, zipped up and looked at Carolyn looking at me in silent fear. The spider the size of Africa leapt from my head, sprung to the tent roof and ran the full length. Carolyn was now screaming so loud I thought we were under attack from an alien invasion. I reached out my hand to grab it and suddenly realised we were in Australia! Spiders bite here, and are quite partial to white Pommie flesh. I grabbed a pillowcase, scooped up the spider and evicted the lot. I'm okay with creepy crawlies but what were most disturbing were its size and the way it leapt off me. Camping in the outback bush and on the beaches in Western Australia is so remote, it's soul searching. Nobody about, silence broken only by whistling wind from uprising thermals, wildlife and the gentle lapping of turquoise water. Time alone was unique and then when we did see somebody it was disappointing!

We dipped our toe into civilisation once, scoffing complimentary cheese and crackers washed down with a full-bodied red on a wine-tasting tour and found a freebie dessert in a chocolate factory.

The heat was sweltering, the rain like no other and the wind was the sort you wouldn't go out in with a toupee. And people, the introductions and kindness just kept coming. The Italian honeymooners on a Honda Goldwing who had never heard of Chitty Chitty Bang Bang but insisted we took their address in Florence and come to stay for a bowl of pasta. Setting up camp at Walpole, the secretary of the Australian Land Rover owners' club, who didn't actually own one and drove round in a Japanese Land Cruiser, with the feeble excuse they were just not reliable and left oil on the drive, really did his best to get us to return back to Perth. It came with a very kind invitation of a real bed and Aussie cuisine. Meeting the club of Toyota-driving Land Rover enthusiasts sounded like treason to me, but hey! After spending over two hours engaged in conversation we finally got the tent from the back of the car and started to erect it. Carolyn said, 'Is this important? I found it on the floor by the brake pedal.' One shiny ball bearing was handed over. 'Don't know, depends where it came from,' I said.

The first of February was a significant milestone so to celebrate we opened a bottle of white port we had saved from our wine-tasting adventure. The bumpy corrugated dirt road was the start of things to come and was just like driving endlessly on a cattle grid. The unmade outback road shook the heart out of us and the guts out of Chitty. Thirty odd kilometres and down an incredibly steep track we arrived at Two Peoples Bay. Completely isolated, there was not a soul about. There was a tiny stretch of grassy bank to pitch the tent on and the foreshore swept away into the distance. The coral white sand squeaked with every footprint like freshly fallen snow and was lapped by crystal-clear water. The horizon disappeared towards the Southern Ocean and the next stop was Antarctica. Small electric-blue jellyfish baked in the sun. Thousands had been washed ashore, their metre-long tentacles wrapping driftwood and sand as if in a sixties collage. I scooped a new arrival back into the sea and Carolyn said, 'What's the point in that? There are bloody thousands of them, vicious things.' 'Yeh, but I saved his life,' I said. 'Your bonkers,' she fired back. 'No, there's this story about a starfish … Oh, it doesn't matter,' I said, flicking another two back into the water. For two days we sat, talked, paddled and drank port and the simplicity was etched firmly on our minds and will last for ever. A fat and fluffy Magpie-sized bird that sounded remarkably like R2-D2 rudely interrupted dawn and the silence. As pleasing as it was, it was far too early and the force would be coming his way if he didn't shut up.

Fed and watered, Albany gave us the opportunity to stock up on bread, milk and oil in preparation to tackle the Great Victorian Desert. However, before that we had Esperance to pass through. Sixty kilometres this side of the town we stumbled over Quagi beach, and a few nights here couldn't go amiss. The beach was what Australia was famous for and again so isolated. We found a sheltered spot on the upper beach, surrounded by salt-loving bushes and out the sandblasting wind. Chitty engaged four wheel drive and made minced meat of the soft sand. It would be so easy to opt out of life's responsibilities here and watch the world go by. That is until the mosquitoes turned up along with the March flies or Marchies, as they're known. These elephant-sized horse fly lookalikes have a fixed proboscis the size of a North Sea oilrig, and pain, I'd rather be trampled by wildebeest. It wasn't long before we realised why nobody else was camping there. We entered town early to seek an internet café to hopefully find a local campsite and to get some advice on the Nullarbor. E-mails came fast and furious including one from 'Aussy Kent'. He was a Chitty nut claiming to have the largest collection of Chitty Chitty Bang Bang memorabilia in the southern hemisphere and had followed our travels on the web. We now had web viewers in Canada, the United States, Iran and India and Kent down under who insisted we took a detour to his home in Castlemaine in Victoria. Chitty was surrounded by people when returning with our shopping including one local lady over the moon with the car and Carolyn's tan saying, 'Look at you, you bitch!' The Esperance Express wanted a few photos so we did our bit then noticed the piece of paper stuck under the windscreen wiper: 'We had seen you at Northwood House on the Isle of Wight last summer, good luck with your travels.' How nice, what a shame we missed them.

We spent five hours talking before we could finally put up the tent but as usual we enjoyed it. One guy brought us a freshly made cappuccino from a full Italian espresso machine installed in his caravan and a sweet old couple invited us to stay the night if we made it to the state of Victoria. 'So where are you heading?' came the usual question. 'Oh, the Nullarbor, eh? It's a big old country this, you know.' Yes, I did know because I had actually looked at the map and 18 million of the 20 million or so Australians had told me on an hourly basis. 'Water, yep you need plenty of water and fuel don't be one of those Pommie drongos whingeing 'cos it's too bloody hot and you got lost in the sand.' The advice was always good beneath the bravado and as ever they instilled a genuinely healthy fear which only made me question what we were about to tackle. I wanted more, so I said, 'Thanks for that. God, I am so glad for the information. Have you crossed it many times?' 'Who me, well no, no not yet, it's a big country this, can't just whiz over east you know, but anyway most Aussies haven't.' In fact, so far everybody we've met had sound advice on something they hadn't done just yet Well, I can understand their concerns for the Brits, after all it amazes me how Cook ever found Australia in the first place.

Chapter 49 **F**lat roads and Mad Max moments

Back in the good old days, Norseman made its mark. Lawrence Sinclair claimed his horse, Norseman, hoofed at the ground and unearthed gold. Too much grog or a blinding stroke of luck I'd say. It sparked a full-scale gold rush. This was literally a one-horse town by name and nature and its lasting impression was one of stark loneliness. A crackpot who claimed he was Jesus Christ and a group of aboriginal people sat inebriated outside the only pub. I shouldn't be hard on this place because it felt raw and had a real feeling of Walk about Creek surrounding it. The collection of single storey houses lined the only, hot, sun-baked through road and advertised the cheapest petrol you'd find on the Nullarbor. The white-haired pump attendant was always keen to banter with a fellow lost Pom countryman. He boasted of his years in Oz and the fact he had married a right ripper. 'Oh yeh, she'll be right, the last Tasmanian devil that's her.' A colourful postcard was stuck under my nose of a cartoon showing the outback and the legendary naked woman running across the road. 'There you go, mate, watch out for the Nullarbor Nymph,' he said with a cheeky smile. 'That can't be real,' I said. 'Yep, your right on that front me, old mate, nobody's got tits that big,' he said grinning even more. It was obviously a long and lonely drive for the road train trucker. 'Watch out for those road trains, they'll eat you alive,' he went on. 'You wanna see what they do to caravans; no bull, these things rip 'em to pieces.' What was he going on about? I thought.

Why now? I just didn't get it, sixteen litres and that was it. The petrol splashed back like a geothermal geyser, soaking my sleeve, because a suction airlock had occurred. The desperately needed fuel, which I was about to pay for, was flooding out of the breather pipe. Gallons siphoned themselves all over the forecourt. In haste I grabbed the inch-thick pipe pulling it upwards to stem the flow. This sent a torrent all over the rear of Chitty and down the back of my neck. I was a walking incendiary device but more to the point I couldn't fill the tank. Don't ask me why but every

500 miles or so the fifty-litre tank blocked and would only accept fifteen or sixteen litres. Chitty still had the brass reserve fuel container holding another fifty and I had the two jerrycans topped up, but if ever I needed to be full, it was now. I was really concerned and Carolyn was holding her nose as I smelt. 'Have a good 'un and remember road trains; yeh some of those drivers are right bad mongrels,' was his farewell message.

Mesmerising is the best way to describe the road, and straight. The Romans would have loved this place, black parched tarmac shimmered in a quivering heat haze, and the road warped into the horizon, shaped with the curves of a woman's hourglass figure. Dipped sections disappeared into bouncing light reflecting the red dust and surrounding bush in an 'oh, it really happens' mirage moment. We were both grinning from ear to ear at the delights of the real 100 per cent and original outback. The true vast expanse hit us as Carolyn, myself and Chitty embarked on crossing the unforgiving Great Victorian Desert, known as the Nullarbor. Carolyn was deep in thought and my mind was going over and over wondering if I had enough fuel Would the water last? Had I got enough engine oil, gearbox oil, brake fluid, and would the clutch fluid last until the next service station? 'What are you thinking, Wigs?' I said after two or three hours. 'Oh, how Ben and Michelle are back home and just how beautiful all this is. I can't believe they say it's full of nothing, it's for ever changing. What about you?' 'I was wondering where those three silver ball bearings had come from, down there by my feet!'

We drove away from the sunset, it would have been nice to say we drove into it, but as usual we were heading east. It was time to find a place to kip down, so randomly in the middle of nowhere I turned right into the flat dusty bush. Chitty rumbled over short dry scrub for a good kilometre and we parked up to the nearest thing resembling a tree. We made camp and I decided to light a fire. From day one Carolyn had ribbed me for bringing three kettles, especially my pride and joy the Kelly kettle from Ireland. This was a real bushman's teapot and I was going to use it here come what may. Within a few minutes boiling water from twigs and paper made a perfect cuppa and I was really proud. 'See I told you,' I said smugly. 'Yes dear,' came her sarcasm. I really didn't want to be one of those stupid Pommie tourists and set light to the undergrowth, burning down Western Australia in a wild forest fire, and I was slightly paranoid to say the least. I know, after dousing with water, I'll dig a hole and bury the embers, I thought. In this never ending wilderness I took to digging a small hole about two feet from the tent Carolyn had just put up. Six inches down a rock was in the way so I dug it out' 'Oh! Oh heck, oh dear, oh dear, oh dear,' I whispered to myself. Humongous and crouching in fear was a black hairy tarantula spider. What a dilemma. I couldn't tell Carolyn; she'd scream, want me to kill it, then we would have to pack up the tent and move to the next continent. Um, getting a photo, forget it. Two feet from the tent I carefully replaced the rock and filled in the hole and said, 'More tea, Vicar?'

Living in an overcrowded country, it felt so strange to have no boundaries. I walked into the bush half expecting to look over the next wave of low lying scrub and find a housing estate or at least a cul-de-sac. Over every fence or hedge in England is something and here there was nothing. I looked back for a brief moment and a wave of fear engulfed me. Which way was back? The bush was just head height and I hadn't a clue. Walking, walking, walking and a sigh of relief at the sound of washing pots. The air was still, the night sky pitch-black and the Milky Way was star-filled. Sitting together and looking up was probably one of most memorable night entertainments we had ever had. Reflective and sobering, we put everything into perspective and hearing what sounded like footsteps down to the wildlife or wind. The night had left a strong impression and Carolyn and I were in no hurry to leave.

Nullarbor is Latin for no tree and yep there weren't any. There were lots of dead kangaroos though; I counted thirty-one on the roadside being eaten by pterodactyl-sized buzzards. I don't want to keep on the theme of dead things but today's drive en route to Balladonia was a bit stressful. Reaching the brow of a hill, the other side welcomed us with a recently overturned lorry. This was a place where you always stopped if someone needed assistance and fortunately a ute, a pickup truck, was on the case. We hadn't passed any vehicles for hours and now there were two. The double-decker lorry, which had swerved off the road, had been carrying livestock. Sadly about thirty sheep lay dead. The poor things were scattered everywhere, on the road, lying in the bush and hanging in the lorry side railings; blood and guts were everywhere. The driver looked in shock and was pacing up and down with one hand holding a towel against his head. The ute owner was on his radio and I wondered how on earth somebody got out here to sort this lot. Truth be known there're a pretty hardy bunch out here. With an exchange of words we headed on, passing three rather worried-looking sheep running along the road bound for Adelaide. The road widened to the size of a runway complete with navigational landing lines, just after a yellow warning sign saying 'Royal Flying Doctor Service airstrip'. No guesses to whom ute man was ringing.

Not too far off the main road was Cactus Beach. There was not much there, not even a cactus. The sand dunes had flowed into Arabian landscapes with the constant winds off the Southern Ocean. The bright, white powder mountains and deep blue sky made a vivid contrast David Hockney fashion. Beautiful, lonely and windy but more pressing and to the point the place had a toilet. It might be a civilised country but we were well in the outback and you gotta go somewhere. Pit toilets stunk, were full of bluebottles and what ever you did you didn't look down because something would be alive. The corrugated iron 'dunnie' was the norm but today we were in for a treat. Nestled in the sand was a small stone circle with no roof and a driftwood timber door. Once sat on the throne the wall was as high as your chest. This was slightly off putting, even though the view was great. Fortunately, there was not a soul in sight but from afar a man sitting reading the newspaper with a three-foot wall around him would look quite comical and clearly occupied. Why they ever bothered to put a lock on the door I'll never know, and yes, sadly heaven knows why, I locked it!

Australia's straightest stretch of road ran for 146 kilometres, not a kink, curve or the slightest bend, and we were on it. This was a real Mad Max moment. It was teasing and enticing to go down hard on the accelerator and take the opportunity to really floor it. No cars, no police and a runway longer than the distance from London to Coventry. We went for it. In fact, we'd been going for it for the last six months, that is foot to the floor and we were doing 40 mph. Okay, so we were in Chitty and we were not flying but the road train with three trailers was.

A white Kenworth truck emerged over the hot distorted horizon and within a minute or so my rear-view mirror was filled with its bulk. This man was driving on the wrong side of the road, stopping for no one, ready to overtake. Three emus ran alongside the road then darted into the scrub just before the enormous truck thundered past. Debris of mangled aluminium and white panelling dotted the roadside every few kilometres or so. I was struggling to imagine who on earth would come so far for illegal fly tipping when just as the truck closed in all became apparent. You know how you jump out of your skin as an idiot on a loud motorbike overtakes surprisingly from behind, and you politely thank him for the warning, well that's nothing. Juggernaut man chewed me up, rolled me on his tongue and spat me out along with Carolyn, Chitty and one not so quick emu. The explosion of noise, jumbo jet suction and vortex of wind rush shook the living daylights out of us. Chitty literally shifted sideways, our ears popped and the bonnet bellowed upwards. Four chrome latches jumped free and the now weathered and salt-encrusted M&S leather belts took the strain, two inches of slack held the bonnet vibrating madly. The second trailer wagon passed and Chitty didn't need wings and by the time the third road train attachment bulldozed past, luggage was lifting and flapping in the wind, the roof was straining and flexing against the brass windscreen. And that fly tipping; fragile aluminium boxes on wheels just simply imploded. All that was left of caravans after road train road rage. I now realised why there were so many steel ball bearings lying on the floor mat. The steering wheel had taken the toll of thousands of kilometres over Indian potholes and Aussie outback and was now flapping about madly. The steering column bearing was shot and the caravan-eating road train had driven in the final nail.

Midway across this unbelievably vast continent the Great Australian Bight became close to the road. At times the flat plateau ended abruptly, chiselled vertically to meet a wild and furious sea below, and a few hundred kilometres more the edge was softened by white sand dunes of epic proportions. The strong, prevailing Antarctic winds took 10 mph off our top speed and whistled through the cab. Yesterday I had burnt my legs against the engine bay bulkhead in the sweltering heat and today we had both donned our fleeces and windproof raincoats. Without the concerns of vanity as nobody could see us, the rock concert ringing in our ears was dampened by toilet paper rolled up and stuck in each ear. Looking like that was a small sacrifice to stop the biting wind from perforating our ear drums. I didn't mind leaning into the wind but when it relented, then I nearly fell out of the car, and I'm not kidding it was that strong. We had to gulp air to breath. I shall never take car windows for granted again.

A motorbike coming the other way had just passed us. We had waved frantically and so had he. Two minutes later he overtook us and disappeared over the horizon ahead of us. Another two minutes he came back towards us again with his crash helmet slung over one arm, holding the handlebars and a video camera stuck to his face. 'I suppose we'd better wave,' said Carolyn.

Chitty spluttered to a grinding halt. The sixteen litres had gone and so had the reserve fifty litres of fuel in the brass tank on the rear. Carolyn filed her nails while I topped up with the last of the two twenty-litre jerrycans and quickly calculated at about four miles to the litre Chitty was good for another eighty miles. This was slightly unnerving as according to the last road sign at Eucla the Nullarbor roadhouse was at least another 200 kilometres. We hadn't helped the situation much by sightseeing thirty miles or so down a sandy track seaward in search of a grand view that looked just like all the others. Miles, kilometres and litres were doing my head in. All I knew was we had a long way to go on a sniff.

Chapter 50 **So what day is it today?**

The quiet star-gazing nights in the outback made every stop worth savouring. Joey-filled kangaroos hopped past our tent and as far as we were both concerned this could last for ever. Cool morning wake-ups gave us a window away from the daily heat.Chitty was packed like a sherpa's mule and we fired her up before the temperature started to rocket. Today something was different; a slightly unusual distant but distinctive rumble accompanied the tuneful purr of Chitty's engine. Faint, and almost unnoticeable, unless you had spent six months listening to the four cylinder harmonies eight hours a day. I popped the bonnet and couldn't place the sound, but towards the front was my guess. 'Water pump, Wigs, I reckon it's the pump.' 'How do you know that?' she asked. 'I don't, but its one thing we haven't got. Don't worry sweetheart, it'll probably be fine,' I said full of optimism. Bloody hell, I thought to myself, I really hope it's not the water pump, not out here.

Horizons gave way to more horizons and the drive across Australia felt like a lifetime, one we both wished would never end. For the first time in our lives we were truly alone, no schedules or timetables, no deadlines or decisions. The world rushes by, but out here time stood still and we were savouring every moment. The fuel gauge sat on empty; the speedo needle flapped and fluctuated between 10 and 50 mph, yet Chitty just kept going. In an eye-blurring heat haze the roadhouse warped into view and a sigh of relief ebbed out as if we had both been holding our breaths for the last eighty kilometres. Font size and type face can be a bit misleading to say the least as the map pinpointed this settlement the size of Fremantle. Fremantle was big and allegedly so was this place – well, a hut with a fuel station. Once I had taken on board the oil reserves of a Third World nation I asked a weather-beaten faced man in his seventies if he knew anything about Land Rovers. 'Do I know anything about Land Rovers? I'll tell you this me old mate,' he said with here comes a war story intake of breath. 'Series two Landys cut the outback roads of Australia. We sat compass in hand, took a bearing and drove for weeks with a bulldozer behind.' 'Well, I just wondered whether you thought this slight rumble up front was a problem,' I said, hoping for a bit of support. The old guy returned with a stethoscope in hand, complete with a screwdriver fixed on the end. He listened very carefully to the engine, placed the tip here and there. 'Yep, it's your water pump, it is leaking.' 'Oh no.' 'Where are you heading,' he asked. 'Oh, we're off to Brisbane.' 'Brisbane eh, oh she'll be right,' he said positively in a strong Aussie accent. Well, he showed all the signs of somebody who knew what he was talking about, but Brisbane was still well over 1,500 kilometres away. The silence was broken by three aboriginal lads pulling up in a rust bucket with a smashed windscreen; without a word they disappeared out the back returning with a crate of beer. I smiled at them and smiles were returned with a twangy 'all right mate' and then they were gone. 'How do they get away with it, bloody alcos?' a pony-tailed Kiwi said, loitering on the veranda. 'We wouldn't get away with driving a smashed-up car, tanked up all day, worthless bloody alcoholics,' he went on again. Our friendly old man piped up, 'They weren't alcoholics before whites turned up, think about it.'

Dust stirred in the midday heat, and a small whirlwind scooted across the forecourt as I turned the key. Leaping from his cab an eager Kenworth truck driver smiled and introduced himself as Bruce. Well, what d'ya know, Bruce eh, I thought. 'Jeeesus mate, she's a beauty, what the, what is, where are you,' said the unshaven trucker in vest and jeans, stumbling over his words. I did the usual and explained all. 'Seriously, blinding, no air con and all,' he went on and on. 'Yous guys gotta be pretty tough to do that with no air con.' Oh come on, I thought, yes it's hot but you're the hardened outback Aussie who eats Poms for breakfast. 'Credit to ya. I'll tell you what, mate, she's a tough old bird,' he said pointing to Carolyn. Compliment received we were soon back heading east.

When it came to my concerns I thought a lot and said nothing. Carolyn had enough worries over missing her family so the car's wellbeing was down to me. I was still putting a litre of oil in the engine every day, I checked and topped up the front and rear axles with gear oil and used the same in the transfer and gearbox which I had nicknamed Niagara. Each morning I refilled the clutch reservoir, which because of its location was only possible by a five-year-old gymnast or in my case a lot of pain, and topped up the brake fluid which actually didn't leak, just kept spilling out through the cap seal. All steering wheel bearings had departed and now the water pump was working my imagination to the full, but hey on the plus side the replacement carburettor and the new steering arm were working well and so far we hadn't had a puncture. As for finance, a wave of fear descended over me every time the thought entered my head. We truly were on a pot noodle budget now and reaching Brisbane looked slim. We had no income, no savings and no way of repaying a credit card bill. The carefree image we had left back in the UK made it far too embarrassing to ask home for a loan so the only options on the table were to leave Chitty in Australia or to stop eating and drive like a snail. God, I was hungry.

Ceduna was back into civilisation and the end of the Nullarbor. Sad but we still weren't half way across Australia yet. Iron Knob was the next main town, which I couldn't say without smirking like a schoolboy. Carolyn just kept raising her eyebrows disdainfully.The idea of not much money made us stupidly ostrich-like, heads well and truly in the sand ignoring the problem. Kimba had a shop so we pulled in for milk and more Bushells teabags. Most welcome to this town signs were quite moderate; Kimba had a sign claiming the halfway point across the continent worthy of a photo and a great backdrop to Chitty. Carolyn had picked up a gold-plated kangaroo paperweight for ten dollars and thought it might be a replacement for the Spitfire plane we had stolen. Over the road was a guy, head down angle-grinding steel, and after a quick chat he drilled a hole in the base and Kimba the Kangaroo was commissioned to ride on Chitty's bonnet as the new mascot. A small local bakery caught my eye and the thought of fresh bread sounded great. 'Hi, have you got any hot cross buns?' I asked politely. 'No, it ain't Easter,' came the abrupt reply from a large man with a Kevin Keegan footballer's perm. 'Oh, um, I'll have that loaf of bread then, please.' 'Is that your wife out there?' the baker said looking through his window at Carolyn sitting in the car. 'Um yes,' I answered. 'She's a pretty girl, you're a lucky man.' Oh thanks.' 'Yeh, you know what, my wife's bloody ugly, yeh and she's fat, that's four bucks please,' he said. How strange, how funny and how nice the bread smelt. The day had come to an end after driving thirty kilometres and setting up camp on sand dunes behind a beach. The sunset was postcard idyllic and we had fresh bread and a nice cup of tea while paddling a few yards from the tent.

The daily routine was fine tuned like a Steinway grand piano. Carolyn folded the tent and I refilled anything on Chitty that held oil. East soon became south-east as we followed the coastal road towards Adelaide. The road was now full with traffic; heads turned and we caused a stir whenever we parked. Free camping was now becoming a challenge so if we had to pay we were going to make the most of a good bath. A white-haired hippy left over from the sixties shook my hand and smiled his well-tanned and weathered face with genuine affection. 'So where are you from.' 'The Isle of Wight,' Carolyn replied proudly. 'Well I'll be, I've just been watching a video of Hendrix at the 69 festival on the Isle of Wight.' 'Wow, have you?' I replied. 'Sixties, mate, it was a ripper. I can't remember a thing.' Yep, that sounded about right for anybody living through it. 'I'll tell you what, it's normally seventeen dollars a night, for you ten bucks,' he said, pleased with the island connection. Carolyn whispered in my ear: 'He said eight dollars fifty to those other guys.' 'Is that right eight fifty each as that's nineteen dollars, two more than the seventeen,' Carolyn said. 'No girly, ten for both, unless you wanna pay eight fifty each,' he said slightly bemused. 'Keep quiet, Wigs, it's ten. We're from the Isle of Wight so it's ten,' I said trying to recover the situation.

On our pitch about twenty campers turned up and we talked for two hours before a luggage bungee was unleashed, away from the line of sight. The group of five or six caravaners and 4X4 drivers, all new residents from South Africa, invited us over for beer and a barbie. The two of us sat among the crowd around a huge star-lit campfire. One guy handed me a Budweiser and asked us to tell them about our trip. We talked and talked and talked and at one in the morning and a handful of Budweisers later we staggered back to the tent after a memorable evening and a round of applause. Loads of beer, full stomachs and a bed for the night, they were the best ten dollars we had spent for ages. Before we departed one of the friendly South Africans told me about a great car show which was on our route. 'It's a blinder mate, you gotta go, it's next Saturday.' I liked the idea, I'm always interested in old cars, so I replied, 'Next Saturday you say, um, so what day is it today?' 'God, you really have been away a long time,' came the unexpected answer.

Chapter 51 **Collectormaniac**

The word always got out but earlier than usual that morning, 6 a.m. Crawling out of the tent in T-shirt and boxers I came face to face with an audience. 'Oh blimey, good morning,' I said, caught a bit offguard. Standing in front were about thirty people, mums, dads, grandparents and a selection of kids. 'I hope you don't mind,' said a quietly spoken mother 'Well, you see, the campsite owner's children go to school with ours and they said Chitty Chitty Bang Bang was in town.' We didn't mind but it was a bit of a shock. They had all come early before school in case they missed us. Carolyn concerned about her hair hid in the tent. I stood unshaven, bleary eyed and barefooted on the dew-damp grass and talked for half an hour.

Breakfast done and the next strange thing happened. A bus full of old people sailed past Chitty clearly visible from the road they waved and disappeared over the brow of the hill. Two minutes later the bus had turned round and driven on to the campsite and parked up next to us. The bus leant towards us as the windows were filled with wrinkled and smiling faces, waving and taking photos. It was a surreal moment and quite fun until it dawned on us Carolyn still hadn't done her hair and I was still standing in my boxer shorts eating toast.

Phillip Island just off Melbourne was a tourist Mecca for penguin viewing and we did our bit. However, the island had more on offer for us. The capital was Cowes, twinned with, yes you guessed it, Cowes back home on the Isle of Wight, and boasted the delights of the Isle of Wight pub. They were just as surprised to see our rally trip number plate labelled IOW as we were to be there, so we all took photos.

Castlemaine, named after the beer which isn't brewed there any more, was a town that had been following us across the globe. Kent always left a travel blog entry and had been e-mailing us ever since Chitty hit the press. He was Chitty bonkers, a complete fanatic and by the sound of his outlandish claims had the largest Chitty Chitty Bang Bang collection in the southern hemisphere. He sounded like a complete anorak and the closer we came to the east coast Kent's e-mailing went into overdrive.

We had come this far so we just had to divert and call in and see him. Deep down we were very wary. Kent's enthusiasm echoed down the phone so we agreed to meet first thing that morning at the town's central camping ground. What does a Chitty nut look like I thought? We couldn't have been more wrong; yes he was a nut, a complete fruit and nut, but a genuinely nice guy. Kent was tall with a full head of hair and glasses. He had a ruddy complexion and sported the smile of an eager boy scout at camp.. About fifty, wearing formal trousers and a black freshly unpacked Chitty stage show T-shirt and holding the pressed steel Australian GEN11 number plates he had bought but hadn't a car to fix them to, Kent introduced himself and was bursting with excitement. His formalities included handshaking, embracing and a kiss on the cheek for Carolyn. When I suggested a ride in Chitty, I was instantly elevated to a higher being. 'Oh can I?' said Kent drooling like a six-year-old on Christmas Eve. Carolyn upped the volume on the CD sound track and out blasted the theme tune to Chitty Chitty Bang Bang and Kent sang his heart out, clenching his fist as he sang into an imaginary microphone and knowing all the words. This middle-aged man was beside himself; he shouted out and waved to everybody he knew and everybody he didn't. Carolyn and I both smiled from ear to ear and really felt we had made his day. Deed done, we found ourselves in Kent's kitchen scrutinising his unbelievable collection. 'See, this is the first edition, and hang on this is the 266 model, I've got twenty of them,' Kent rambled on. Red and yellow everywhere, there were more wings than at terminal four. Carolyn was fascinated. His wife, yes he had one, went to bed, I yawned a bit and his cat nodded off. He then pulled out one of only three in the world plastic Chitty pedal cars from the sixties and solemnly said, 'After riding in yours, this just doesn't do it for me any more.' There was a slight embarrassed silence and I could see Carolyn sympathetically wanted to mother this middle-aged collectormaniac.

Over the Snowy Mountains Chitty's water pump rumbled into Sydney. The steering wheel had more play than a primary school break and oil stained the old town cobbles at the city's birthplace, The Rocks. A deep sigh of relief engulfed us both as we took in the amazing view of the iconic Opera House as we passed over the Sydney Harbour Bridge.

There was a wave of excitement knowing we had really done it, Sydney wasn't the end by any means but it felt as if it should have been, The Solent News Agency was hot on our trail and wanted photos for the Daily Express with the white sails of the Opera House in the background. We pulled up to a frosty faced security guard who pointed out it was private property and was extremely unhelpful to say the least. A flotilla of limousines and blushing brides around Circular Quay had established a great photo vantage point just under the bridge and fortunately for us everyone assumed we were part of the wedding regalia. Chitty's wings were fitted, which we had carried across the world just for this purpose, and the swarming Sydney siders and tourists made a great resource of helpful photographers. We hadn't a tripod and Carolyn and I both needed to be in shot. 'I can see what you need,' said a tall young man with John Lennon glasses and a beret pulled down to one side of his face. His slim, scantily clad model stood by holding his camera the size of the Hubble telescope while he negotiated my lesser mortal Nikon. The narrow overcrowed streets gave the city a strong sense of established character and made for concentrated driving. There was a lot to Sydney including the cost of living and camping fees that were driving us north. After a welcome break and real food at Chatsworth compliments of Bub and Scott, our emigrant relations from the Isle of Wight, we took to the Pacific Highway.

Chapter 52 **P**oke in the eye with a mobile phone

Crossing the Australian continent from the windswept west and deserted beaches to the vibrant east of cosmopolitan city siders and Wicked Camper van-driving backpackers gave a unique sense of fulfilment. Hermit crab living was as insecure as it was rewarding; the world had embraced us but our guard was always up. If there was a place to truly relax, it was here. No longer did I feel the brass bell needed to be hanging from Chitty's roof to raise the alarm and I could now sleep without my adjustable spanner under my pillow. With a good 15,000 miles under our belts we were feeling pretty confident, the water pump rumbled for England and after a hard day's drive we took time out in the Dickie Beach campsite just north of Brisbane. Our best friends Scott and Gill had made a new life down under a few years ago so popping in for a cup of tea was top of the list, especially as Scott was the butt of shopfloor jokes for even mentioning our endeavour and a visit was needed to set the record straight. 'I very much doubt that,' Scott's foreman had said in a typical cynical Pom-bashing verbal assault.

The Sunshine Coast was a great place to catch up on a bit of washing and route planning. The campsite had just emptied out after a bank holiday so Carolyn disappeared to the laundry room saying, 'Watch my phone.' Her mobile was on charge adjacent to where I was sitting with maps sprawled out on the grass. We could follow the coastal road north all the way up to Cairns and Cape York, or maybe we could cut through the centre heading up towards Darwin and ship on from there. Then I heard Carolyn call out, 'Where's my phone?' 'What?' I answered. 'Where's my phone,' Carolyn's panicked voice came back. 'Um, it's … it was there, heck, it's …' I said knowing I hadn't been paying attention. God, this was a disaster. As a mother this was Carolyn's link to the kids, not only did her top spec Sony Ericsson hold all her contact details but it stored treasured family photos. 'The cleaner, yes the cleaner's probably got it,' I jabbered on feeling bloody awful and hoping it was a possibility. I was clutching at straws. 'I told you to watch my phone,' she said with a quivering voice.

Nothing I could say was going to put things right. I knew how much she valued her links with home and I needed to find it. Carolyn ran one way, me the other looking for the buggy-driving cleaner. At reception they confirmed the worst. It hadn't been handed in. 'That's my lifeline, my kids, I was only gone a minute,' Carolyn said, eyes welling up with tears. She tried to talk more but the emotion was too much. Home, Ben and Michelle had pulled at her heartstrings the entire trip and her phone was her security blanket. And I had lost it. Carolyn knelt on the grass with her head in her hands and bawled her eyes out. I really felt terrible and so concerned.

Now you don't need to be a Sherlock Holmes to notice two odd-looking lads trying to climb over the perimeter fence. One skinny Aussie lad in his early twenties looked shiftier than a Transit van parked outside Barclay's. The other guy stood well over six foot, was well built and had a South Pacific Islander look. He was ugly, they were both bloody ugly. I ran straight over and shouted, 'Er, you got my mobile phone?' and then received the normal defensive, creative bull and verbal abuse. The big lad was obviously just for show, his eyes instantly looked down and said nothing. The skinny lad, now halfway over the fence, chose to ignore me. Instinctively I went to grab his bag but a swift kick came my way. 'I haven't got your effing phone,' he grunted. Carolyn calmly walked up to him and said, 'Look, mate, I only want the SIM card. It's my family. You can have the phone.' Jumping down he said, 'I told you I haven't got your effing phone.'

Society had installed in us both the notions of political correctness, we had no clear evidence and were unsure of our accusations in a foreign country, and so we pondered, dithered and felt helpless. The cleaner arrived too late. 'Yep, I saw the mongrel with it, wrapping the flex around his hand,' he said. Anger and passion-filled to the point of disbelief, I couldn't believe I had let them walk away. Carolyn rang the police and I swapped my flip-flops for my walking boots and jumped the fence. I ran and ran and ran and found nothing, which was just as well as I didn't really know what I was going to do if I found them. We talked over and over about it and I just couldn't come to terms with the fact I had lost her phone to a couple of thieving yobs and then allowed them to walk away.

The police in Carolyn's words were bloody useless, so coming to terms and moving on was the only thing to do.

With a bright new day I wandered over the road to get a pint of milk. Oh no, quick hide, stand still, you lemon. I couldn't believe it, it was him. Oh my God. My heart was racing. Hell, what do I do? Call the police? No, yes, um. I didn't believe what I was seeing: he was texting on what I thought was Carolyn's phone. Wearing my hat and sunglasses, he had no idea who I was. He was surrounded by five or six lads, all in T-shirts and board shorts. I passed by close enough to get a good view of the phone and I was as nervous as hell. They were all laughing and joking as they loitered outside the local café and I was furious, shaking like a leaf not knowing what to do. Ah sod it, I'd spent fifteen years being told to get lost by shoplifters knowing I had the company's reputation at stake and a job to lose. I just couldn't let him walk away again. Not having had a fight since primary school, I stepped back and ran as fast as I could with aim of grabbing the phone. I was so angry and fired up I hit him with my whole body trying to grab the phone out of his grubby hand. The force of running across the pavement sent him and me down a flight of stairs. The phone hit the ground and bounced on the steps. I shouted a load of incoherent gobbledygook and fumbled for the phone. As I looked up his mates looked on as he smacked me clean in the face. I thought to myself, strangely that didn't hurt as much as I imagined it would. Now we are both locked in a full-scale punch up. The world of tourists and Dickie Beach had had the gentle silence shattered as I allowed him to perfect his fighting skills on my torso. My blood was boiling and I ripped his shirt off his back and wrestled him to the ground. Cheers and chanting fill the distorted airwaves as I reached for the phone lying close by. My heart sank when Carolyn's mobile was kicked across the ground by a misguided supporter and into the hands of ugly's sidekick, who snapped it up and legged it. Helped to my feet by a local surfing dude the size of California's governor Arnold Schwarzenegger, I brushed myself down to a wave of rather rude abuse. My heart sank at the thought of the phone slipping through my fingers for a second time. Clearly still in shock, my ugly opponent dithered and then started to goad me with the fact he still had the phone. But hey I wasn't the one with a ripped shirt, a broken chain and blood coming out my nose. Okay, so I'd got a cracking black eye developing but I really did feel so much better, that was until the café owner telephoned the police from her mobile and said, 'You will know the young lad and he's fighting with a middle-aged man.' Middle aged, I'm not middle aged yet, am I? God, was that how they saw me? Feeling incredibly stupid and embarrassed I limped back to my wife in search of recognition for attempting to put things right.

See the minute you let your guard down, some dingbat took advantage. I just couldn't help reflecting on the countries we had passed through and the potential areas of risk we had found ourselves in and of all places it happened here. Mind you we had been truly humbled on our journey and frankly 99 per cent of the people we had met were great, genuinely nice people, off to work, raising families, who couldn't do enough for us. Sadly, you get the bad 1 per cent everywhere.

Chapter 53 **B**ackpacking backchat

After nearly ten months away, serious thoughts of the route home started to fill our road conversations. Leaving the Sunshine Coast northwards I pulled in to a rather smart BMW motorbike dealer. Carolyn and I had watched the series the Long Way Round for inspiration before we left and I fancied a look at the style of bikes they had used. Intimidating was not the word. I felt like a schoolboy who was retrieving a football from just behind the 'Please keep off the grass' sign. All the salesmen were engaged in serious deal making and I was starting to justify my own financial well-being. I could afford one if I really wanted one, I thought, on a loan, of course, over 300 years but they didn't know that. We both tiptoed over the marbled floor and stood against a vast expanse of glass next to the BMW GS 1200 Adventure. 'Can I help,' said a corporate-looking salesman. He was of stocky build, grade one haircut and very smartly dressed in BMW-branded clothing, 'Fancy doing a Charley Boorman, do ya?' 'Um, yes, that would be nice. I have to say I like the idea,' I replied. Then in typical Aussie to Pom patronising fashion he said, 'Yeh, buddy, it's a nice idea, but it ain't a game. It's not like popping down your local, it's a big old country this you know.' I considered asking the price for the all singing all dancing model, knowing I couldn't even afford a tank of fuel, and then thought not. 'Ewan and Charley,' talking as if he knew them personally, 'went through a blinding training regime, counterterrorism, self-defence, off-road riding skills and all that paperwork, serious stuff, buddy,' he went on. God, I've only come into to look at a bike and to daydream a bit. 'So how much are the bikes fully loaded, two of them. We're thinking of riding back to the UK,' I said defiantly. 'I'll get the price for you but it's not that simple, see, importing, exporting, luggage, fixers, visas, passports and homework. It's good to do some homework.' I only wanted a brochure. He disinterestedly handed me a current price list. I really wanted to say something. 'Go on,' said Carolyn. 'Tell him about Chitty and the trip.' 'Naa, probably wouldn't believe us anyway.' As we stepped up into Chitty the salesman ran over bouncing with a new lease of enthusiasm. 'Wow, what is she?' he asked. 'It's a Chitty Chitty Bang Bang car. We've just driven it overland from the UK and thought we might go home on a motorbike,' I stated proudly, landing one just below the belt. By the look on his face, he had heard something via the media about us. 'Yes, we have just driven through France, Belgium, Luxembourg, Germany, Austria, Italy, Greece,' pausing for breath I continued, 'Turkey, Iran, United Arab Emirates, India, Malaysia, Thailand, Burma, Cambodia, Singapore, shipped into Perth and have driven from the west coast to the east of Oz and here we are, and now we're heading north. Cheerio,' I said. Just as I engaged first, pulling out on to the highway north, the man reached into his shirt pocket, pulling out a business card, and said, 'My name's ...' Too late he had had his chance and muffed it.

Just north of the Sunshine Coast is Fraser Island, the world's largest sand island.   Inskip Point Rainbow Bay were on the doorstep of the vehicle barge that gave access to the island. I engaged Chitty's four wheels and ploughed through deep-rutted soft sand, pulling up on a deserted windswept beach. Soon tea was boiling and a campfire was in full swing. Carolyn was washing her hair, pouring leftover washing-up water with a creal bowl. The sun was over the yardarm and a not so shy dingo was sniffing round. We kept our scraps to ourselves. There were stark warnings everywhere not to feed them as a young lad had sadly lost his life. I quickly threw another log on the fire. In the fading light a bloke of about twenty turned up and said, 'Jesus, mate, how did you get here?' 'Sorry, oh hello, what?' 'How did you get up here in that?' he said, looking confused. 'Oh, it's Chitty Chitty Bang Bang, we flew in,' I replied in jest. 'What? Only I'm stuck in the sand and I've been trying to get out for the last hour,' he said, looking for help. 'Oh, I see. Chitty's built on a Land Rover,' I said explaining our success. It wasn't long before Chitty had the ageing Nissan Patrol pulled out of the sand. Carolyn and I felt really good about that and I thought I would save this story for the next Aussie who gave me a hard time about owning a Land Rover.

A short ferry crossing costing an arm and a leg took us over to Fraser Island with its crystal-clear freshwater lakes and perfect white sand. The interior is kauri tree rain forest.   Camping here was spot on apart from the tourists. Yes, we had been spoilt and sharing Australia's outback was taking a bit of getting used to. It seemed either we were getting older or we had spent too much time alone. I had been a backpacker once and had loved it but Fraser was packed solid with them. For 300 dollars each, eleven young souls were packed in like sardines in a well-worn Toyota Land Cruiser. They make for the beach and partied for three days. Mixed in together, nationalities from all over the world bonded with common interests which normally revolved around lager. A convoy of cosmopolitan-filled salt-corroded Land Cruisers complete with roof racks and backpacking luggage rushed past sending sand and salt spray into the air.

Once back on the mainland Carolyn needed a bit of shopping and I pulled into the Rainbow Beach service station to reinflate the tyres after off-roading. On cue the returning fleet of Toyotas emptied out bleary-eyed travellers while they were topped up with fuel before heading back down to Brisbane, trendily referred to as Bris-Vegas. Chitty was gleaming in the sunshine and soon we had an audience. Three young Swedish girls came straight over for a photo. They formed a pose round the headlights and cuddled Chitty. 'She is so sweet and pretty, what is her name?' I gave them the story and they were enthralled at our journey. 'Hello, we are from Norway,' said a tall blond lad and his mate. 'Ya know we have a beautiful folk story about a friendly car in Norway and it looks just like this one. Can I ask you how come the car is here?' I went into a quick rundown of the adventure and they both thanked me for telling it. The two lads took a few snaps and shook my hand and then disappeared into the shop. Well, after the Swedes and the Norwegians in came the Germans, a group of four well-groomed young men all in Bermuda shorts and incredibly interested in the engineering. 'How many cylinders has the auto?' asked the first. 'What is its top speed?' asked the next. I could have talked for hours; they wanted to know so much and remarked how brave they thought we were. Then just as I finished the last front tyre, a lad jumped down from a Land Cruiser wearing just his brightly coloured boxer shorts. A grade one skinhead with tattoos covering most of his upper body, a few with the hallmark of 'I did this one with a compass at school', English was my first thought. The brash delivery and coarse language shattered the vocal sound of a beautiful northern accent. Walking straight up to me, he looked at me as if I was a Martian. 'Er, mate, is this Chitty Chitty Bang Bang?' 'Yes sort of, it's a replica,' I said. 'Er, it's got British plates, bloody English number plates. How did you get it here?' he said, rocking side to side barefooted on the hot tarmac. 'Oh we drove it overland from the UK,' I replied. 'F*** off, ya didn't,' he said in a startled John Cleese manner. 'No really we did.' 'F*** off.' 'No, we really really did. How else would we get here? Have a look at the stickers on the back,' I said, inwardly laughing at the response. Oh how we Brits do let ourselves down.

Chapter 54 **N**ot quite the end

The day was drawing to an end. The sun was low in the sky and burning a deep red glow across the horizon. Today was ending, just like the very first day that our trip had started, with not knowing where we were going to sleep tonight. We had endless possibilities matched by an endless imagination, which had matured over the last year. We were missing home, friends and family but we still wanted more. The only obstacle was money. We had come away with £15,000 that we had borrowed for a new kitchen we hadn't got, and on a very rough calculation after shipping Chitty home and paying out for two flights for us, it didn't leave much. Allowing for fuel and a few weeks' worth of pot noodles, we had £40 left and that was it. Not even enough to get an airport taxi home from Heathrow to the Isle of Wight. Yes, we had unused credit cards but we would need a job to service them. A job, now there was an idea. Maybe we could do the odd Aussie wedding or kids' party or maybe we could just pick fruit. Chitty purred along at 45 mph on a cooling and lonely road north, the water pump had made Brisbane like the old boy said it would, the steering wheel column had lost all its ball bearings and the oil was still leaking from everywhere which held oil. Chitty's new carburettor was working well and so far we hadn't had a single puncture. We had rented out our home, given up our jobs and embarked on a hare-brained adventure just because somebody said we couldn't and in a car we built ourselves. This was one of the most insecure things we had ever done, but so rewarding. I had known we would break down somewhere but I hadn't cared because it was all part of the adventure, and to be fair, Chitty had never actually stopped going, I had just panicked a lot. I had known we would run out of money but, despite it all, we had made it down under on a wing and a prayer. We had had our minds filled with amazing people, places and experiences, which would last a lifetime. We had crossed seventeen countries that had left their mark on our hearts and we had smelt, touched and savoured every moment. Despite being still hungry for more, the note my brother had e-mailed me had for the first time started to make sense: 'A man travels the world in search of something and returns home to find it.' Yes it made sense but not just yet.

As the silhouette of low-lying bush disappeared against a reddening sky and tired eyes gave way to the rhythms of nature, I said, 'So Wigs, what do you reckon, what next?' Holding the wheel steady I put my hand on top of hers and gave it a gentle squeeze. 'What about America, do you fancy that; what about Route Sixty-Six?' 'What about money?' came back the reply. 'What about money, we'll sort that, but what about Canada then? We could ship her there, then we would have done the world.' I said. 'Yes, that sounds good, I'd like to see Canada,' Carolyn said. 'I know, what about Timbuktu?' I said enthusiastically. 'Timbuktu, where the hell is that?' she laughsed. 'It's in Africa. Yes, Timbuktu. Let's face it we have been on the road to Mandalay and that's pretty iconic, now we need to go from here to Timbuktu. I'll tell you what, when we find a place to camp I'll have a look at the atlas and you put the kettle on.'

Glossary

Chitty was built in the true spirit of the film, not because we planned it but more because that is just how we are ... sadly! We genuinely didn't have much money so we built it from whatever came our way. I went into the garage with a collection of bits and came out with a Chitty.

Land Rover long wheelbase, series 3, from 1973. Including a few days' MOT £100.

Singer sewing machine: turning wheel to hold on the spare tyre. Found in the garage.

Marks & Spencer brass lamp stands x two: used for the headlights, the front bumper and the bonnet mascot support. £9 each reduced in the sale from £80 each.

Auntie Gertie's piano: brass piano hinge to hold the two bonnet bits together, inlaid wood veneer used on the dashboard.

Chrome metal fittings from a glass bathroom shelf: used on the rear of Chitty.

Marks & Spencer brass tea light stands: body for dashboards lights and switches.

Marks & Spencer leather belts (Menswear 44-inch waist) x two: bonnet straps.

Mitsubishi Gallant 1990: rear light bulbs and wiring to rewire part of the electrics.

Brass industrial steam valve gauges: used to house the original Land Rover dashboard clocks and speedo.

Shop-fitting electric door housings: aluminium used to create the floor.

Toyota MR2 pop up headlight: hidden under rear seat for an electrically operated drinks cabinet.

Glossary

Victorian mirror: ornate wooden carvings used on the dashboard and glovebox.

Brass fifty-litre fuel tank: Beaulieu auto jumble £50 because Carolyn bargained it down from £200.

Lucas 'King of the Road' brass gas lamps: £60 a pair because they were unpolished (£300 polished).

Snake's head horn: Beaulieu auto jumble.

Brass windscreen: from an old MG, very old!

RAC and AA badges (period): from my Grandad.

Iroko timber: Clare Lallow's, Cowes, Isle of Wight, for boat tail.

Sheets of aluminium: , Newport Steel, Isle of Wight, for bonnet and flooring.

Brass Victorian door handle.

B&Q interior door handle (broken and cheap): glovebox handle.

Last thought

The one thing that continued to tickle us most was the sheer surprise and delight when we explained we had built Chitty and the concept of having driven overland to Australia seemed incomprehensible. ' Where did you get it?' ' I built it.' 'Wow, you built it?' 'Yes, I built it.' 'How did you get it here?' 'I drove it.' 'That's nice. Who did you fly with?'